This Great Company

This Great Company

Sermons by Outstanding Preachers

of the Christian Tradition

Selected and edited by David Poling

Foreword by Keith Miller

Keats Publishing, Inc.

New Canaan, Connecticut

Acknowledgments

"Ambassador of the Word" by Fulton J. Sheen, from *If I Had Only One Sermon to Prepare,* edited by Joseph Fort Newton. Copyright 1932 by Joseph Fort Newton; renewed 1960 by Josephine Newton Hooven. New York, N.Y.: Harper & Row, Publishers, Inc. Used by permission of the publishers.

Sermon XII from *A Selection of the Most Celebrated Sermons of John Calvin.* Philadelphia, Pa: Thomas Cowperthwait and Co., 1817.

Sermon III from *A Selection of the Most Celebrated Sermons of Martin Luther.* Philadelphia, Pa.: Thomas Cowperthwait and Co., 1817.

"The Great Assize" by John Wesley, from *The World's Great Sermons,* edited by S. E. Frost. Garden City, N.Y.: Halcyon House, 1943.

"War and Peace" by Henry Ward Beecher, from *The World's Great Sermons,* edited by S. E. Frost. Garden City, N.Y.: Halcyon House, 1943.

"The Egyptians Dead upon the Seashore" from *Sermons* by Phillips Brooks. New York, N.Y.: E. P. Dutton and Co., 1893.

"The Lord's Supper, the Sample of the Christian Life" from *Sermons Preached in Manchester* by Alexander Maclaren. New York, N.Y.: Funk and Wagnalls Co., 1902.

"The Man at Bethesda" from *The New Crusade* by Charles Edward Jefferson. New York, N.Y.: Thomas Crowell and Co., 1902.

"A New Year's Benediction" from *Sermons* by Charles Haddon Spurgeon. New York, N.Y.: Robert Carter and Brothers, circa 1860.

"The Religion of Public Opinion" from *Lectures to Professing Christians* by Charles Grandison Finney. Oberlin, O.: E. J. Goodrich, 1880.

"What Think Ye of Christ?" from *Twelve Select Sermons* by Dwight Lyman Moody. Old Tappan, N.J.: Fleming H. Revell Co., 1890.

"Old Wells Dug Out" from *Old Wells Dug Out* by Thomas DeWitt Talmage. New York, N.Y.: Harper and Bros., 1874.

"Nothing but Slag" from *Borrowed Axes and Other Sermons* by Russell Herman Conwell. Valley Forge, Pa.: Judson Press, 1923. Used by permission of the publishers.

"Christ Regenerates Even the Desires" from *Sermons on Living Subjects* by Horace Bushnell. New York, N.Y.: Charles Scribners, 1870.

"The Message of the Church to Men of Wealth" from *Sermons Preached at Brighton* by Frederick William Robertson. New York, N.Y.: Harper and Bros., 1850.

"Blinding the Mind" from *Things That Matter Most* by John Henry Jowett. Old Tappan, N.J.: Fleming H. Revell Co., 1913. Used by permission of the publishers.

"Work" from *The Simple Things of the Christian Life* by George Campbell Morgan. Old Tappan, N.J.: Fleming H. Revell Co., 1907. Used by permission of the publishers.

"As Jesus Passed By, or Follow Me" from *As Jesus Passed By* by Rodney (Gipsy) Smith. Old Tappan, N.J.: Fleming H. Revell Co., 1900. Used by permission of the publishers.

"The Immortal Life" by Joseph Fort Newton, from *If I Had Only One Sermon to Preach on Immortality,* edited by William L. Stidger. Used by permission of the publishers.

"The Claims of the Church upon Christians" from *University Sermons* by Henry Sloane Coffin. New Haven, Conn.: Yale University Press, 1914. Used by permission of the publishers.

"Loving Your Enemies" from *Strength to Love* by Martin Luther King, Jr. Copyright 1963 by Martin Luther King, Jr. New York, N.Y.: Harper & Row, Publishers, Inc. Used by permission of the publishers.

"Unto You Is Born This Day a Saviour" from *Deliverance to the Captives* by Karl Barth, translated by Marguerite Wieser. Copyright 1961 by SCM Press, Ltd. New York, N.Y.: Harper & Row, Publishers, Inc. Used by permission of the publishers.

Words of Thanks

A writing experience such as *This Great Company* involves people and places and I want to recognize those who had a vital part in this collection of historic sermons. My appreciation to librarians at Yale Club of New York; The College of Wooster, Wooster, Ohio; and most especially to Miss Sarah Elizabeth Firor of the Hutchins Library of Berea College, Berea, Kentucky. These friends, as well as the staff and pastor's secretary, Mrs. Lois Jackson, of the First United Presbyterian Church, Albuquerque, New Mexico, assisted me in countless ways.

David Poling
EASTER 1976

Contents

Foreword

The church has been busy absorbing all kinds of theological, social and liturgical storms and experiments during recent years. David Poling has sensed, correctly I think, that ministers and laymen are stopping to ask themselves once more: "What is it we have to *say* to a broken, nervous world about the good news of Jesus Christ? And how can we best communicate it?"

To help in this renewed interest in proclaiming the Christian message, David has done a valuable service to us all in bringing together some powerful sermons by men from different social backgrounds, historical periods and denominational groups.

The striking thing to me, as to the editor, is not the great differences one would suspect, but the amazing similarities in the relevance to our own problems and needs. Also, I am impressed by the almost universal drive of the preachers to settle for nothing less than driving their truth into the motivational bloodstream of their audience—rather than simply presenting logical arguments which might be intellectually accepted or rejected.

Whatever shapes the communication of the Gospel will take in the years before us—and I think it will take many shapes—I believe that those whose voices will travel deepest and furthest into the human predicament will be standing on the shoulders of great biblical preachers like many of those whose sermons you are about to read.

Keith Miller
Port Aransas, Texas

Introduction

To edit a collection of great sermons is a fearful task. It really takes a lot of nerve to pull together several dozen sermons from three centuries and say to those interested, "Here are the best from the finest." Your first mistake or error is the assumption that one person can judge the outstanding preachers of the Christian faith. Having reached that conclusion, one is now able to pull out of such powerful preaching a single representative sermon. . . . What began in nerve ends up in folly!

Yet our publisher was correct in his insistence that a gathering of great sermons should be in print, now. The change and upheaval within the Christian Church calls for a return, even a recovery, of preaching. The convulsions of the 1960s shook every institution in sight, and the Church received some major blows to the body. And should the Christian community have something to say to this decaying, secular world, it will be from the Bible and the preaching of the Word of God. It was Halford Luccock, professor and friend, who must have sensed such an hour as this when he wrote:

> The great renewal of Christianity, its recurring springtimes, which make the most stirring chapters of history, have been accompanied, often started, by preaching.

Combining nerve and foolishness, but also the conviction that the hour is right for preaching to emerge once again, we present this treasury of sermons. One regrets immediately the host of outstanding clergymen who, for limits of space, have not been included. We also apologize for brevity and some necessary condensations, again because of limits of space.

The individual sermon selections represent the viewpoint of the editor, not a committee or poll. Should they appear in grand disorder it is by editorial design. They defy the categories of time or theological party labels. All unite to make *This Great Company* what it is—a fellowship pointing to the enduring good news. A sermon by Brooks or Beecher or Finney is here because it not only reflected upon the preacher, but appealed to my own sense of time and place. One is immediately impressed with the application of so many texts and themes to our own time. But it should be that way if biblical preaching is honest and vivid. The Bible speaks to our day as well as to the sixteenth century. It belongs to our life as the living Word. These clergymen have shown its timelessness.

In reading and studying so many sermons in preparation for this book, one realizes that some material "reads" better than others. Illustrations do have a way of jumping out of old pages. Outline and form do become apparent. Movement and direction are sought. Some preachers should be read out loud if we are to catch the full impact of the man and his message. Gipsy Smith and Billy Sunday would be in the category of power communicated through "spoken sermons." Joseph Fort Newton and Leslie Weatherhead have a smooth literary flow that is pleasing to the eye as well as the ear.

A book of great sermons should be prized by those who are preaching as well as by those who listen and shape the life of the Church. Our horizon should be extended, our vision broadened, by the excellence of this evangelical treasure-house. The very exposure to these men of faith is indeed a growing experience in true religion.

And something more happens here among the giants of the pulpit. Vocabulary and delivery. You will be impressed many times by the rich employment of words and phrases. Here were scholars and saints who worked long and late in preparing their weekly material. Is it too much to expect that our own skill with words, our development of vocabulary, our construction of sentences will improve and enlarge? We hope so, and a recovery of the force of speech as well.

Public speaking needs, in twentieth-century America, a good dose of professional tonic. The sanctuary, the senate, the university lecture hall—all are desperate for some better voices, higher themes, sharper delivery. Here we have the true professionals in action, from the pulpit, before "live" audiences, giving of their best

The success of this book will be in leading us all to a recovery of preaching, which will strengthen the world as much as the Church. It seemed appropriate to have Fulton Sheen's advice at the beginning and his quotation in our Introduction:

> On the last day we will not be asked how many came to hear us preach, but how many we brought to Christ. We are ambassadors of the Word of God, and that Word is everlasting truth.

David Poling

This Great Company

Fulton John Sheen/
Ambassador of the Word

THE beloved disciple John, in the quiet and peace of Patmos Isle, soared on the wings of Revelation into the very flame and fire of God, and there discovered the source and fountainhead of all preaching in those words which he sets down at the very beginning of his Gospel, "In the beginning was the Word and the Word was with God." The Word is the intelligence of God which reaches to the abyss of all things that are known and can be known. The Word alone articulates the very secrets of the life of God, divines his nature, declares his holy praise; and we, the preachers on earth, are but the broken syllables of that Word, diminutive letters of that Utterance, and the feeble reflection of that great light which came on earth as the light illuminating the darkness of men.

The preacher who is conscious of his dependence on the divine Word surpasses in dignity the most sublime orators who in their highest reaches have been the supreme organs and mouthpieces of people. Moses was the voice of his country; Demosthenes in the *Philippics* the voice of Greece; Cicero in his Cataline orations the voice of Rome; Mirabeau, of the constitution; O'Connell, of Ireland; Pitt, of England: all were the expressions of great peoples and great nations. But the Christian orator surpasses all of these, for his mission is not to be merely the voice of his country; he is the voice of God, and the echo of the Word.

In this symposium on preaching the two following questions have been submitted to me for discussion: first, what is the best way for the preacher to approach the modern mind? and second, how do I personally prepare my sermons?

In answer to the question, what is the best approach to the modern mind, it might be well to inquire just what is precisely the nature of this rather vague something called "the modern mind." It will hardly be disputed that the modern mind is not Christian in the sense that it was

Christian fifty years ago. A Christian today does not generally mean what it has meant traditionally: namely, one who believes in the divinity of Christ. There is many a modern preacher today who would remonstrate with you very mildly if you told him that he was not a Christian in the latter sense, but would become extremely angry if you told him he was not a gentleman. If the term "modern" be taken not merely in the chronological sense of the term but as expressive of a mood or spirit, the modern mind may then be defined as that religious mentality which holds to the sufficiency of human reason without divine revelation, and the sufficiency of human activity without divine grace. If this be the modern mind, how can it be approached by a Christian preacher? In the last analysis there are only two approaches, for there are only two possible adjustments in life; one is to suit our life to dogmas, the other is to suit dogmas to our life. In other words, one must either live as one thinks or think as one lives. In the face of the modern mood the preacher must decide for himself whether he will come down from the cross in response to the appeal of that mood, or whether he will remain there like Christ and draw the whole world to himself. He must very definitely decide whether he is going to make Christianity fit men, or whether he is going to make men fit Christianity. There is no other fundamental issue.

To me, the approach which sacrifices a Christian principle of the modern mind is unthinkable, for this reason: that if it were adopted as a general principle in other fields, it would lead into very grave error. Simply because everybody is doing a certain thing, such as breaking traffic laws, it does not follow that legislators must make a religion out of that particular violation. The public opinion of the mob is very often wrong, just as it was wrong when it chose Barabbas instead of our divine Saviour. It must forever be kept in mind, regardless of how much the modern mind insists on changing morals and beliefs to suit new conditions, that right is right if nobody is right, and wrong is wrong if everybody is wrong. The surrender of Christian principles for the sake of popularity may win a few adherents, but deep-seated in the human heart is a positive disrespect for anyone who is untrue and disloyal to principles. Men who ask for sacrifice are respected more than those who ask for an easier life. Chrysostom has lived because he did not bow to Eudoxia, and Ambrose is immortalized because he did not sacrifice an iota of the law of Christ to Theodosius. Bossuet was respected even by the young Louis XIV, at whom he thundered. If the great tradition of these noble men of Christ is to be continued, then preachers must not follow the democratic principle of giving ghosts to the congregation simply because they want ghosts, and expelling hell fire because they do not like the sound of the Word in their ears.

What is needed in the face of this cheap claptrap which caters to the weaknesses of men instead of leading them on to the vitality of the sacraments, and which goes down with them into the abysses instead of leading them on to Tabors, is something of the fearlessness of the greatest man born of woman who was not afraid to thunder out before a king that it was unlawful for him to live with his brother's wife. When

Salome danced she typified public opinion, which is keeping pace with the times; and as she danced two men lost their heads. John the Baptist lost his head literally, for he believed that the principle concerning the sanctity of marriage could not be sacrificed to suit a modern whim. Herod lost his head figuratively, for he believed that public opinion was right, and that a man could change his morals as he changed his clothes. Becoming a really great preacher means leading men instead of following them, and it also means losing one's head John's way rather than Herod's.

But it may be asked, is there not some legitimate adaptation to be made for our own times? Each age has its own spirit, and much of that spirit is good. Unquestionably there is a lawful adjustment to the modern mind, but it is an adjustment of *method,* and not of *content.* It is perfectly fitting, for example, for men to change their hats as the style changes, and not to wear helmets when everyone else is wearing a derby. But it certainly does not mean changing our head every time we change our hat. The nature of things is fixed, like the spots of a leopard.

Within the sphere of method four distinct approaches to the modern mind may be mentioned among many others possibly more important. The first approach in preaching to the modern mind is to establish a common denominator with it. That common denominator or common interest may be either the news of the day, scientific advancements, current economic, moral and ethical problems, which are more or less variable, or it may be psychological needs and aspirations which are fixed and constant.

A second method of approach to the modern mind is to show how a Christian truth fits in with human life. I say "fits in," because the modern world has lost its capacity for solid thinking. It no longer seeks for proofs, but seems far more interested in learning just how far any truth or doctrine can be integrated with life. In other words, it is not nearly so necessary to prove the fundamental truths of Christianity now as it was some years ago for the reason that the minds of our day do not seek proof. What they do look for, however, is a harmonious adjustment and mechanical clicking of one part of the mental universe with every other part. This craving for organic unity of doctrines offers a very fertile field for those preachers who have to offer a religion which itself is consistent and organic.

A third way of soliciting the attention of the modern mind is to give a discourse or sermon starting with the statement of some modern objection against traditional Christianity. Upon hearing it the modern mind will immediately have its interest aroused, and will follow the answer given with much more avidity than if the preacher opened with an attack upon the content of that objection. For instance, at the present time there is considerable interest shown in psychoanalysis and its relation to religion. A Christian preacher could very well begin with the assertion of that fact, and then, by separating the wheat from the chaff, could lead his hearers on to a better understanding of what is meant by sacramental confession, concluding with the idea that psychoanalysis is just the revelation of a mind, whereas sacramental confession is the revelation of a will which craves for pardon from the God offended. In that same connection a preacher might solicit the attention of his hearers by the mention of some new theory in the field of morals or religion, and then by a very clever turn of the argument show that the new theory is only a new label for a very old error. In each instance the actual or the current is used as the bait with which to catch the modern mind on the hook of the true fisherman, who is Peter.

A fourth and never-failing approach is with the life of our blessed Lord, who will never cease to interest human hearts. If there has been any decline in such interest, it is only because preachers have been preaching a kind of emasculated Christ, talking about him as if he were just a mere man, a Buddha or Plato, without ever referring to that great redemptive act by which he purchased the freedom of the human race. It is my own personal belief that there is nothing which will so quickly touch the hearts of men, regardless of whether they are moderns or ancients, as the passion of our blessed Lord, which passion reached its climax when he lay spread on the cross as a great and wounded eagle, in order that we who are slaves might begin to enjoy the glorious freedom of the sons of God.

The second question presented for consideration was regarding my preparation of sermons. In answer to this, I will set down as the most important elements of preparation prayer and contemplation. Just as the cock flaps his wings before crowing, so too the preacher must meditate before ever opening his mouth. In the biological order there is no such thing as spontaneous generation; life must generate life. With equal truth this fact prevails in the order of spirit. If ever the preacher is to generate the divine life he must have divine life. As Horace put it in his own pagan way, "If you wish me to weep, you must weep first." The source is always higher than the fountain, and the Christian preacher who has prepared himself either at the foot of the crucifix or kneeling before his Eucharistic Lord is one who has already begun to cast forth sparks capable of enkindling faith and fire in the hearts of his hearers. The great master Thomas Aquinas has stated that truth in his *Summa,* and his statement deserves to be enscribed on every pulpit: *Ex plenitudine contemplationis derivatur praedicatio.*

I have estimated that for the preparation of the seven Lenten sermons which I give every year I spend about four hundred hours, mostly in contemplation. At the end of those hours I have only a few scrap notes, but the sermons themselves are ready to be delivered. There is only one very small detail left to do, and that is to write them.

Next in importance in preparation is the orderliness and sequence of points. I do not believe that the mind can hold over three points in a sermon, and these should be stated at the very beginning of the sermon in order that the hearer may be better able to follow the development of the points and retain them in his memory. It is advisable not to have the points unrelated and disconnected, but to tie them up in a unified manner.

In the development of each point it should be kept in mind that psychological cognition is prior to faith, and that some intellectual or rational principle must precede emotion. Otherwise, the emotion will be like a rib without a backbone. Too much sentiment is like a golden key—it is beautiful, but opens no doors. The intellectual principle should be accompanied by a concrete example illustrating that principle, taken, if possible, from the life of our blessed Lord. Thus, if developing the point that there are only two classes of people that find Christ, namely, the very learned and the very simple, one could illustrate it by an appeal to the wise men and the shepherds—those who knew they did not know anything, and those who knew they knew nothing.

So much for the construction of the sermon. There remains the actual delivery of it, and this will depend a great deal upon the individual temperament. Personally, I do not believe that a sermon should ever be memorized. I have made it a point in five years of radio broadcasting never to use a manuscript, even when talking in a studio. What is lacking in exactness or verbiage is certainly gained in the sincerity of the message. Finally, the sermon should conclude not with some vague appeal or with an injunction that "If you do this, then you will hear the words 'Come to me, ye blessed, to my Father,' " but with the strongest line of the whole sermon. I have made it a point in the preparation of my sermons to spend more time in writing the last line or last paragraph than the whole body of the discourse.

In conclusion, one point the preacher should always keep in mind is that he is using the gifts of God, and that those who crowd to hear him or are thrilled by his words are really solicited more through the kindness of God than through himself. I often think as I see great crowds beneath the pulpit, many of whom feel that I am doing very effective work for the cause of Christ, that perhaps some old woman hidden behind the pillar, who understands not a single word I say, is doing more good for the salvation of the world than I am. There is only one message in the world worth preaching and that is Christ, and him crucified. On the last day we will not be asked how many came to hear us preach, but how many we brought to Christ. We are ambassadors of the Word of God, and that Word is everlasting truth. Modern moods and vagaries and even the very heavens themselves will pass away, but his Word will not pass away. In the great struggle with the forces of Pan, which are paganism, the preachers of the Word need never fear the outcome. Popularity may not always come their way, but when the smoke of battle is cleared, the most precious thing in the world will be their heritage, and that will be victory. For if truth wins, we win; but if truth—ah, but truth can never lose.

Fulton J. Sheen, Bishop of Newport (1895–) *Bishop Sheen is one of the most articulate spokesmen for the Christian Church. He is easily the most popular Roman Catholic in the United States and has reached an enormous audience over radio and television. As theologian, teacher, author and preacher, he has never flagged in spreading the Word. His books are many and* Peace of Soul *and*

Religion without God *have been best-sellers. In this volume we have his sermon "Ambassador of the Word," with its special message for preachers. The vitality of the man and the force of his message are most apparent today—and this sermon reprinted here was delivered more than forty years ago. It seemed appropriate to begin this collection with the theme of such a sermon—almost a backdrop against which to perceive the impact and reach of others who are part of this volume.*

John Calvin/**Sermon XII**

10 *For there are many unruly and vain talkers, specially they of the circumcision;*
11 *Whose mouths must be stopped, who subvert whole houses, teaching things which they ought not, for filthy lucre's sake.*
12 *One of themselves, even a prophet of their own, said, The Cretians are always liars, evil beasts, slow bellies.*

TITUS 1:10-12

S T. PAUL saith, "there are many unruly and vain talkers and deceivers," in the towns and country of Crete. He maketh mention of this to Titus, who was then in that island, that he might be careful in appointing men to govern the church, who would reprove those that rose up against the truth of God and endeavored to trouble the church. As dangers and necessities increase, men ought to provide remedies. So, when we see wicked men strive to bring confusion into the church, we must be careful and zealous, and endeavor to keep all things in their proper order. St. Paul informeth us that there were many rebels even among the faithful, and such as attempted to preach the Gospel, who were given to vain prattling and filthy lucre, teaching that which did not edify.

When we see the church of God so troubled by the wicked, it is the duty of ministers to strive to keep things in a proper condition: they must be armed, not with a material sword but with the word of God, with wisdom and virtue, that they may be enabled to resist the ungodly. When we see so many turn from the right way, let us be careful, and endeavor to have the church of God provided with good rulers, that Satan raise not up stumbling blocks among us. When St. Paul speaketh of these vain deceivers, he mentioneth the Jews in particular, who were the flower of the church, the firstborn of the house of God. We know that the Gentiles were as wild branches, which God of his grace grafted into the stock of Abraham. Although we see that the Jews were anciently the true heirs of salvation, and that the inheritance of life belonged to them, yet notwithstanding, St. Paul notes them as being the greatest disturbers of the church.

When the wicked sow tares, whether it be of false doctrine or wicked talk, to turn the faithful from the right way, if we dissemble, or make as though we saw them not, the weak will become infected, and many will be deceived; thus there will be a general plague: but if we point out such men, they will be shunned, and therefore will do but little evil. When we see men who do nothing but pull down, and endeavor to cause trouble in the church, we must labor to bring them into the right way; but if they remain steadfast in their wickedness, we must make them known; we must disclose their filthiness, that men may abhor them, and separate themselves from their company.

Shall we leave the church of God among thieves and wolves, as it were, and let the whole flock be scattered, and the blood of our Lord Jesus Christ trodden underfoot? Shall we suffer all order to be abolished, the souls which have been redeemed destroyed, and in the meantime shut our eyes and be silent? If we act thus, are we not cowards? Let us therefore endeavor to bring back those who have strayed, who are not utterly past hope—especially if their faults be secret. But when they fall into such wickedness as to make confusion in the church, we must use a different remedy: we must show them what they are, and hold them up to the view of the world, that they may be avoided. We must not spare them, because the whole salvation of the people of God is in danger.

We must not be moved by favor toward the person of anyone, and say, "this man is worthy of commendation, he is yet to be regenerated." We must not think so much upon those men who seem honorable and privileged at the present day, as upon our duty. We have already shown that the Gospel came from the Jews—that they were the holy root, the chosen people, the church of God. Therefore, when they had such prerogatives, might they not have expected some privileges? It is evident that by this they were enabled to do the more evil. They need not use this goodly title, only to say, "We are the firstborn of the house of God." But they might say: "we are the people whom God hath chosen to himself; we are the stock of Abraham, who were adopted from all ages; we are they to whom God revealed himself, and it is through our means that you have the doctrine of salvation at this day." When they made use of such sayings as these, was it not enough to astonish the minds of the weak?

Let us therefore remember that when persons of honor and dignity have been in credit a long time, and then become deceivers, and endeavor to sow tares and destroy the building of God, we must withstand them the more courageously, for they are far more dangerous than those of lower rank. If an ignorant man, who is but little known, be wicked, and disposed to do evil, he cannot pour out his poison afar off, for he is, as it were, fettered. But he that is of reputation and intelligence, who setteth himself on high that he may be seen afar off, who can boast of his credit, and so forth, that man, I say, will be armed like a madman; and if he be suffered, he may do much hurt.

Let us mark well when we see men who are honorable, whether it be on account of the office they fill, or the reputation they have had for a long time. In other places where St. Paul speaketh of those that pervert the truth of the Gospel, and put forth errors and false doctrine, he calleth them heretics; but in this place he calleth them "unruly and vain talkers and deceivers," who will not be ruled by truth or reason. There are no worse enemies than traitors, who, under color of God's name, come and make divisions in the church, and endeavor to destroy that which God hath established. We see some who will not say, at first, that the doctrine we preach is false; for they would be ashamed to speak in this manner, were they ever so impudent; but they will labor to bring the people into a dislike of it; this we frequently see. I would to God we were entirely rid of such infection and filth.

If these vain talkers and deceivers be let alone, if we take no notice of them, what will become of the church? Will not the devil win all? And shall we not be guilty of betraying the flock, and of destroying that which was built up in God's name? We must therefore consider that we have to fight not only against the papists and Turks, who utterly reject the doctrine we preach, but against home enemies who go about maliciously and traitorously to bring to nought those things which are well devised and established, that Jesus Christ may not reign in full power; who endeavor to corrupt the Word, that in the end, the sincerity of religion may be destroyed.

We ought to withstand such enemies courageously, but we are so far from it, that everyone seemeth to thirst after nothing so much as to be wittingly poisoned. If we doubted the purity of any meat, we should quickly abstain from it, for the love and care of this frail life leadeth us to it. But when God telleth us that it is poison to turn aside from his Word, from the reverence we ought to bear him and from the zeal with which we ought to be inflamed, we make no account of it. Some care for nothing but to hear vain curiosities; others have a longing to see the servants of God vexed and this doctrine troubled, that they may triumph at it. Thus they join hands with heretics, as we have frequent examples. But the faithful must be put in mind of that which God teacheth them: if they wish to stand safe and sound, they must be watchful and shun false doctrine. Yea, and when they perceive that Satan goeth about secretly, endeavoring to corrupt the Word of God which is preached to them, it is the duty of everyone to employ himself and be faithful, that he may withstand the temptations of the adversary—for St. Paul spake not only to Titus, but to the people generally.

Now let us observe what is added: "they subvert whole houses." If one man only were misled by them, it would be too much; for men's souls ought to be precious to us, seeing our Lord Jesus Christ hath esteemed them so highly, that he spared not his own life, but freely gave it for our

salvation and redemption. But when we shall see whole houses sub-
verted, that is, every one without exception, it is far more detestable.
When St. Paul spake of the horrible crimes of deceivers, he mentioned
vain babbling and foolish imaginations; he spake also of certain traditions the Jews brought out of their law, of which they had a wrong
understanding. Are we not then sufficiently warned? If we be turned
from the right way, whom shall we blame for it? If Satan be suffered to
deceive us, and we be given over to a reprobate state, it is no more than
we deserve; because we have not used the remedy God hath provided
for us.

After St. Paul hath thus spoken, he addeth, it is "for filthy lucre's
sake." We therefore see that as soon as we are carried away with
covetousness, seeking after the goods of this world, it is impossible for
us to preach the Gospel in its purity. St. Paul saith that he preached the
Gospel in its purity, and held it forth in simplicity. Let all those therefore
that teach the church follow the example of the apostle; let them take
heed to themselves, knowing that if they will serve God purely, they
must be content with what he hath given them, and cast off all desire of
riches. They must come to this conclusion, that they are rich enough if
they are enabled to edify the church of God; if the Lord causeth their
labor to become profitable, they must be content therewith. This is what
St. Paul meant to set forth in this place. The island of Crete, which at
present is called Candia, formerly contained about one hundred cities or
towns. St. Paul informeth us that the nation had indulged themselves in
wickedness for a long time, and therefore have an evil name. He saith,
"One of themselves, even a prophet of their own, said, 'The Cretians are
always liars, evil beasts, slow bellies.' "

Such reproaches as these seem to take away all their reputation. Some
imagine that St. Paul here showeth himself to be their enemy; for he
writeth to Titus, not secretly, but that his letter might be read and
published, that the Cretians might know what he said concerning them.
Notwithstanding his rebukes, he had the pastoral charge of them. Thus
we may learn that although a man may desire the salvation of a people
and love them sincerely, yet he will not cease to point out the faults of
which they are guilty; and indeed we cannot show that we love those
whom God hath committed to our charge unless we labor to correct the
faults and diseases wherewith we see them infected. A good shepherd,
therefore, though he rebuke the people sharply, must love them better
than his own life.

It being the duty of those who are called to preach the Word of God to
use plainness and point out the errors of the faithful, they must not be
offended or grieved when they are told of their faults. Many at this day
think the Gospel is not well preached unless they are flattered; that is,
they think men do not preach the Word of God unless they cover their
sins and endeavor to please them, but we here see another kind of
divinity. Ministers, when they see any kind of wickedness among those
who are committed to their charge, must not conceal it; it must be made
known. It is better to put those to shame, who have been negligent and
sleepy, than to hoodwink them, that they may become more blind.

The surgeon who hath a wound to heal cutteth away all the rotten flesh; or if there be any apostume, he purgeth it to the quick, to take away all the infection and corruption. So must the ministers of the Word of God do, if they wish to discharge their duty faithfully toward those committed to their care; and those of the faithful must bear such correction patiently, knowing that it is necessary that they should be thus handled. They must not murmur against those who seek their salvation, for what shall it profit us to be honorable in the eyes of the world, if in the meantime God abhorreth us? But there are many who are displeased if they are told of their faults. If he who hath authority to teach points out the wickedness that reigneth among them, they will be displeased with him and mock him.

We see how justice is corrupted and what favors are granted. Men speak of wickedness in their houses, in their shops, in the streets and in the marketplace; but if it be mentioned in the pulpit, if wickedness be made known by the preaching of the Word of God, we see them displeased and full of malice. There is no man but what can say, "such a sin is common; such a man hath done such a fault." Everyone may see what sins reign among the people; and yet those who are appointed to watch over them dare not reprove them, although their office requireth it of them.

It is said the Word of God is like a two-edged sword, which pierceth the most secret thoughts, separating joint and marrow. Yea, it reacheth even to the bottom of the heart, and maketh known whatever sins lurk within us. If we wish to be taken for Christians, we must have quiet and contented minds, and not be angry when we are reproved for our faults. When we have any apostume about us, we must be willing to have it lanced; when the sore is ripe and raging, let us be willing to receive the remedy, knowing it is for our profit. It is said by our Lord Jesus Christ, that he will send the Comforter—"And when he is come, he will reprove the world of sin and of righteousness and of judgement." Therefore, if we will not bow down our necks and receive God's yoke—that is to say, if we do not condemn ourselves and suffer him to exercise spiritual jurisdiction over us, by those whom he hath appointed to preach his word—we shall be condemned. This is the cause why the papists speak evil of us. St. Paul exhorteth us to walk uprightly, and to have a good conscience before God.

If we wish not to be condemned by infidels, we must be meek and patient, and show ourselves ready and willing to receive instruction from the Word of the Lord. When our faults are made known to us, we must confess them. We are commanded throughout the Scripture to reprove the wicked; but it is a common practice in these times for men to cast off all correction, and take free liberty in all manner of sin and iniquity, being under no subjection. But those who wish to pass for Christians must not behave themselves in this manner. St. Paul saith, "Admonish one another," and again, "Reprove sin." To whom doth the Holy Ghost speak in these two places? To all the faithful without exception. For although God hath chosen some to whom he hath given a special charge to admonish, exhort and reprove those that do amiss, yet, notwithstanding, he chargeth every man to set himself against sin and wickedness.

If this be lawful for those who have no public charge, what must the minister do, whom God hath expressly charged to fill this office? There are bastard Christians among us at this day who know not God, nor obey his Word; therefore they will not bear correction. St. Paul reproveth the Cretians by putting them in mind of the witness of their own prophet, who saith, "The Cretians are always liars, evil beasts." When God maketh known our faults and reproveth us, he doth it for our salvation; we ought therefore to be displeased with ourselves, and confess our sins with the deepest humility. We gain nothing by being stubborn: it is of no use; for if we will not bow, God will break us in pieces.

It seemeth that God wrought a miracle in sending the Gospel into Crete. Although the people were very wicked, yet, notwithstanding, the Lord in his goodness visited them. We may therefore perceive that God hath no regard to our worthiness when he calleth us to be first in his church, but he oftentimes does it to set forth the brightness of his mercy. If, when we were cast away, he reached out his hand and took us to himself, he deserveth so much the more honor and praise.

We have deserved nothing at his hands; and if we have received the Gospel, it is not by reason of our own virtue; for nothing can move God to call men to himself, and make them know his will, but his free mercy. Let us therefore learn to glorify our God in the spirit of humility; and if he hath chosen us, and forsaken others, and we wish to remain in possession of so great a blessing, let us examine our lives daily. When we see that there is nothing in us but wretchedness, and that we can do nothing but provoke him to anger, let us prevent his wrath by condemning ourselves. When every man judgeth himself, then shall we be justified before God, who will not only purge us from all our wretchedness, but cause his glory to shine more and more, that we may have occasion to call upon him as our Father, and proclaim to the world that he hath redeemed us by the merits of his Son, that we may become his inheritance.

John Calvin (1509–1564) *This leader of the sixteenth century Reformation, who was born in France and died in Geneva, often referred to himself as a "simple layman," yet his ministry was world-changing within the Christian community. Calvin prepared for the law and his theological works show the precision of his earlier training. Presbyterians trace their beginnings to this slim preacher and his chief publication,* The Institutes of the Christian Religion.

Martin Luther/**Sermon III**

23 *And he turned him unto his disciples, and said privately Blessed*
are the eyes which see the things that ye see:

24 *For I tell you, that many prophets and kings have desired to see*
those things which ye see, and have not seen them; and to hear
those things which ye hear, and have not heard them.

25 *And, behold, a certain lawyer stood up, and tempted him,*
saying, Master, what shall I do to inherit eternal life?

26 *He said unto him, What is written in the law? how readest thou?*

27 *And he answering said, Thou shalt love the Lord thy God with*
all thy heart, and with all thy soul, and with all thy strength,
and with all thy mind; and thy neighbour as thyself.

28 *And he said unto him, Thou hast answered right: this do, and*
thou shalt live.

29 *But he, willing to justify himself, said unto Jesus, And who is my*
neighbour?

30 *And Jesus answering said, A certain man went down from*
Jerusalem to Jericho, and fell among thieves, which stripped him
of his raiment, and wounded him, and departed, leaving him half
dead.

31 *And by chance there came down a certain priest that way: and*
when he saw him, he passed by on the other side.

32 *And likewise a Levite, when he was at the place, came and*
looked on him, and passed by on the other side.

33 *But a certain Samaritan, as he journeyed, came where he was:*
and when he saw him, he had compassion on him,

34 *And went to him, and bound up his wounds, pouring in oil and*
wine, and set him on his own beast, and brought him to an inn,
and took care of him.

35 *And on the morrow when he departed, he took out two pence,*
and gave them to the host, and said unto him, Take care of him;
and whatsoever thou spendest more, when I come again, I will
repay thee.

36 *Which now of these three, thinkest thou, was neighbor unto him*
  that fell among the thieves?

37 *And he said, He that shewed mercy on him. Then said Jesus*
  unto him, Go, and do thou likewise.

LUKE 10:23–37

I HOPE that you rightly understand this Gospel, it being preached every year; notwithstanding, occasion now offers, and we shall treat of it again. First, the evangelist saith that Christ took his disciples aside and said unto them secretly, "Blessed are the eyes which see the things that ye see: for I tell you that many prophets and kings have desired to see those things which ye see, and have not seen them; and to hear those things which ye hear, and have not heard them." To see and hear, is to be understood in this place, simply of the outward seeing and hearing; to wit, that they saw Christ come in the flesh, heard his sermons and were present at those miracles that he did among the Jews. The Jews saw the same according to the flesh, yea, and felt them also; yet did they not truly acknowledge him for Christ, as the apostles did; and especially Peter, who in the name of all the rest did confess him, saying, "Thou art Christ, the son of the living God." We grant, indeed, that there were some among the Jews who acknowledged him, as did the apostles, but the number of them was very small; wherefore he taketh his apostles severally unto himself.

Many prophets and kings have seen Christ, howbeit, in the spirit; as the Lord himself saith to the Jews, of Abraham, "Your father Abraham rejoiced to see my day: and he saw it, and was glad" (John 8:56). The Jews thought that he had spoken of the bodily seeing; but he spake of the spiritual seeing, whereby all Christian hearts did behold him before he was born; for if Abraham saw him, undoubtedly many other prophets in whom the Holy Ghost was, saw him also. And although this seeing saved the holy fathers and prophets, yet did they always with most inward and hearty affection desire to see Christ in the flesh, as is plainly shown in the prophets. Wherefore the Lord saith unto his disciples, which saw him both in the flesh and in the spirit, "Blessed are the eyes which see the things which ye see," as if he had said: now is the acceptable year and time of grace; the matter is so weighty and precious that the eyes are said to be blessed which see it; for now was the Gospel preached openly and manifestly both by Christ and also by his apostles; whereupon he here calleth them all blessed which see and hear such grace, which I have preached much and a long time to you. I would to God that ye keep that which I have spoken fresh in memory.

When the Lord spake these things, a certain lawyer stood up, showing himself, as he thought, to be some great one who, tempting the Lord, saith, "Master, what shall I do to inherit eternal life?" This lawyer was endued with wisdom and not unskillful in the Scriptures, which even his answer declares. Yet in this place he is proved a fool; yea, he is brought to shame and ignominy, for Christ taketh away all his glorying in one word; believing that he had observed the whole law, and that he was chief one, with respect to others, as undoubtedly he was, he thought himself sufficiently worthy by reason of his godliness and learning to be conversant with the Lord. But what doth the Lord in this case? The following text declares: "And he said unto him, what is written in the law? how readest thou? he answered and said, Thou shalt love the Lord thy God with all thy heart, and with all thy soul, and with all thy strength and with all thy mind, and thy neighbor as thyself. Then he said unto him, thou hast answered right; do this and thou shalt live." Methinks the Lord gave this good man a hard lesson; he deals very plainly with him, and puts him to shame openly, before all. He proves that he had done nothing, who, notwithstanding, thought that he had done all things.

If I had time, many things might be spoken of the two commandments; for they are the chief and greatest commandments in Moses, on which the whole law and all the prophets hang, as Christ himself saith in Matthew. If we consider the commandments of Moses, they have respect altogether unto love: for this commandment, "Thou shalt have no other gods before me," we cannot otherwise declare or interpret than this, thou shalt love God alone. So Moses expounded, where he saith, "Hear, O Israel: the Lord our God is one Lord: and thou shalt love the Lord thy God with all thine heart, and with all thy soul, and with all thy might" (Deuteronomy 6:4, 5) from whence the lawyer took his answer. But the Jews think that this commandment extends no farther than that they should not set up or worship idols. And if they can say and witness that they have one God only, and worship none but him, they think they have observed this commandment. After the same sort did this lawyer understand it, but that was an evil and wrong understanding thereof.

We must otherwise consider and understand this precept, "Thou shalt have no other gods before me." Thou, it saith, with all that thou art, but especially it requireth all thine heart, soul and strength. It speaketh not of the tongue, not of the hand or the knees, but of the whole man, whatsoever thou art and hast. That no other god may be worshipped by me, it is necessary that I have the true and only God in my heart; that is, I must love him from my heart, so that I always depend upon him, trust in him, repose my hope in him, have my pleasure, love and joy in him, and daily remember him. If we take pleasure in anything, we say, it doth me good inwardly at the heart; and if any speak or laugh, and do it not in good earnest, neither from his heart, we are apt to say, he speaks or laughs, indeed, but it comes not from the heart. The love of the heart in the Scriptures signifies a vehement and special love which we ought to bear toward God. They who serve God with mouth, hands and knees only, are hypocrites; neither hath God any care of them, for he will not have part, but the whole.

The Jews outwardly abstained from idolatry, and served God alone in mouth; but their hearts were far removed from him, being full of diffidence and unbelief. Outwardly they seemed to be very earnest in serving God, but within they were full of idolatry. Whereupon the Lord said unto them, "Woe unto you, scribes and Pharisees, hypocrites! for ye are like unto whited sepulchres, which indeed appear beautiful outward, but are within full of dead men's bones, and of all uncleanness. Even so ye also outwardly appear righteous unto men, but within ye are full of hypocrisy and iniquity" (Matthew 23:27, 28). These are those wicked ones who glory in the outward thing, which go about to justify and make themselves good by their own works, after the manner of this lawyer. Consider how great the pride of this man was; he cometh forth as though he could not be blessed or rebuked of the Lord. He thought, yea, it seemed to him, that the Lord would commend and praise his life before the people. He thought not to learn anything of the Lord, but sought only his own commendation; he would willingly have had Christ set forth his praise, toward whom the eyes of all were bent, and who was an admiration to all. So all hypocrites outwardly pretend to excellent, great and weighty works.

They say that they have respect neither to glory or praise; but in their hearts they are full of ambition, and wish that their holiness were known to the whole world. Like unto this lawyer are all they which most grievously offend against the first commandment, and think that God is to be loved no more than the sound of the words, and that thereby it is fulfilled. The commandment therefore remains in their mouth, and doth as it were float above the heart and pierceth it not. But I must go farther; I must so love God that I can be content to forsake all creatures for his sake, and, if required, my body and life: I must love him above all things, for he is jealous, and cannot suffer anything to be loved above him, but under him he permits us to love anything. Even as the husband suffers his wife to love her maids, the house, household things and such like, howbeit he suffers her not to love anything with that love wherewith she is bound to him, but will have her leave all such things for his sake. Again, the wife requireth the same of her husband. In the same manner, God suffers us to love his creatures; yea, therefore are they created and are good.

The sun, gold and silver, and whatsoever by nature is fair, procures our love, which makes it dear to us; neither is God offended thereat. But that I should cleave to the creature, and love it equally with him, he will not suffer; yea, he will have me both deny and forsake all these things when he requires it of me, and will have me to be content although I never see the sun, money or riches. The love of the creature must be far inferior to the love of the Creator. As he is the Sovereign, he requires that I love him above all other things; if he will not suffer me to love anything equally with him, much less will he suffer me to love anything above him. You see now what I think it is to love God with all the heart, with all the soul and with all the mind. To love God with all the heart is to love him above all creatures; that is, although creatures are very amiable and dear to me, and that I take great delight in them, yet must I so love them, that I contemn and forsake them when my Lord requires it of me.

To love God with all the soul is to bestow our whole life and body at his pleasure; so that if the love of the creature or any temptation assail us or would overcome us, we may say, I had rather part with all these than forsake my God; whether he cast me off, or destroy me, or whatsoever through his permission shall come upon me, I had rather leave all things than him. Whatsoever I have and am, I will bestow, but him I will not forsake. The soul, in the Scriptures, signifies the life of the body, and whatsoever is done by the five senses—as eating, drinking, sleeping, waking, seeing, hearing, smelling, tasting and whatsoever the soul worketh by the body. To love God with all the strength is for his cause to renounce all the members and limbs of the body, so that one will expose to peril both flesh and body, before he will commit that which is unjust against God. To love God with all the mind is to do nothing but what will please him.

You perceive now what is contained in this commandment of God. Thou, thou, saith he, and that wholly—not thy hands, not thy mouth, not thy knees alone, but every part of thee. They who do these things, as it is said, do truly fulfill it: but no man lives on earth that doth so; yea, we all do otherwise. Wherefore the law doth make us all sinners; not so much as the least jot or point thereof is fulfilled by them that are most holy in this world. No man cleaves with all his heart to God, and leaves all things for his sake. How can it be that we should love God when his will is not settled in our mind? If I love God, I cannot but love his will also. If God send sickness, poverty, shame and ignominy, it is his will, at which we murmur; our minds are carried hither and thither; we bear it very impatiently. We, like this Pharisee and lawyer, lead an honest life outwardly; we worship God, we serve him, we fast, we pray, we behave ourselves in outward appearance justly and holy. But God doth not require that of us, but that we should bend ourselves to do his will with pleasure and love, cheerfully and lovingly. Whatsoever the Lord saith to the lawyer, he saith to us all; to wit, that we have yet done nothing, but that all things remain yet to be done. All men are therefore guilty of death and subject to Satan. All men are liars, vain and filthy; and to whatsoever they pretend, it is worth nothing. We are wise in worldly matters, we scrape together money and goods, we speak fairly before men, and cunningly propound and set forth our case. What doth God care for these things? He requires us to love him with our whole heart, which no man living is able to perform of himself; therefore it is inferred that we are all sinners, but especially those whose life hath a goodly outward show only.

Having discussed the former part of the text, namely, the preaching of the law, now follows the other part, which is the preaching of the Gospel—which declares how we may fulfill the law, and from whence that fulfilling is taken, which we shall learn of the Samaritan.

What doth the lawyer after the Lord had thus dealt with him? He, says the evangelist, willing to justify himself, spake unto the Lord, and asked him, "Who is my neighbor?" He asked not who is my God? As if he said, I owe nothing to God, neither do I want anything of him: yea, it seems to me that I do not owe anything to man; nevertheless, I would be willing to know who is my neighbor. The Lord, answering him, brings forth a good similitude, whereby he declares that we are all neighbors one to another—as well he that giveth a benefit as he that receiveth or needeth one—although by the text it seems to appear that he only is a neighbor who bestows a benefit upon another. But the Scripture makes no difference: sometimes calling him our neighbor who bestows a benefit, and sometimes him that receives it.

By this similitude the Lord inferreth, "Go, and do thou likewise," so that the lawyer had offended not only against God but also against man, and was destitute of love both to God and his neighbor. This wretched man is brought into such a situation that he is found to be altogether evil, even from the head to the feet. How came it to pass that he being so skillful in the Scripture, was not aware of this? He led a pharisaical, hypocritical and counterfeit life, which had no regard to his neighbor or to succor and help others; but sought thereby only glory and honor before men, and thought by negligent and dissolute living to get to heaven. But ye have heard very often that a Christian life consisteth in this: that we deal with faith and the heart in things that pertain to God, but use our life and works toward our neighbors. But we must not wait until our neighbor seeks a benefit and requires something of us; but according to our duty must prevent his asking, and of our own accord offer our liberality to him.

We will now see what is contained in the parable. The Samaritan, in this place, is without doubt our Lord Jesus Christ, who hath declared his love toward God and man. Toward God, in descending from heaven, being made incarnate and fulfilling the will of his Father. Toward man, wherein, after baptism, he began to preach, to work miracles, to heal the sick. Neither was there any work that he did which concerned himself only, but all were directed to his neighbors; being made our minister, when notwithstanding he is above all, and equal with God. But he did all these things knowing that they pleased God, and that it was the will of his Father. When he had fulfilled the commandment that he loved God with all his heart, he committed his life and whatsoever he had to the will of his Father, saying: Father, behold all that I have is thine; I leave for thy sake the glory and honor which I have had among men, yea, and all things, that the world may know how much I love thee.

This is that Samaritan, who, without being desired by prayers, came and fulfilled the law; he alone hath fulfilled it, which praise none can take from him: he alone hath deserved it, and to him only it appertaineth. He, being touched with pity, has compassion on the wounded man, binds up his wounds, brings him to an inn, and provides for him. This pertaineth to us: the man which lieth wounded, beaten, spoiled and half dead, is Adam; yea, and we also. The thieves which wounded and left us in this deplorable situation are the devils. We are not able to help ourselves, and should we be left in this situation, we should die through anguish and distress; our wounds would become festered, and our afflictions exceedingly great.

This excellent parable is set before us to show us what we are, and what is the strength of our reason and free will. If that wretched man had attempted to help himself, his case would have been made worse; he would have hurt himself, he would have opened his wounds anew by exertion, and so would have fallen into greater calamity. Again, if he had been left lying, without assistance, his case would have been the same. So it is when we are left to ourselves; our studies and endeavors amount to nothing. Sundry ways and divers means have been invented to amend our lives, and get to heaven: this man found out this way, another that; whereby innumerable sorts of orders have increased; and letters of indulgences, pilgrimages to Saints, and so forth, which have always made the state of Christianity worse. This is the world, which is represented by this wounded man: he being laden with sins, fainting under a heavy burden and not able to help himself.

But the Samaritan who hath fulfilled the law is perfectly sound and whole. He doth more than either the priest or Levite. He binds up his wounds, pours in oil and wine, sets him upon his own beast, brings him to an inn, makes provision for him, and, when he departs, diligently commends him to the host, and leaves with him sufficient to pay his expenses—none of which either the priest or Levite did. By the priest is signified the holy fathers which flourished before Moses; the Levite is a representation of the priesthood of the Old Testament. All these could do nothing by their works, but passed by like unto this priest and Levite; wherefore, though I had all the good works of Noah, Abraham and all the faithful fathers, they would profit me nothing.

The priest and Levite saw the miserable man lie wounded, but they could not help him; they saw him lie half dead, but could not give him any remedy. The holy fathers saw men drowned and plunged all over in sin; they also felt the sting and anguish thereof, but they could make the case no better. These were the preachers of the law, which shows what the world is: namely, that it is full of sin, and lieth half dead and cannot help itself with its utmost strength and reason. But Christ is that true Samaritan, who is moved with the case of the miserable man: he binds up his wounds, and having great care of him, pours in oil and wine, which is the pure Gospel. He pours in oil when grace is preached; when it is said, O miserable man, this is thy incredulity, this is thy condemnation; thus art thou wounded and sick; but I will show thee a remedy: join thyself to this Samaritan, Christ the Saviour; he will help and succor thee.

The nature of oil, as we know, is to make soft and mollify; so the sweet and gentle preaching of the Gospel makes the heart soft and tender toward God and our neighbors. Sharp wine signifieth the cross of affliction, which forthwith follows: there is no cause for a Christian to seek the cross, for it sooner hangs over his head than he is aware of. As Paul witnesseth, "All that will live godly in Christ Jesus shall suffer persecution" (II Timothy 3:12). This is the cognizance and badge of this King; and he that is ashamed of it, pertaineth not to him. Moreover, the Samaritan puts the wounded man upon his own beast: this is the Lord Jesus Christ, who supports us, and carries us upon his shoulders. There is scarce a more amiable and comfortable passage in the whole Scripture than that where Christ compares himself to a shepherd, who carrieth again the lost sheep upon his shoulders to the flock.

The inn is the state of Christianity in this world, wherein we must abide for a short time; the host is the ministers and preachers of the Gospel, whose charge is to have care of us. This, therefore, is the sum of the text: the kingdom of Christ is a kingdom of mercy and grace; Christ beareth our defects and infirmities; he taketh our sins upon himself, and bears our fall willingly; we daily lie upon his neck, neither is he weary with bearing us. It is the duty of the preachers of this kingdom to comfort consciences, to handle them gently, to feed them with the Gospel, to bear the weak, to heal the sick; they ought fitly to apply the Word according to the need of everyone.

This is the duty of a true bishop and preacher, not to proceed by violence, as is the custom of some bishops at the present day, which vex, torment and cry out, he that will not willingly, shall be compelled to do it. We must in no wise proceed in this manner; but a bishop or preacher ought to behave himself as a healer of the sick, who dealeth very tenderly with them, uttering very loving words, talking gently, and bestowing all his endeavors to do them good. A bishop or minister ought to consider his parish as a hospital, wherein are such as are afflicted with divers kinds of disease. If Christ be thus preached, faith and love come together, which fulfill the commandment of love.

Martin Luther (1483–1546)   *Great preaching began the Reformation, and Martin Luther was surely the greatest of those who mounted the pulpit in the sixteenth century. His returning of Christianity to the Holy Scriptures, and of the faithful to the Word of God, was bound up in his own personality and vision. He translated the Bible into German, wrote music that we sing today and poured out a river of outstanding sermons. During his lifetime he changed the course of Western Europe and, most especially, the Christian Church.*

John Wesley/
The Great Assize

We shall all stand before the judgment seat of Christ.
ROMANS 14:10

How many circumstances concur to raise the awfulness of the present solemnity! The general concourse of people of every age, sex, rank and condition of life, willingly or unwillingly gathered together, not only from the neighboring but from distant parts; criminals, speedily to be brought forth and having no way to escape; officers, waiting in their various posts to execute the orders which shall be given; and the representative of our gracious sovereign, whom we so highly reverence and honor. The occasion, likewise, of this assembly, adds not a little to the solemnity of it: to hear and determine causes of every kind, some of which are of the most important nature; on which depends no less than life or death; death that uncovers the face of eternity! It was, doubtless, in order to increase the serious sense of these things, and not in the minds of the vulgar only, that the wisdom of our forefathers did not disdain to appoint even several minute circumstances of this solemnity. For these also, by means of the eye or ear, may more deeply affect the heart: and when viewed in this light, trumpets, staves, apparel, are no longer trifling or significant, but subservient, in their kind and degree, to the most valuable ends of society.

But, awful as this solemnity is, one far more awful is at hand. For yet a little while, and "we shall all stand before the judgment seat of Christ." "For, as I live, saith the Lord, every knee shall bow to me, and every tongue shall confess to God." And in that day "every one of us shall give account of himself to God."

Had all men a deep sense of this, how effectually would it secure the interests of society! For what more forcible motive can be conceived to the practice of genuine morality, to a steady pursuit of solid virtue, and a

The Great Assize

21

uniform walking in justice, mercy and truth? What could strengthen our hands in all that is good, and deter us from all that is evil, like a strong conviction of this, "The judge standeth at the door," and we are shortly to stand before him?

"God will show signs in the earth beneath," particularly he will "arise to shake terribly the earth." "The earth shall reel to and fro like a drunkard, and shall be removed like a cottage." "There shall be earthquakes" not in divers only but "in all places"; not in one only, or in a few, but in every part of the habitable world, even "such as were not since men were upon the earth, so mighty earthquakes and so great." In one of these "every island shall flee away, and the mountains will not be found."

At the same time, "the Son of man shall send forth his angels" over all the earth; "and they shall gather his elect from the four winds, from one end of heaven to the other." And the Lord himself shall come with clouds, in his own glory, and the glory of his Father, with ten thousand of his saints, even myriads of angels, and shall sit upon the throne of his glory. "And before him shall be gathered all nations, and he shall separate them one from another, and shall set the sheep [the good] on his right hand, and the goats [the wicked] upon the left." Concerning this general assembly it is that the beloved disciple speaks thus: "I saw the dead [all that had been dead], small and great, stand before God. And the books were opened [a figurative expression plainly referring to the manner of proceeding among men], and the dead were judged out of those things which were written in the books, according to their works."

The person by whom God will judge the world is his only-begotten Son, whose "goings forth are from everlasting," "who is God over all, blessed forever." Unto him, being "the out-beaming of his Father's glory, the express image of his Person," the Father "hath committed all judgment, because he is the Son of man"; because, though he was "in the form of God, and thought it not robbery to be equal with God, yet he emptied himself, taking upon him the form of a servant, being made in the likeness of man"; yea, because, "being found in fashion as a man, he humbled himself [yet further], becoming obedient unto death, even the death on the cross. Wherefore God hath highly exalted him," even in his human nature, and "ordained him," as man, to try the children of men, "to be the judge both of the quick and dead," both of those who shall be found alive at his coming and of those who were before gathered to their fathers.

And every man shall there "give an account of his own works"; yea, a full and true account of all that he ever did while in the body, whether it was good or evil.

Nor will all the actions alone of every child of man be then brought to open view, but all their words; seeing "every idle word which men shall speak, they shall give account thereof in the day of judgment"; so that "by the words" as well as works, "thou shalt be justified; and by thy words thou shalt be condemned." Will not God then bring to light every circumstance also that accompanied every word or action, and if not altered the nature, yet lessened or increased the goodness or badness of them? And how easy is this to him who is "about our bed, and about our path, and spieth out all our ways"? We know "the darkness is no darkness to him, but the night shineth as the day."

"Then the King will say to them upon his right hand, 'Come ye, blessed of my Father. For I was hungry, and ye gave me meat; thirsty, and ye gave me drink; I was a stranger, and ye took me in; naked, and ye clothed me.'" In like manner, all the good they did upon earth will be recited before men and angels; whatsoever they had done either in word or deed, in the name or for the sake of the Lord Jesus. All their good desires, intentions, thoughts, all their holy dispositions, will also be then remembered; and it will appear that though they were unknown or forgotten among men, yet God noted them in his book. All their sufferings, likewise, for the name of Jesus, and for the testimony of a good conscience, will be displayed, unto their praise from the righteous judge, their honor before saints and angels, and the increase of that "far more exceeding and eternal weight of glory."

After the righteous are judged, the King will turn to them upon his left hand, and they shall also be judged, every man according to his works. But not only their outward works will be brought into the account, but all the evil words which they have ever spoken, yea, all the evil desires, affections, tempers which have or have had a place in their souls, and all the evil thoughts or designs which were ever cherished in their hearts. The joyful sentence of acquittal will then be pronounced upon those upon the right hand, the dreadful sentence of condemnation upon those on the left, both of which must remain fixed and unmovable as the throne of God.

It remains only to apply the preceding considerations to all who are here before God. And are we not directly led so to do by the present solemnity, which so naturally points us to that day when the Lord will judge the world in righteousness? This, therefore, by reminding us of that more awful season, may furnish many lessons of instruction. May God write them on all our hearts.

How beautiful are the feet of all those who are sent by the wise and gracious providence of God to execute justice on earth, to defend the injured and punish the wrongdoer! Are they not the ministers of God to us for good, the grand supporters of the public tranquillity, the patrons of innocence and virtue, the security of all our temporal blessings? And does not every one of these represent not only an earthly prince, but the Judge of the earth? Him, whose "name is written upon his thigh, King of kings, and Lord of lords"? Oh that all these sons of the right hand of the Most High may be holy as he is holy, wise with the wisdom that sitteth by his throne, like him who is the eternal Wisdom of the Father. No respecter of persons, as he is none, but rendering to every man according to his works: like him inflexibly, inexorably just, though pitiful and of tender mercy! So shall they be terrible, indeed, to them that do evil, as not bearing the sword in vain. So shall the laws of our land have their full use and due honor, and the throne of our king be still established in righteousness.

John Wesley (1703–1791) *John Wesley was raised in the tradition of the Church of England. Educated at Oxford, he held early assignments as pastor in America before returning to England to lead, with his brother, Charles, the resurgence of the Christian faith. After 1738 when he experienced a clear conversion, he devoted himself to organizing the Methodist Church. His impact on England was staggering. Wesley often preached out of doors, in open fields, before the shafts of coal mines, along docks and warehouses. He brought the Word of God wherever people would gather.*

Henry Ward Beecher/
War and Peace

And many people shall go and say, Come ye, and let us go up to the
mountain of the Lord, to the house of the God of Jacob; and he will
teach us of his ways, and we will walk in his paths: for out of Zion
shall go forth the law, and the word of the Lord from Jerusalem.
And he shall judge among the nations, and shall rebuke many
people: and they shall beat their swords into ploughshares, and
their spears into pruninghooks: nation shall not lift up sword
against nation, neither shall they learn war any more.

ISAIAH 2:3, 4

DOES it not seem strange to you, when you look back upon the long line of nations, civilized or semicivilized, and read their literature, their poetry and their philosophies, and see on every side only a spirit of rivalry and of military glory—does it not, then, seem strange that the one sweet voice that is lifted up like a chant or a hymn, through all the ages, was the voice of the old Hebrew people? They were themselves not unwarlike; they were a people of fierce passions, whom it required ages to discipline; and yet their prophets, instead of being the leaders of the people to believe that war was the favorite pastime of the gods, and that it was the mark of honor among men to be eminent in military skill and prowess, taught that when God should rule, the earth would be at peace; and that when the ways of God should be observed, and the law should go forth from Zion, it would be then the time when all people should turn from military occupations, and bestow themselves upon remunerative industrial and civil pursuits.

This passage which I have read is the exultant prediction that a day shall come to pass when the nations shall be governed by God's will. That is, national laws and national policies shall yet be controlled, not by the lowest passions of mankind as largely as hitherto, but by the highest moral sentiments. A day is coming when public sentiment shall demand that public men shall be nobler morally; when all public laws shall be couched and framed in the highest moral interest of the whole; and when the policy of nations shall conform to the beneficent policy of Divine providence. When that shall take place, there will be universal peace; and this peace will turn the resources of nations into wealth-producing channels.

The time has come, or at least is now near, when there shall be an organization of nations for the peace of the world. We have an organization in every town or village in this land by which no one man is allowed to let loose his passions as he pleases. The good of every citizen in the town requires that the lawless forces of men shall be regulated. The law undertakes to do for men what in a savage or barbarous condition they undertake to do for themselves. But the time is coming when nations shall organize for the same purposes that villages and towns do now, and when it shall be as unlawful for a nation to let loose its avaricious and vindictive desires in the community of nations, without their leave, as it is for a man to let loose his personal passions in the midst of civilized men, without law, and without the leave of a magistrate.

I do not believe that the use of physical force to maintain the great moral ends of justice, liberty and national life can yet be dispensed with. The time is coming when it can be dispensed with, but that time has not come yet. I agree with the most advanced men that the ideal of Christianity is absolute peace; I believe that the ideal of Christianity is to suffer evil rather than inflict evil; but Christianity has not yet come to its ideal. You cannot bring communities up by the ears. You may say to the individual man, "You are bound to develop to the uttermost"; but he cannot develop thus all at once. Since God ordained that men and society should come up by growth, you cannot force them up. Growth, of necessity, requires time. The ideal of Christianity is final and universal peace, and it is the duty of nations to dispense with physical force as fast and as far as possible; but you cannot dispense with it suddenly, and disband all armies and police organizations, and leave the world to think that there is no government. To do that would be to leave the world to brutality, and make the tyrant more tyrannical, and the lawless more lawless. Until society is stronger in the direction of the social, intellectual and moral elements, we must use an inferior instrument. We must use the hand till the head and the heart are right. Christianity is so large that we are to grow into it gradually; but as fast as possible nations should take hold of its principles.

I take the ground that the time has come when by suitable efforts the war spirit may be abated, and men in the main set against it. The time has come when the forces of nations may be so combined as to reduce the temptations of war. Nations can be so organized as to prevent any unruly member from going to war, as rightfully as municipal bodies in towns and villages can prevent any citizen from going into a fight at the expense of the peace of the whole community. The peace of the world, in other words, is not to be subject to the whim or caprice of any single nation, any more than the peace of a nation is to be subject to the whim or caprice of any man or body of men in it.

We have seen dueling go out of practice almost entirely. It has been thought that two men might go out and settle their differences by the use of deadly weapons, but that idea is fast going out of date. It is thought that two nations have a right to fight national duels to settle their difficulties; but this sort of dueling is just as wrong as the other, and just as really and as easily vincible. There should be, therefore, such steps taken as, for instance, the organization of a national congress, for enacting international law, and administering that law between nation and nation. At present the law of nations is crude, and a large part of the ground between nation and nation is not covered by national enactments. But we have come to a time when I think we might begin, at last, to form a national congress, that shall enact laws which shall be for the good of all nations, and by which all nations alike shall be bound. There are some international laws, which pertain more largely to commerce than to anything else; but I think the time has come for a more thorough work through the organization of a national congress. There must be a determination to so educate the whole people that the current of public sentiment will run in that direction. If the people remain ignorant on the subject, or indifferent to it, it will be in vain to undertake to institute and carry out this reform; but if the people are instructed, and aroused to feel that their interests lie in peace, then vox populi will be vox Dei—a proverb which has been as little understood and as much abused as any proverb in the world. If by saying that the voice of the people is the voice of God, you mean that the people have the power to know a truth as God has power to know it, that is hideously false; for the vast mass of the common people have almost no power to comprehend the truth. But when the truth is found out and made known to the great mass of the common people, and they accept it, and lift up their voice, and give it power, then the voice of the people is indeed the voice of a heaven full of gods. And we must get the power of the people to enforce the laws which may be enacted by an international congress.

On the church of God rests, primarily, this work. I do not undertake to say, I am far from saying, that a church should turn aside from its work of individual evangelization, of preaching the Gospel from man to man, in the society where it exists; yet the church universal has a large sphere. It is bound to stand foremost in making reformatory laws, in tempering brutal penalties, and in infusing sympathy and love into men, instead of separating them by sharp theological prejudices. The church of God, as a representative of Christ, must go forth, not to preach will, nor even conscience, but a Gospel which shall employ that will and that conscience in the world as instruments by which to secure peace and harmony among nations, as well as individuals. God's church is hereafter to promote more widely and efficiently those institutions and laws and governments which shall diffuse through civil economy everywhere the essential spirit of humanity.

Henry Ward Beecher (1813–1887) *A powerful and persuasive man, Beecher preached at Plymouth Congregational Church in Brooklyn for forty years. He championed many causes and concerns within the national life. A colorful orator, his opposition to slavery was well-known through his voice as well as his pen. The famous Lyman Beecher Lectures on Preaching, at Yale, honored his father.*

Phillips Brooks/The Egyptians Dead upon the Seashore

And Israel saw the Egyptians dead upon the seashore.

EXODUS 14:30

I T was the Red Sea which the children of Israel had crossed dry-shod, "which the Egyptians essaying to do were drowned." The parted waves had swept back upon the host of the pursuers. The tumult and terror, which had rent the air, had sunk into silence, and all that the escaped people saw was here and there a poor drowned body beaten up upon the bank, where they stood with the great flood between them and the land of their long captivity and oppression. It meant everything to the Israelites. It was not only a wonderful deliverance for them, but a terrible calamity for their enemies. It was the end of a frightful period in their history. These were the men under whose arrogant lordship they had chafed and wrestled. These hands had beaten them. These eyes they had seen burning with scorn and hate. A thousand desperate rebellions, which had not set them free, must have come up in their minds. Sometimes they had been successful for a moment; sometimes they had disabled or disarmed their tyrants; but always the old tyranny had closed back upon them more pitilessly than before. But now all that was over; whatever else they might have to meet, the Egyptian captivity was at an end. Each dead Egyptian face on which they looked was token and witness to them that the power of their masters over them had perished. They stood and gazed at the hard features, set and stern, but powerless in death, and then turned their faces to the desert, and to whatever new unknown experiences God might have in store for them.

It is a picture, I think, of the way in which experiences in this world become finished, and men pass on to other experiences which lie beyond. In some moods it seems to us as if nothing finally gets done. When we are in the thick of an experience, we find it hard to believe or to imagine that the time will ever come when that experience shall be wholly a thing of the past and we shall have gone out beyond it into other fields. When we open our eyes morning after morning and find the old struggle on which we closed our eyes last night awaiting us; when we open our door each day only to find our old enemy upon the doorstep; when all our habits and thoughts and associations have become entwined and colored with some tyrannical necessity, which, however it may change the form of its tyranny, will never let us go—it grows so hard as almost to appear impossible for us to anticipate that that dominion ever is to disappear, that we shall ever shake free our wings and leave behind the earth to which we have been chained so long. On the long sea voyage the green earth becomes inconceivable. To the traveller in the mountains or the desert it becomes very difficult to believe that he shall some day reach the beach and sail upon the sea. But the day comes, nevertheless. Some morning we go out to meet the old struggle, and it is not there. Some day we listen for the old voice of our old tyrant, and the air is still. At last the day does come when our Egyptian, our old master, who has held our life in his hard hands, lies dead upon the seashore; and looking into his cold face we know that our life with him is over, and turn our eyes and our feet eastward to a journey in which he shall have no part. Things do get done, and when they do, when anything is really finished, then come serious and thoughtful moments in which we ask ourselves whether we have let that which we shall know no longer, do for us all that it had the power to do, whether we are carrying out of the finished experience that which it has all along been trying to give to our characters and souls.

For while we leave everything behind in time, it is no less true that nothing is wholly left behind. All that we ever have been or done is with us in some power and consequence of it until the end. Is it not most significant that these children of Israel, whom we behold today looking the dead Egyptians in the face and then turning their backs on Egypt, are known and appealed to ever afterwards as the people whom the Lord their God had brought "out of the land of Egypt, out of the house of bondage"? In every most critical and sacred moment of their history they are bidden to recall their old captivity. When God most wants them to know him, it is as the God of their deliverance that he declares himself. The unity of life is never lost. There must not be any waste. How great and gracious is the economy of life which it involves! Neither to dwell in any experience always, nor to count any experience as if it had not been, but to leave the forms of our experiences behind and to go forth from them clothed in their spiritual power, which is infinitely free and capable of new activities—this is what God is always teaching us is possible, and tempting us to do. To him who does it come the two great blessings of a growing life, faithfulness and liberty—faithfulness in each moment's task, and liberty to enter through the gates beyond which lies the larger future. "Well done, good servant: thou hast been faithful over a few things. Enter thou into the joy of thy Lord."

All this is true, but it is very general. What I want to do this morning is to ask you to think about the special experience to which our text refers, and consider how one truth is true of that, and of what corresponds to it in all men's lives. It was the end of a struggle which had seemed interminable. The hostility of Hebrew and Egyptian had gone on for generations. However their enmity may be disguised or hidden, the tyrant and the slave are always foes. If hope had ever lived, it had died long ago. Patient endurance, grim submission, with desperate revolt whenever the tyranny grew most tyrannical—these had seemed to be the only virtues left to the poor serfs. Not to be demoralized and ruined by their servitude, to keep their self-respect, to be sure still that they were Abraham's children and that Abraham's God still cared for them, patience and fortitude—these must have been the exhortations which they addressed to their poor souls as they toiled on in the brickyard or by the river.

It does not prove anything, if you please, about our present life, but it certainly sets us to asking new questions about it, perhaps to believing greater things concerning it, when in our typical story we behold all this changed. Behold, the day came when the chains were broken and the slaves went free. Are, then, our slaveries as hopeless as they seem? Are we condemned only to struggle with our enemies in desperate fight, and shall we not hope to see them some day dead like the Egyptians on the seashore?

Surely it is good for us to ask that question, for nothing is more remarkable than the way in which, both in public and personal life, men accept the permanence of conditions which are certainly someday to disappear. The whole of history, which teaches us that mankind does conquer its enemies and see its tyrants by and by lying dead on the seashore, often appears to have no influence with the minds of men, all absorbed as they are in what seems a hopeless struggle. But look around! Where are the Egyptians which used to hold the human body and the human soul in slavery? Have you ever counted? The divine right of rulers, the dominion of the priesthood over the intellect and conscience, the ownership of man by man, the accepted inequality of human lots, the complacent acquiescence in false social states, the use of torture to extort the needed lie, the praise of ignorance as the safeguard of order, the irresponsible possession of power without corresponding duty, the pure content in selfishness—do you realize, in the midst of the cynical and despairing talk by which we are surrounded, can you realize, how these bad tyrants of the human race have lost their power over large regions of human life? They are dead Egyptians. Abominable social theories which fifty years ago—in the old days of slavery, in the old days of accepted pauperism—men stated as melancholy but hopeless truisms are now the discarded rubbish of antiquity, kept as they keep the racks and thumbscrews in old castle dungeons for a tourists' show.

Is there anything more wonderful than the way in which men today are daring to think of the abolition and disappearance of those things which they used to think were as truly a part of human life as the human body, or the ground on which it walks? Ah, my friends, you only show

how you are living in the past, not in the present, when you see nothing but material for sport in the beliefs of ardent men and brave societies which set before themselves and humankind the abolition of poverty, the abolition of war, the abolition of ignorance, the abolition of disease, the sweeping away of mere money competition as the motive power of life, the dethronement of fear from the high place which it has held among—aye, almost above—all the ruling and shaping powers of the destiny of man. I recognize in many a frantic cry the great growing conviction of mankind that nothing which ought not to be need be. I hear in many hoarse, ungracious tones man's utterance of his conviction that much which his fathers thought was meant to cultivate their patience by submission is meant also to cultivate their courage by resistance till it dies. "The Egyptian must die." That is the assurance which is possessing the heart of man.

When any evil does finally perish, then there is something infinitely pathetic in the remembrance of the way in which mankind for generations accepted it as inevitable and drew out of its submission to it such blessing and education as pure submission to the inevitable is able to bestow. The poor man, who thinks his poverty, and the ignorance and servitude which his poverty entails, all right, comforts himself by saying that God made him poor in order that he might be patient and learn to possess his soul in self-respect. By and by when the iniquity of the system under which he has lived gives way and he finds himself admitted to the full rights and duties of a man—what then? Infinitely pathetic, as it seems to me, is the recognition that he wins of the great love and wisdom with which God would not let even that darkness be entirely fruitless of light; but while He was making ready for the fuller life of which the poor man never dreamed, at the same time fed him in the wilderness with manna which the wilderness alone could give, so that no delight of freedom to which he afterwards should come need make him wholly curse or utterly despise the regions of darkness and restraint through which he came to reach it.

Is it not thus that we may always explain at least a part, the best part, of that strange longing with which the world, when it has entered into any higher life, still finds itself looking back to the lower life out of which it has passed? It is not properly regret. It is not a desire to turn back into the darkness. The age of real faith does not covet again the chains of superstition. The world at peace does not ask to be shaken once more by the earthquakes of war. But faith does feel the beauty of complete surrender which superstition kept for its sole spiritual virtue; and peace, with its diffused responsibility, is kindled at the thought of heroic and unquestioning obedience which the education of war produced. Still, let superstition and war lie dead. We will not call them back to life; but we will borrow their jewels of silver and jewels of gold as we go forth into the wilderness to worship our God with larger worship. Do you not feel this in all the best progress? Do you not see it in the eyes of mankind, in the depths of the eyes of mankind always, as it turns away from the dead forms of its old masters and goes forth into the years to be;

the hoarded power of the past glowing beneath the satisfaction of the present and the fiery hope of the unknown future?

Ah, well, there is always something fascinating in thus dwelling on the fortunes of the world at large, peering, like fortune-telling gipsies, into the open palm which she holds out to all of us. It is fascinating, and is not without its profit. But just as, I suppose, the shrewdest gipsy may often be the most recklessly foolish in the government of her own life, so it is good for us always to turn speedily and ask how the principles which we have been wisely applying to the world, apply to that bit of the world which we are set to live.

Do we believe—you and I—in the death of our Egyptians? What is your Egyptian? Some passion of the flesh or of the mind?—for the mind has its tyrannical passions as well as the flesh. Years, years ago, you became its captive. Perhaps you cannot at all remember when. Perhaps, like these children of Israel, you were born into its captivity. It was your father, or your father's fathers, that first became its slaves. When you first came to know yourself, its chains were on your limbs. As you grew older you knew that it was slavery, but it was such a part of all you were and all you did that you accepted it. That has not made you cease to struggle with it, but it has made you accept struggle hopelessly, as something never to be outgrown and left behind. You have looked forward into the stretch of years, and in prophetic imagination you have seen yourself an old man still wrestling with the tyranny of your covetousness or your licentiousness or your prejudice, getting it down, planting your foot upon its neck, even compelling it to render you, out of the unceasing struggle, new supplies of character; absolutely fixed and determined never to give up the fight until you die—to die fighting. All this is perfectly familiar. Countless noble and patient souls live in such self-knowledge and consecration. But there comes something vastly beyond all these, when the soul dares to believe that its enemy may die, that the lust or the prejudice or the covetousness may absolutely pass out of existence, and the nature be absolutely free—sure no doubt to meet other enemies and to struggle till the end, but done with that enemy forever, with that Egyptian finally dead upon the seashore.

When that conviction takes possession of a man, his fight is a new thing. The courage not of desperation, but of certain hope, fills every limb and gives its force to every blow. The victory which the soul believes is coming is here already as a power for its own attainment.

Has a man a right to any such hope as that, or is it the mere dream of an optimistic sermon? I dare appeal to you and ask you whether, in your own experience, God has not sometimes given you the right to such a hope. Are there no foes of your youth which you have conquered and left dead, passing on to greater battles? I am not speaking of the vices which you have miserably left behind, merely because the taste is exhausted and the strength has failed—vices which you would take up again if you were once more twenty years old. Those are poor victories. Those are no victories at all. But I mean this: whether you are a better or a worse man now than you were twenty years ago. Are there not at least some temptations to which you yielded then to which you know that you can never yield again? Are there not some meannesses which you once thought glorious which now you know are mean? Are there no places where you once stumbled where now you know you can walk firm? I pity you if there are not. Other enemies which you then never dreamed of, you have since encountered, but those enemies are done with. The Moabites and Midianites are before you and around you, but the Egyptians are dead. And in their death your right and duty are to read the prophecy of the death of every power which stands up between you and the Promised Land.

The appeal is not only to experience. It is to the first Christian truth concerning man. I have preached it to you a thousand times. I will preach it again and again until the end. The great truth of Christianity, the great truth of Christ, is that sin is unnatural and has no business in a human life. The birth of Christ proclaimed that in one tone; his cross proclaimed it in another. And that which is unnatural is not by any necessity permanent. The struggle of all nature is against the unnatural, to dislodge it and cast it out. That beautiful struggle pervades the world. It is going on in every clod of earth, in every tree, in every star and in the soul of man. First to declare and then to strengthen that struggle in the soul of man was the work of Christ. That work still lingers and fails of full completion, but its power is present in the world. When he takes possession of a nature he quickens that struggle into life. No longer can that nature think itself doomed to evil. Intensely sensitive to feel the presence of evil as he never felt it before, the Christian man instantly and intensely knows that evil is a stranger and an intruder in his life. The wonder is not that it should some day be cast out; the wonder is that it should ever have come in. The victory promised in the sinless Son of man is already potentially attained in the intense conception of its naturalness. This is Christianity.

Phillips Brooks (1835–1893) *Probably most noted for his carol, "O Little Town of Bethlehem," Phillips Brooks was rector of Trinity Church, Boston, in 1869 and later Bishop of Massachusetts, in 1891. Students continue to study his Yale Lectures on Preaching. Dozens of volumes of his sermons were published during the years he preached.*

Alexander Maclaren/The Lord's Supper, the Sample of the Christian Life

This do in remembrance of me.
I CORINTHIANS 11:24

Whatsoever ye do, in word or deed, do all in the name of the Lord Jesus.
COLOSSIANS 3:17

One of the saddest things about the Christian life is that it seems to ourselves to be split up into two separate parts, which we find it very hard, if not altogether impossible, to unite. We feel as if we lived in two different worlds. We have our moments of devotion and our hours of utter worldliness. We begin, for instance, the day with thankful acknowledgment to God for his mercies; and howsoever sincere that may be, we know too well that it is going to be followed by a day of unthankful reception of them. We kneel down in the morning and ask God to guide us; and then we go out into the world and take guidance of idleness and vanity and selfishness. We confess our sins and ask forgiveness; and then we rise from our knees and take our fellow servant by the throat and say, "Pay me that thou owest!" In a word, on the clear mountaintop we stand in the light of God's face; and then we come down into the plain, and the earthly vapours shut out the blue. I suppose the best of us feel this apparently inevitable severing of our lives into two unlike portions.

Is that distinction, then, between sacred and profane, a valid one? Is there any reason why a man's prayers should be more devout than his business? Is there any need why the sanctity of life should be curdled together, as it were, into Sundays and acts of special worship, and not be diffused through the whole of life? Look at these two passages: one of them taken out of the words for the institution of the holiest act of

Christ's church, "This do in remembrance of me"; the other of them taken out of a series of plain, simple practical directions to people, to do their work rightly in ordinary life—and yet the two commands are precisely the same. "Whatsoever ye do in word or deed, do all in the name of the Lord Jesus," is exactly the same thing as saying, "This do in remembrance of me." And surely it is a very beautiful and very significant fact that thus the very same consecration is claimed for the most trivial acts of daily life, a hundred times repeated, as is claimed for that sacred communion of the body and blood of our Lord Jesus Christ. I need not dwell here, in passing, upon the complete refutation of all notions of an awful and separated sacredness as attaching to the act of the commemoration of our Lord's death, which such a parallel, as is evidently in the Apostle's mind here, gives. I pass that altogether. My purpose now is only to try to set before you, in a few thoughts, the relation which the ordinance of the Lord's Supper, as the commemoration of the death of Christ, bears to the common acts of our common life. It is just this. The Communion of the Lord's Supper is meant to be *a sample of, and not an exception to, our common days; and in the rite there lies a mighty power to make the whole of the rest of life like itself.* These are the two points I wish to present to you this morning. The former of them is the one on which I want to dwell at the greatest length—the parallel betwixt the daily life of a Christian man and this sacred act of communion at the table of our Lord.

In the first place, I would notice that all the objects around us are to be regarded by us as being symbols and memorials of our Lord. Bread and wine are very common things; the act of eating and drinking is not a very elevated one; a supper table is by no means a very holy place. And when Christ selected such a place, such a time, such an act, such common materials, as being the fitting embodiments of the grandest and most precious truths of his Gospel, in addition to all the other things that he did by such a selection, he did this furthermore—he showed us that all material things as well as that bread and wine which he chose for the special purpose were fitted and were intended to impart the same symbolic and memorial teaching which these two are specially selected to do. The bread and the wine have an adaptation to speak to us about Christ's flesh and Christ's blood, about Christ's sacrifice, about eating and drinking it as the sustenance of our spirits; but they are not more adapted—or at least not in a different way, though in a different degree—than the rest of the common objects that lie round about us.

I need not at all seek to enter on the reasons upon which the statement rests, that all created things are to be the symbols and memorials of our Lord. There is one mind in the universe, one Spirit working through all things; and all creatures, on their various platforms and in their different degrees, receive the impression of the same will, and are set to testify of the same Lord. The unity of the Maker, the all-pervading influence of one Divine Spirit, make everything sacred, and make the whole world a series of manifold meanings, and put every object to witness to some Divine truth. The whole universe stands here not only to say to us,

"Look, there are works of design, there must be a designer; there are certain qualities which you may infer as existing in the Maker of all these things"; but to say to us, "Look, there, in these creatures, is a mirror in which you may see—not only capable of being inferred, but shadowed and typified—the Divine Spirit that made them, the laws of his being, and the revelation of himself." All things that are, are the shadow and image of heavenly things. The highest lesson they can teach is to remind us of, and to symbolize for us, the uncreated and everlasting Wisdom and Love and Beauty which lie beneath them and ripple up through them.

But I need not dwell on this. The language of every nation under heaven has confessed it. The teaching of all the wise has embodied it. The natural impulse of us all is to find shadows and symbols of spiritual life in natural existence. He who spake as never man spake, spake in parables, and, knowing all things, took bread and said, "This is my body." Surely, besides all the other purposes of that institution there is this also to teach us to see everywhere emblems of him. Every day we walk amidst the "outward and visible signs of an inward and spiritual grace," and in that meaning of the word "sacrament," the true and Christian view of this wonderful world is that it is all one great sacrament. All the elements stand as types of spiritual things. The sunshine is to speak to us of "the light of the world," the life of men. The wind blows, an emblem of that Spirit, which, though he comes low and soft as befits a comforter, can rise and wax into a tempest against all "the lofty and lifted up." The water speaks of the stream of life and the drink for thirsty souls, and the fire of his purity and of his wrath. All objects are consecrated to him. The trees of the field, in a thousand places, speak of the "root of David," and the vine of which we are all branches. The everlasting mountains are his "righteousness," the mighty deep his "judgments." All the processes of nature have been laid hold of by him. The gentle dew falls a promise, and the lashing rain forebodes another storm, when many a sand-built house shall be swept away. Every spring is a prophecy of the resurrection of the dead, every harvest a promise of the coming of his kingdom and the blessed issues of all service for him. All living things, in like manner, testify of him. In that sense, as in others, he is lord over the fish of the sea, and over the fowls of the air and over the beasts of the field. The "eagle stirring up its nest," the "hen gathering her chickens under her wings," speak of him, his functions and his relations to us. The "Lion of the tribe of Judah" and the "Lamb of God" were his names.

All occupations of men, in like manner, are consecrated to reveal him. He laid his hand upon the sower and the vine-dresser, upon the ploughman and the shepherd, upon the merchant and the warrior, upon the king and the prophet and the judge, upon the teacher and the lawgiver, as being emblems of himself. All relations between men testify of him. Father and mother, brother and friend, husband, parent and children—they are all consecrated for this purpose. In a word, every act of our life sets forth some aspect of our Lord and of our relation to him, from the moment when we open our eyes in the morning—as those do who, having slept the sleep of sin, awake unto righteousness; all through the busy day, when our work may speak to us of his that worketh continually, and our rest may prophesy to us of the "rest that remaineth for the people of God"; and our journeyings may tell of the journey of the soul to God, and our home may testify of the home which is above the skies—up to the hour when night falls, and sleep, the image of Death, speaks to us of the last solemn moment, when we shall close the eyes of our body on earth, to open those of our soul on the realities of eternity; when we shall no more "see through a glass darkly, but face to face." All things and all acts and this whole wonderful universe proclaim to us the Lord our Father, Christ our love, Christ our hope, our portion and our joy! Oh brethren, if you would know the meaning of the world, read Christ in it. If you would see the beauty of earth, take it for a prophet of something higher than itself. If you would pierce beneath the surface and know the sanctities that are all about us, remember that when he took bread and wine for a memorial of him, he did not profane thereby, but consecrated thereby, all that he left out, and asserted the same power and the same prerogative, in lower degree, but as really and truly, for everything which the loving eye should look upon, for everything which the believing heart should apprehend. All is sacred. The world is the temple of God. Everywhere there are symbols and memorials of the living God.

Once more: not only are all objects around us regarded as being memorials of him, but every act of our life is to be done from the same motive as that Holy Communion. "This do in remembrance of me," or, as Paul expresses it, "discerning the Lord's body." Do this, not only because you are in danger of forgetting, but do this because you remember. Do this, not only in order that your reminiscences may be strengthened, but do it because they are strong. Seeing the Lord's body, discerning his presence, loving that which you discern—do this! And, in like manner, "Whatsoever ye do, in word or deed, do all in the name of the Lord Jesus." Do all, that is to say, for the sake of the character, as revealed to you, of him whom you love; do it all, giving thanks unto God and the Father by him. And then, in the parallel passage at the close of the same chapter, "Whatsoever ye do, do it heartily," that is one principle; and next, as the foundation of all real heartiness, do it "as to the Lord." This is the foundation, and the limitation as well; for it is only when we "do it heartily, as to the Lord," that earnestness is kept from degenerating into absorption, and that a man, whilst working with all his might and "diligent in business" shall also be "fervent in spirit." The motive is the same; in the Communion it is the remembrance of the Lord, in the ordinary life it is "in the name of the Lord Jesus." Brethren, is that sacred motive one which you and I keep for select occasions, and for what we call special acts of worship? I am afraid that the most of Christian people do with that divine reason for work, "the love of Christ constraineth me," as the old Franks (to use a strange illustration) used to do with their long-haired kings—they keep them in the palace at all ordinary times, give them no power over the government of the kingdom, only now and then bring them out to grace a procession, and then take them back again into their reverential impotence. That is very like what Christian people do, to a very large extent, with that which ought to be the rule of all their life and the motive of all their work. We sit down to that communion, and we do it "in the name of the Lord Jesus"; we commemorate him there. When we come to pray, we speak to him and in his name. Our high tides of devotion do not come so often as the tides of the sea, and then for the rest of our time there is the long stretch of foul, oozy, barren beach when the waters are out, and all is desolation and deadness. This is not what a Christian man ought to be. There is no action of life which is too great to bow to the influence of "This do in remembrance of me"; and there is no action of life which is too small to be magnified, glorified, turned into a solemn sacrament, by the operation of the same motive. Are we doing that, Christian men— living on one principle from Sunday morning to Saturday night? Or are we having one principle for Sunday and another principle for Monday; one principle for the ordinary tenor of our uneventful days and another principle for the crises and the solemn times? Do you and I keep our religion as princes do their crown jewels—only wearing them on festive occasions, and have we another dress for weekdays and working days? Do we keep our love of Christ here in our pews, with our hymnbooks and our hassocks? Or do we take it out into the street and the marketplace with us, and work it out day by day, hour by hour, in patient endurance, in loyal love, in simple faith, finding that there is nothing little if Christ's name be crossed over it, and nothing too great if it be approached in his strength.

Alexander Maclaren (1826–1910) *This Scottish Baptist preacher served a distinguished pulpit for nearly forty-five years. His sermons demonstrate the style that made him famous as a professor as well as a preacher.*

Charles Edward Jefferson/
The Man at Bethesda

A certain man was there, which had an infirmity thirty and eight years.

JOHN 5:5

THIRTY-EIGHT years is a long time. It is a long time to any man. It is a longer time to a man who is sick. And to a sick man who has no friends, it is longer still. To the man at the pool of Bethesda, time had become interminable. All days to him were alike, chill and drab and hopeless.

Strange to say, no one had ever seen this man. For years he had lain at one of the prominent centers of Jerusalem. Men constantly passed the spot where he was lying, but one one ever saw him. Merchants and traders, vinedressers and shepherds, scholars and church officials—the keen-eyed men of their day and generation—came and went, but not one of them ever saw this man. This was because every man was thinking of himself. One had bought a piece of ground, another had bought five yoke of oxen, another had married a wife, and so none of them had time to come to this man's assistance. And that is why they could not see him. We do not readily see a man who is likely to stop us when we are in a hurry. He was invisible even to the crowd of invalids in the midst of whom he lay. His fellow sufferers, as they hobbled or shuffled by him, did not see him, for their eyes were fixed upon the bubbling water which was to bring them swift relief. Sickness does not always open the heart and refine the spirit; it may close the one and dull the other. Invalidism is a soil in which the flowers of paradise sometimes grow with marvelous luxuriance and celestial bloom, but just as often it is the soil in which flourish brambles and briers and all the poison weeds of an abnormal selfishness. The sick men at Jerusalem had organized their life around the principle which lay at the foundation of the civilization of their day.

Every man for himself: that was their motto. And the reason why no invalid saw this hopeless cripple was because he was at the rear end of the procession. Year after year the blind and the halt and the withered, like so many priests and Levites, passed by on the other side, and no good Samaritan ever came.

It is not a pleasant picture and yet we ought to look at it, for it gives us a bird's-eye view of the world which Jesus came to save. To the Hebrews, God had sent prophets in a long succession, teaching them the ways of mercy; but the servants, one after another, had been killed, and the husbandmen of the vineyard had refused to bring forth fruit. The episode at the pool of Bethesda is an awful commentary on the moral degradation of the Hebrew people. A sick man lies for years within the sight of water which he believes will heal him, and in all the great and pious city there is not one hand reached out for his relief. Day after day, week after week, month after month, the sacrifices and anthems and prayers of an elaborate worship went on in the temple, but not a man in all the priesthood seemed to know that there was a brother man a few yards away who had something against him. While the fire was kept burning on the temple altar, the fire of hope in a human heart, the divinest fire on earth, was left to flicker feebly and at last go out. The man at the end of the procession lay in darkness and the shadow of death.

But in the fullness of time on a never-to-be-forgotten day, a man comes down to the pool of Bethesda who has a genius for seeing men. Running his swift glance over the faces of the crowd, his eyes rest at last on the wan face of the man at the end of the procession. He looks at him; he comes toward him; he speaks to him; he asks him a question. The man pours out the dismal story of his woe, but before the last dark syllable has died on the air the man is on his feet—so swiftly has infinite mercy come to his relief.

The story is significant because illustrative of the disposition and habit of the world's Redeemer. What he did at Bethesda he always did, and does and will forever do. How large a part of all his public career can be covered by this picture of Bethesda! "The Son of Man is come to seek and to save that which was lost." "They that are whole have no need of a physician, but they that are sick." "I come to call not the righteous, but sinners, to repentance." So he said and says, and will say forever. He began his ministry by holding up an ideal sketched by Isaiah's master pen, and said to the people who knew him best, "This day is the Scripture fulfilled in your ears. For the spirit of the Lord is upon me because he has anointed me to minister to the world's neglected." Strange to say, this announcement of his program stirred up opposition at the very start. But he never wavered or turned back. He said he would preach the Gospel to the poor and he did it. The poor were the victims of the cruelty and scorn of the rich. He befriended them. There were men who were morally and spiritually poor who had lost treasure in comparison with which a purse is but trash. He was especially kind to these. The poorest people in all Palestine were the

Samaritans. For four hundred years they had been ostracized and hated by the Jews. The capital of Samaria was called a city of fools. A Samaritan was not considered so good as a dog. For many generations the Samaritans had been steadily ignored. A Samaritan was at the end of the procession, and so it was to a Samaritan that the first clear disclosure of his Messiahship was made. The Samaritan chosen to receive the revelation was not a man, but a woman, for a Samaritan woman was lower down in the scale than a Samaritan man. She was nothing but a toy or a slave, in whose soul the rabbis had no interest.

And so Jesus preached his Gospel first of all to a Samaritan woman. She was not a lady, but a jaded, ignorant woman, mentally unfurnished and morally bankrupt. She had neither education nor character nor reputation. Of all the human beings who were at that time upon the stage of action, this woman was as low as the lowest. To her first of all he announced the fact that he was the Messiah, and to her he explained what kind of worship is acceptable to the Eternal. A certain woman was there who had an infirmity for a long time, and when Jesus saw her he had compassion on her and said to her, "Wilt thou be made whole?" His heart went out always to the Samaritans. The religious teachers of his day were experts in handling Scripture, but they were blind to the needs of men; so one day he told a story in which a man naked and half dead is neglected by a priest and a Levite and rescued by a Samaritan who chances to pass that way. To the complacent and self-satisfied scribe who listens to the story, Jesus says, pointing to the figure of the Samaritan, "Go, do thou likewise." His tenderness for the Samaritans was never forgiven by the Jews. When Jesus attempted to preach in the streets of Jerusalem, men hooted at him and stabbed him with the venomous taunt, "You are a Samaritan and have a devil!"

In Galilee and Judea the men lowest in the social scale were Publicans. They were the customhouse officers of Palestine. They collected Jewish money for Caesar's treasury, and hence were counted renegades and traitors. Like all reputed traitors, they were treated with contumely and scorn. Jesus' heart went out to the Publicans. He ate with them in their homes. Men in consternation asked his disciples the reason why their Master ate with Publicans. So unusual a phenomenon demanded instant explanation. By and by it became a remark tossed from mouth to mouth, "He is a friend of Publicans."

But the frowns and criticisms of the good people of his day never swerved Jesus from his course. He was the steadfast friend of the unpopular and of all upon whom society refused to smile. One day when passing through the city of Jericho, the most unpopular man in all the town climbed into a tree to see him. He was rich, and he was a Publican. Jesus looked up into his face and said, "Come down, Zaccheus; I will dine with you today." He said it in the hearing of a great crowd. He said it, remember, in the priestly city of Jericho, where social lines were drawn more tightly than anywhere else in all Palestine, and where class hatred was most venomous, because sanctified by the sanction of the professed leaders of religion. There were two men in

Palestine who were especially conspicuous and noteworthy—at the one end of society stood the Pharisee, at the other end stood the Publican. Jesus pictures both men praying in the Temple, and lo, the Publican goes home justified rather than the Pharisee! Oh, the divine audacity of this man! He erects twelve thrones, and on each throne he places a man who shall judge one of the twelve tribes of Israel; and when the world looked to see who the men were, behold one of them was a Publican! And there the Publican has sat for nineteen centuries, and there he will sit to the end of time, reminding us ever of the consoling fact that out of the world's neglected and outcast classes can come, and will forever come, regenerating forces for the redemption of the race.

But why need I dwell on these things? The time would fail me if I should tell you of the lepers whom he healed, of the blind men to whom he gave sight, of the insane men among the tombs to whom he gave a sound mind, of the miserable outcasts whom he loved back to life again. What is the New Testament but a description of Bethesda, the house of mercy, with Jesus at the center of it, saying to the most helpless and hopeless of all the impotent folk that lie there, "Rise and walk"? The French artist, Tissot, seized upon the core of the Gospel when he painted the picture of Jesus—wearing the crown of thorns, sitting on the steps of a ruined temple, holding his bleeding brow—over the shoulders of two poor peasants, who, footsore and weary, have sat down there in the gloom of their great desolation.

And what he did he told his followers to do: "Go to the lost sheep, heal the sick, cleanse the lepers, raise the dead, cast out demons; when you give a dinner, invite the people overlooked by others; if you want to be great, you must be the servant of all." When John the Baptist, shut up in prison, began to wonder why Jesus did not march straight onward and seize the reins of power, he sent a messenger, asking, "Art thou he that was to come, or shall we look for another?" Jesus sent back in substance this luminous reply, "Tell John I have tarried behind at the pool of Bethesda with the man who has had an infirmity thirty and eight years. I am caring for the people who are impotent and discouraged at the end of the procession." That was the proof that he came down from Heaven. To take care of the man for whom nobody cares and to give strength to the man who has lost courage and hope, God himself cannot do a diviner thing than that! Some great deliverer standing at the pool of Bethesda saying to the man who is without a friend or a hope, "Rise and walk," is the world's ideal Messiah, the one for whom weary ages have looked long and waited. "Follow me," "Follow me," "Follow me," so he said to all who were willing to listen, and when they looked up they saw him going always toward Bethesda. The disciple must be like his Master, and the servant must obey his Lord. "Why call ye me Lord if ye do not the things which I say? Ye are my friends if ye do whatsoever I command you. I have given you an example."

Knowing that in a little while the world would see him no more, he breathed the ruling ideas of his soul into a few simple words, which will shine like constellations with steady and saving light on the world's dark path forever. The "lost sheep," the "lost coin," the "lost son," the half-dead traveler between Jerusalem and Jericho, the neglected beggar at the gate—are these not the fixed stars by which humanity must guide its course? All through his life our Lord could not look upon a crowd without being moved with compassion for them. He loved men from the beginning, he loved them to the end. The last day he spent in the temple he gave immortality to a poor lonely woman who had timidly dropped two bits of copper into the treasury. He noticed her because she was at the end of the procession of all who gave gifts. On the cross he threw around the poor benighted soldiers, neglected servants of Caesar's court, as they drove the nails through his hands, the healing folds of a loving prayer. And when at last he stepped from this world into paradise, he carried a robber in his arms. "Therefore God has highly exalted him and given him a name which is above every name, that at the name of Jesus every knee should bow and every tongue confess that Jesus Christ is Lord, to the glory of God the Father."

Charles Edward Jefferson (1860–1937) *One of the great New York City preachers, Dr. Jefferson was called to serve the Broadway Congregational Church in 1898. His influence was felt among secular groups as well as within church circles.*

Charles Haddon Spurgeon/A New Year's Benediction

But the God of all grace, who hath called us unto his eternal glory by Christ Jesus, after that ye have suffered awhile, make you perfect, establish, strengthen, settle you.

I PETER 5:10

I HAVE this morning taken this text as a New Year's blessing. You are aware that a venerable minister of the Church of England always supplies me with the motto for the new year. Ripening as he is for eternal glory, he prays much before he selects the text, and I know that it is his prayer for you all today. He constantly favors me with this motto, and I always think it my duty to preach from it, and then desire my people to remember it through the year as a staff of support in their time of trouble, as some sweet morsel, a wafer made with honey, a portion of angel's food, which they may roll under their tongue, and carry in their memory till the year ends, and then begin with another sweet text. What larger benediction could my aged friend have chosen, standing as he is today in his pulpit, and lifting up holy hands to preach to the people in a quiet village church? What larger blessing could he implore for the thousands of Israel than that which in his name I pronounce upon you this day, "But the God of all grace who hath called us unto his eternal glory by Christ Jesus, after that ye have suffered awhile, make you perfect, establish, strengthen, settle you."

In discoursing upon this text, I shall have to remark: first, *what the apostle asks of heaven;* and then, secondly, *why he expects to receive it.* The reason of his expecting to be answered is contained in the title by which he addresses the Lord his God, "The God of all grace who hath called us unto his eternal glory by Christ Jesus."

*What the apostle asks for
all to whom this epistle
was written*

He asks for them four sparkling jewels set in a black foil. The four jewels are these: *Perfection, Establishment, Strengthening, Settling.* The jet-black setting is this: "After that ye have suffered awhile." Worldly compliments are of little worth; for as Chesterfield observes, "They cost nothing but ink and paper." I must confess I think even that little expense is often thrown away. Worldly compliments generally omit all idea of sorrow. "A Merry Christmas! A Happy New Year!" There is no supposition of anything like suffering. But Christian benedictions look at the truth of matters. We know that men must suffer; we believe that men are born to sorrow as the spark flieth upwards; and therefore in our benediction we include the sorrow. Nay, more than that, we believe that the sorrow shall assist in working out the blessing which we invoke upon your heads. We, in the language of Peter, say, "after that ye have suffered awhile, may the God of all grace make you perfect, establish, strengthen, settle you." Understand, then, as I take each of these four jewels, that you are to look upon them, and consider that they are only desired for you "after that ye have suffered awhile." We must not discard the sufferings. We must take them from the same hand from which we receive the mercy; and the blessing bears date "after that ye have suffered awhile."

The first sparkling jewel in this ring is *perfection*. The apostle prays that God would make us *perfect*. Indeed, though this be a large prayer, and the jewel is a diamond of the first water and of the finest size, yet is it absolutely necessary to a Christian that he should ultimately arrive at perfection. Have ye never on your bed dreamed a dream when your thoughts roamed at large and the bit was taken from your imagination, when stretching all your wings, your soul floated through the Infinite, grouping strange and marvelous things together, so that the dream rolled on in something like supernatural splendor? But on a sudden you were awakened, and you have regretted hours afterward that the dream was never concluded. And what is a Christian, if he does not arrive at perfection, but an unfinished dream? A majestic dream it is true, full of things that earth had never known if it had not been that they were revealed to flesh and blood by the Spirit. But suppose the voice of sin should startle us ere that dream be concluded, and if, as when one awaketh, we should despise the image which began to be formed in our minds, what were we then? Everlasting regrets, a multiplication of eternal torment, must be the result of our having begun to be Christians, if we do not arrive at perfection. If there could be such a thing as a man in whom sanctification began, but in whom God the Spirit ceased to work; if there could be a being so unhappy as to be called by grace and to be deserted before he was perfected, there would not be among the damned in hell a more unhappy wretch. It were no blessing for God to begin to bless if he did not perfect. It were the grandest curse which omnipotent hatred itself could pronounce, to give a man grace at all, if that grace did not carry him to the end, and land him safely in heaven. I must confess that I would rather endure the pangs of that dread archangel, Satan, throughout eternity, than have to suffer as one whom

God once loved but whom he cast away. But such a thing shall never be. Whom once he hath chosen he doth not reject. We know that where he hath begun a good work he will carry it on, and he will complete it until the day of Christ.

Grand is the prayer, then, when the apostle asks that we may be perfected. What were a Christian if he were not perfected? Have you never seen a canvas upon which the hand of the painter has sketched with daring pencil some marvelous scene of grandeur? You see where the living color has been laid on with an almost superhuman skill. But the artist was suddenly struck dead, and the hand that worked miracles of art was palsied. Is it not a source of regret to the world that ever the painting was commenced, since it was never finished? Have you never seen the human face divine starting out from the chiseled marble? You have seen the exquisite skill of the sculptor, and you have said within yourself, "What a marvelous thing will this be, what a matchless specimen of human skill." But alas, it was left unfinished. And do you imagine that God will begin to sculpture out a perfect being and not complete it? Do you think that the hand of divine wisdom will sketch the Christian and not fill up the details? Hath God taken us as unhewn stones out of the quarry, and hath he begun to work upon us, and show his divine art, his marvelous wisdom and grace, and will he afterwards cast us away? Shall God fail? Shall he leave his works imperfect? Point, if you can, my hearers, to a world which God has cast away unfinished. Is there one speck in his creation where God hath begun to build but was not able to complete? Hath he made a single angel deficient? Is there one creature over which it cannot be said, "This is very good"? And shall it be said over the creature twice made—the chosen of God, the blood-bought—shall it be said, "The Spirit began to work in this man's heart, but the man was mightier than the Spirit, and sin conquered grace"? Oh, my dear brethren, the prayer shall be fulfilled. After that ye have suffered awhile, God shall make you perfect if he has begun the good work in you.

But, beloved, it must be after that ye have suffered awhile. Ye cannot be perfected except by the fire. There is no way of ridding you of your dross and your tin but by the flames of the furnace of affliction. Your folly is so bound up in your hearts, ye children of God, that nothing but the rod can bring it out of you. It is through the blueness of your wounds that your heart is made better. Ye must pass through tribulation, that through the Spirit it may act as a refining fire to you; that pure, holy, purged and washed, ye may stand before the face of your God rid of every imperfection and delivered from every corruption within.

Let us now proceed to the second blessing of the benediction—*establishment*. It is not enough even if the Christian had received in himself a proportional perfection, if he were not established. You have seen the arch of heaven as it spans the plain—glorious are its colors, and rare its hues. Though we have seen it many and many a time, it never ceases to be "A thing of beauty and a joy forever." But, alas for the rainbow, it is not established. It passes away, and lo it is not. The fair colors give way to the fleecy clouds, and the sky is no longer brilliant with the tints of heaven. It is not established. How can it be? A thing that is made of transitory sunbeams and passing raindrops, how can it abide? And mark, the more beautiful the vision, the more sorrowful the reflection when that vision vanishes, and there is nothing left but darkness. It is, then, a very necessary wish for the Christian, that he should be established. Of all God's known conceptions, next to his incarnate Son, I do not hesitate to pronounce a Christian man the noblest conception of God. But if this conception is to be but as the rainbow painted on the cloud, and is to pass away forever, woe worth the day that ever our eyes were tantalized with a sublime conception that is so soon to melt away.

What is a Christian man better than the flower of the field, which is here today and which withers when the sun is risen with fervent heat, unless God establish him? What is the difference between the heir of heaven, the blood-bought child of God, and the grass of the field? Oh, may God fulfill to you this rich benediction, that you may not be as the smoke out of a chimney, which is blown away by the wind; that your goodness may not be as the morning cloud, and as the early dew which passeth away; but may ye be established, may every good thing that you have be an abiding thing. May your character be not a writing upon the sand, but an inscription upon the rock. May your faith be no "baseless fabric of a vision," but may it be built of stone that shall endure that awful fire which shall consume the wood, hay and stubble of the hypocrite. May ye be rooted and grounded in love. May your convictions be deep. May your love be real. May your desires be earnest. May your whole life be so settled, fixed and established, that all the blasts of hell and all the storms of earth shall never be able to remove you. You know we talk about some Christian men as being old-established Christians. I do fear there are a great many that are old who are not established. It is one thing to have the hair whitened with years, but I fear it is another thing for us to obtain wisdom. There be some who grow no wiser by all their experience. Though their fingers be well rapped by experience, yet have they not learned in that school. I know there are many aged Christians who can say of themselves, and say it sorrowfully too, they wish they had their opportunities over again, that they might learn more and might be more established. We have heard them sing,

I find myself a learner yet,
Unskillful, weak, and apt to slide.

The benediction however of the apostle is one which I pray may be fulfilled in us, whether we be young or old, but especially in those of you who have long known your Lord and Saviour. You ought not now to be the subject of those doubts which vex the babe in grace. Those first principles should not always be laid again by you, but you should be going forward to something higher. You are getting near to heaven; oh, how is it that you have not got to the land Beulah yet? To that land which floweth with milk and honey? Surely your wavering illbeseemeth those gray hairs. Methought they had been whitened with the sunlight of Heaven. How is it that some of the sunlight does not gleam from your eyes? We who are young look up to you old-established Christians; and if we see you doubting, and hear you speaking with a trembling lip, then we are exceedingly cast down. We pray for our sakes as well as for yours, that this blessing may be fulfilled in you, that you may be established; that you may no longer be exercised with doubt; that you may know your interest in Christ; that you may feel you are secure in him; that, resting upon the rock of ages, you may know that you cannot perish while your feet are fixed there. We do pray, in fact, for all, of whatever age, that our hope may be fixed upon nothing less than Jesus' blood and righteousness, and that it may be so firmly fixed that it may never shake; but that we may be as Mount Zion, which can never be removed and which abideth forever.

Thus have I remarked upon the second blessing of this benediction. But mark, we cannot have it until after we have suffered a while. We cannot be established except by suffering. It is of no use our hoping that we shall be well-rooted if no March winds have passed over us. The young oak cannot be expected to strike its roots so deep as the old one. Those old gnarlings on the roots, and those strange twistings of the branches, all tell of many storms that have swept over the aged tree. But they are also indicators of the depths into which the roots have dived; and they tell the woodman that he might as soon expect to rend up a mountain as to tear up that oak by the roots. We must suffer a while, then shall we be established.

Now for the third blessing, which is *strengthening*. Ah, brethren, this is a very necessary blessing too for all Christians. There be some whose characters seem to be fixed and established. But still they lack force and vigor. Shall I give you a picture of a Christian without strength? There he is. He has espoused the cause of King Jesus. He hath put on his armor, he hath enlisted in the heavenly host. Do you observe him? He is perfectly panoplied from head to foot, and he carries with him the shield of faith. Do you notice, too, how firmly he is established? He keeps his ground, and he will not be removed. When he uses his sword, it falls with feeble force. His shield, though he grasps it as firmly as his weakness will allow him, trembles in his grasp. There he stands; he will not move, but still how tottering is his position. His knees knock together with affright when he heareth the sound and the noise of war and tumult. What doth this man need? His will is right, his intention is right, and his heart is fully set upon good things. Why, he needeth strength. The poor man is weak and childlike. Either because he has been fed on unsavory and unsubstantial meat, or because of some sin which has straitened him, he has not that force and strength which ought to dwell in the Christian man. But once let the prayer of Peter be fulfilled to him, and how strong the Christian becomes.

There is not in all the world a creature so strong as a Christian when God is with him. Talk of Behemoth—he is but as a little thing! His might is weakness when matched with the believer. Talk of Leviathan, that maketh the deep to be hoary, he is not the chief of the ways of God! The true believer is mightier far than even he. Have you never seen the Christian when God is with him? He smelleth the battle afar off, and he cries in the midst of the tumult, "Aha! aha! aha!" He laugheth at all the hosts of his enemies. Or if you compare him to the Leviathan—if he be cast into a sea of trouble, he lashes about him and makes the deep hoary with benedictions. He is not overwhelmed by the depths, nor is he afraid of the rocks; he has the protection of God about him, and the floods cannot drown him; nay, they become an element of delight to him, while by the grace of God he rejoiceth in the midst of the billows. If you want a proof of the strength of a Christian, you have only to turn to history, and you can see there how believers have quenched the violence of fire, have shut the mouths of lions, have laughed tyrants to scorn and have put to flight the armies of aliens, by the all-mastering power of faith in God. I pray God, my brethren, that he may strengthen you this year.

The Christians of this age are very feeble. It is a remarkable thing that the great mass of children nowadays are born feeble. You ask me for the evidence of it. I can supply it very readily. You are aware that in the Church of England Liturgy it is ordered and ordained that all children should be immersed in baptism, except those that are certified to be of a weakly state. Now it were uncharitable to imagine that persons would be guilty of falsehood when they come up to what they think to be a sacred ordinance; and, therefore, as nearly all children are now sprinkled, and not immersed, I suppose they are born feeble. Whether that accounts for the fact that all Christians are so feeble I will not undertake to say, but certain it is that we have not many gigantic Christians nowadays. Here and there we hear of one who seems to work all but miracles in these modern times, and we are astonished. Oh that ye had faith like these men! I do not think there is much more piety in England now than there used to be in the days of the Puritans. I believe there are far more pious men; but while the quantity has been multiplied, I fear the quality has been depreciated. In those days the stream of grace ran very deep indeed. Some of those old Puritans, when we read of their devotion, and of the hours they spent in prayer, seem to have as much grace as any hundred of us. But nowadays, the banks are broken down, and great meadows have been flooded therewith. So far so good. But while the surface has been enlarged, I fear the depth has been greatly diminished. And this may account for the fact that while our piety has become shallow our strength has become weak. Oh, may God strengthen you this year! But remember, if he does do so, you will then have to suffer. "After that ye have suffered awhile," may he strengthen you.

And now I come to the last blessing of the four, which is *"settling."* I will not say that this last blessing is greater than the other three, but it is a stepping-stone to each; and strange to say, it is often the result of a gradual attainment of the three preceding ones. "Settle you!" Oh, how many there are that are never settled! The tree which should be transplanted every week would soon die. Nay, if it were moved, no matter how skillfully, once every year, no gardener would expect fruit from it. How many Christians there be that are transplanting themselves constantly, even as to their doctrinal sentiments. There be some who generally believe according to the last speaker; and there be others who do not know what they do believe, but they believe almost anything that is told them. The spirit of Christian charity, so much cultivated in these days, and which we all love so much, has, I fear, assisted in bringing into the world a species of latitudinarianism; or, in other words, men have come to believe that it does not matter what they do believe; that although one minister says "it is so," and the other says "it is not so," yet we are both right; though we contradict each other flatly, yet we are both correct. I know not where men have had their judgments manufactured, but to my mind it always seems impossible to believe a contradiction.

I can never understand how contrary sentiments can both of them be in accordance with the Word of God, which is the standard of truth. But yet there be some who are like the weathercock upon the church steeple, they will turn just as the wind blows. As good Mr. Whitfield said, "You might as well measure the moon for a suit of clothes as tell their doctrinal sentiments," for they are always shifting and changing. Now, I pray that this may be taken away from any of you, if this be your weakness, and that you may be *settled*. Far from us be bigotry removed; yet would I have the Christian know what he believes to be true and then stand to it. Take your time in weighing the controversy; but when you have once decided, be not easily moved. Let God be true, though every man be a liar; and stand to it, that what is according to God's Word one day cannot be contrary to it another day; that what was true in Luther's day and Calvin's day must be true now; that falsehoods may shift, for they have a protean shape; but the truth is one and indivisible, and evermore the same. Let others think as they please. Allow the greatest latitude to others, but to yourself allow none. Stand firm and steadfast by that which ye have been taught, and ever seek the spirit of the Apostle Paul, "If any man preach any other Gospel than that which we have received, let him be accursed." If, however, I wished you to be firm in your doctrines, my prayer would be that you may be especially settled in your faith. You believe in Jesus Christ the Son of God, and you rest in him. But sometimes your faith wavers; then you lose your joy and comfort. I pray that your faith may become so settled that it may never be a matter of question with you whether Christ is yours or not, but that you may say confidently, "I know whom I have believed, and I am persuaded that he is able to keep that which I have committed to him."

Then I pray that you may be settled in your aims and designs. There are many Christian people who get a good idea into their heads, but they never carry it out, because they ask some friend what he thinks of it. "Not much," says he. Of course he does not. Who ever did think much of anybody else's idea? And at once the person who conceived it gives it up, and the work is never accomplished. How many a man in his ministry has begun to preach the Gospel, when some member of the church—some deacon possibly—has pulled him by one ear, and he has gone a little that way. By and by some other brother has thought fit to pull him in the other direction. The man has lost his manliness. He has never been settled as to what he ought to do; and now he becomes a mere lackey, waiting upon everybody's opinion, willing to adopt whatever anybody else conceives to be right. Now, I pray you, be settled in your aims. See what niche it is that God would have you occupy. Stand in it, and don't be got out of it by all the laughter that comes upon you. If you believe God has called you to a work, *do it*. If men will help you, thank them. If they will not, tell them to stand out of your road or be run over. Let nothing daunt you. He who will serve his God must expect sometimes to serve him alone. Not always shall we fight in the ranks. There are times when the Lord's David must fight Goliath singly, and must take with him three stones out of the brook amid the laughter of his brethren, yet still in his weapons is he confident of victory through faith in God. Be not moved from the work to which God has put you. Be not weary in well-doing, for in due season ye shall reap if ye faint not. Be ye settled. Oh, may God fulfill this rich blessing to you.

But you will not be settled unless you suffer. You will become settled in your faith and settled in your aims by suffering. Men are soft molluscous animals in these days. We have not the tough men that know they are right and stand to it. Even when a man is wrong we admire his conscientiousness, if he stands up believing that he is right and dares to face the frowns of the world. But when a man is right, the worst thing he can have is inconstancy, vacillation, the fear of men. Hurl it from thee, O knight of the Holy Cross, and be firm if thou wouldst be victorious. Faint heart never stormed a city yet, and thou wilt never win nor be crowned with honor, if thy heart be not steeled against every assault, and if thou be not settled in thy intention to honor thy Master and to win the crown.

The reasons why the apostle Peter
expected that his prayer
would be heard

He asked that they might be made perfect, established, strengthened, settled. Did not Unbelief whisper in Peter's ear, "Peter, thou askest too much. Thou wast always headstrong. Thou didst say, 'Bid me come upon the water.' Surely, this is another instance of thy presumption. If thou hadst said, 'Lord, make them holy,' had it not been a sufficient prayer? Hast thou not asked too much?'" "No," saith Peter; and he replies to Unbelief, "I am sure I shall receive what I have asked for; for I am in the first place asking it of the God of all grace—the God of all grace." Not the God of the little graces we have received already, but the God of the great boundless grace which is stored up for us in the promise, but which as yet we have not received in our experience. "The God of *all* grace"—of quickening grace, of convincing grace, of pardoning grace, of believing grace—the God of comforting, supporting, sustaining grace. Surely, when we come to him we cannot come for too much. If he be the God, not of one grace, or of two graces, but of *all* graces; if in him there is stored up an infinite, boundless, limitless supply, how can we ask too much, even though we ask that we may be perfect?

Believer, when you are on your knees, remember you are going to a king. Let your petitions be large. Imitate the example of Alexander's courtier, who, when he was told he might have whatever he chose to ask as a reward for his valor, asked a sum of money so large that Alexander's treasurer refused to pay it until he had first seen the monarch. When he saw the monarch, he smiled, and said, "It is true it is much for him to ask, but it is not much for Alexander to give. I admire him for his faith in me; let him have all he asks for." And dare I ask that I may be perfect, that my angry temper may be taken away, my stubbornness removed, my imperfections covered? May I ask that I may be like Adam in the garden—nay more, as pure and perfect as God himself? May I ask that one day I may tread the golden streets, and "with my Saviour's garments on, holy as the Holy one," stand in the mid-blaze of God's glory, and cry, "Who shall lay anything to the charge of God's elect?" Yes, I may ask it; and I shall have it, for he is the God of all grace.

Look again at the text, and you see another reason why Peter expected that his prayer would be heard, "The God of all grace *who hath called us.*" Unbelief might have said to Peter, "Peter, it is true that God is the God of all grace, but he is as a fountain shut up, as waters sealed." "Ah," saith Peter, "get thee hence, Satan; thou savorest not the things that be of God. It is not a sealed fountain of all grace, for it has begun to flow—The God of all grace hath called us." Calling is the first drop of mercy that trickleth into the thirsty lip of the dying man. Calling is the first golden link of the endless chain of eternal mercies. Not the first in order of time with God, but the first in order of time with us. The first thing we know of Christ in his mercy, is that he cries, "Come unto me all ye that are weary and heavy laden," and that by his sweet Spirit he addresses us, so that we obey the call and come to him. Now, mark, if God has called me, I may ask him to establish and keep me; I may ask that as year rolls after year my piety may not die out; I may pray that the bush may burn, but not be consumed; that the barrel of meal may not waste, and the cruse of oil may not fail. Dare I ask that to life's latest hour I may be faithful to God, because God is faithful to me? Yes, I may ask it, and I shall have it too; because the God that calls will give the rest. "For whom he did foreknow, them he did predestinate; and whom he did predestinate, them he also called; and whom he called, he also justified; and whom he justified, them he also glorified." Think of thy calling, Christian, and take courage, "for the gifts and calling of God are without repentance." If he has called thee, he will never repent of what he has done nor cease to bless or cease to save.

But I think there is a stronger reason coming yet, "The God of all grace, who hath called us *unto his eternal glory.*" Hath God called thee, my hearer? Dost thou know to what he has called thee? He called thee first into the house of conviction, where he made thee feel thy sin. Again he called thee to Calvary's summit, where thou didst see thy sin atoned for and thy pardon sealed with precious blood. And now he calls thee again. And whither away? I hear a voice today—Unbelief tells me that there is a voice calling me to Jordan's waves. Oh, Unbelief! it is true that through the stormy billows of that sea my soul must pass. But the voice comes not from the depths of the grave, it comes from the eternal glory. There where Jehovah sits resplendent on his throne, surrounded by cherubim and seraphim, from that brightness into which angels dare not gaze, I hear a voice—"Come unto me, thou blood-washed sinner, come unto my eternal glory." O heavens, is not this a wondrous call?—to be called to glory—called to the shining streets and pearly gates—called to the harps and to the songs of eternal happiness—and better still, called to Jesus' bosom—called to his Father's face—called, not to eternal glory, but to his eternal glory—called to that very glory and honor with which God invests himself forever? And now, beloved, is any prayer too great after this? Has God called me to heaven, and is there anything on earth he will deny me? If he has called me to dwell in heaven, is not perfection necessary for me? May I not therefore ask for it? If he has called me to glory, is it not necessary that I should be strengthened to fight my way thither? May I not ask for strengthening? Nay, if there be a mercy upon earth too great for me to think of, too large for me to conceive, too heavy for my language to carry it before the throne in prayer, he will do for me exceeding abundantly above what I can ask, or even think. I know he will, because he has called me to his eternal glory.

The last reason why the apostle expected that his benediction would be fulfilled was this: "Who hath called us to his eternal glory by Christ Jesus." It is a singular fact that no promise is ever so sweet to the believer as those in which the name of Christ is mentioned. If I have to preach a comforting sermon to desponding Christians, I would never select a text which did not enable me to lead the desponding one to the cross. Does it not seem too much to you, brethren and sisters, this morning, that the God of all grace should be your God? Does it not surpass your faith that he should actually have called *you*? Do you not sometimes doubt as to whether you were called at all? And when you think of eternal glory, does not the question arise, "Shall I ever enjoy it? Shall I ever see the face of God with acceptance?" Oh, beloved, when ye hear of Christ, when you know that this grace comes through Christ, and the calling through Christ, and the glory through Christ, then you say, "Lord, I can believe it now, if it is through Christ." It is not a hard thing to believe that Christ's blood was sufficient to purchase every blessing for me. If I go to God's treasury without Christ, I am afraid to ask for anything, but when Christ is with me, I can then ask for everything. For sure I think *he* deserves it though *I* do not. If I can claim his merits, then I am not afraid to plead. Is perfection too great a boon for God to give to Christ? Oh, no. Is the keeping, the stability, the preservation of the blood-bought ones too great a reward for the terrible agonies and sufferings of the Saviour? I trow not. Then we may with confidence plead, because everything comes through Christ.

I would, in concluding, make this remark. I wish, my brothers and sisters, that during this year you may live nearer to Christ than you have ever done before. Depend upon it, it is when we think much of Christ, that we think little of ourselves, little of our troubles, and little of the doubts and fears that surround us. Begin from this day, and may God help you. Never let a single day pass over your head without a visit to the garden of Gethsemane, and the cross on Calvary. And as for some of you who are not saved, and know not the Redeemer, I would to God that this very day you would come to Christ. I dare say you think coming to Christ is some terrible thing; that you need to be prepared before you come; that he is hard and harsh with you. When men have to go to a lawyer they need to tremble; when they have to go to the doctor they may fear; though both those persons, however unwelcome, may be often necessary. But when you come to Christ, you may come boldly. There is no fee required, there is no preparation necessary. You may come just as you are. It was a brave saying of Martin Luther's, when he said, "I would run into Christ's arms even if he had a drawn sword in his hand." Now, he has not a drawn sword, but he has his wounds in his hands. Run into his arms, poor sinner. "Oh," you say, "May I come?" How can you ask the question? You are commanded to come. The great command of the Gospel is, "Believe in the Lord Jesus." Those who disobey this command disobey God. It is as much a command of God that man should believe on Christ, as that we should love our neighbor. Now, what is a command I have certainly a right to obey. There can be no question, you see. A sinner has liberty to believe in Christ because he is told to do so. God would not have told him to do a thing which he must not do.

You are allowed to believe. "Oh," saith one, "that is all I want to know. I do believe that Christ is able to save to the uttermost. *May I* rest my soul on him, and say, sink or swim, most blessed Jesus, thou art my Lord?" *May* do it, man? Why, you are commanded to do it. Oh, that you may be enabled to do it. Remember, this is not a thing which you will do at a risk. The risk is in not doing it. Cast yourself on Christ, sinner. Throw away every other dependence, and rest alone on him. "No," says one, "I am not prepared." Prepared! sir? Then you do not understand me. There is no preparation needed; it is, just as you are. "Oh, I do not feel my need enough." I know you do not. What has that to do with it? You are commanded to cast yourself on Christ. Be you never so black or never so bad, trust to him. He that believeth on Christ shall be saved, be his sins never so many; he that believeth not must be damned, be his sins never so few. The great command of the Gospel is, "Believe." "Oh," but saith one, "am I to say I know that Christ died for me?" Ah, I did not say that, you shall learn that by and by. You have nothing to do with that question now; your business is to believe on Christ and trust him, to cast yourself into his hands. And may God, the Spirit, now sweetly compel you to do it. Now, sinner, hands off your own righteousness. Drop all idea of becoming better through your own strength. Cast yourself on the promise. Say,

Just as I am without one plea,
But that thy blood was shed for me,
And that thou bid'st me come to thee,
Oh, Lamb of God! I come, I come.

Now, have I made myself understood? If there were a number of persons here in debt, and I were to say, "If you will simply trust to me, your debts shall be paid, and no creditor shall ever molest you," you would understand me directly. How is it you cannot comprehend that trusting in Christ will remove all your debts, take away all your sins, and you shall be saved eternally? Oh, Spirit of the living God, open the understanding to receive, and the heart to obey, and may many a soul here present cast itself on Christ. On all such, as on all believers, do I again pronounce the benediction, with which I shall dismiss you. "May the God of all grace, who hath called us unto his eternal glory by Christ Jesus, after that ye have suffered awhile, make you perfect, establish, strengthen, settle you!" *Amen.*

Charles Haddon Spurgeon (1834–1892)   *Another British Baptist, Charles Haddon Spurgeon was probably the most famous preacher in his day. He began preaching when he was sixteen years old and before he died he had made Metropolitan Tabernacle in London one of the preaching landmarks. More than sixty volumes of his sermons have been published, marking the evangelical impact of his preaching.*

Charles Grandison Finney/
Religion of Public Opinion

For they loved the praise of men more than the praise of God.
JOHN 12:43

THESE words were spoken of certain individuals who refused to confess that Jesus was the Christ, because he was extremely unpopular with the scribes and Pharisees, and principal people of Jerusalem.

There is a plain distinction between self-love, or the simple desire of happiness, and *selfishness*. Self-love, the desire of happiness and dread of misery, is constitutional; it is a part of our frame as God made us, and as he intended us to be; and its indulgence within the limits of the law of God, is not sinful. Whenever it is indulged contrary to the law of God, it becomes sinful. When the desire of happiness or the dread of misery becomes the controlling principle, and we prefer our own gratification to some other greater interest, it becomes selfishness. When, to avoid pain or procure happiness, we sacrifice other greater interests, we violate the great law of disinterested benevolence; it is no longer self-love, acting within lawful bounds, but selfishness.

In my last Friday evening lecture, I described a class of professors of religion who are moved to perform religious exercises by hope and fear. They are moved sometimes by self-love and sometimes by selfishness. Their supreme object is not to glorify God but to secure their own salvation. You will recollect that this class, and the class I had described before as the real friends of God and man, agree in many things; and if you look only at the things in which they agree, you cannot distinguish between them. It is only by a close observation of those things in which they differ that you can see that the main design of the latter class is not to glorify God but to secure their own salvation. In that way we can see their supreme object developed, and see that when they do the same things, outwardly, which those do whose supreme object is to glorify

God, they do them from entirely different motives, and consequently the acts themselves are, in the sight of God, of an entirely different character.

Tonight, I design to point out the characteristics of the third class of professing Christians, who "love the praise of men more than the praise of God."

I would not be understood to imply that a mere regard for reputation has led this class to profess religion. Religion has always been too unpopular with the great mass of mankind to render it a general thing to become professing Christians from a mere regard to reputation. But I mean that where it is not generally unpopular to become a professor of religion, and will not diminish popularity but will increase it with many, a complex motive operates—the hope of securing happiness in a future world, and that it may increase reputation here. And thus many are led to profess religion, when after all, on a close examination, it will be seen that the leading object, which is prized beyond anything else, is the good opinion of their fellowmen. Sooner than forfeit this utterly, they would not profess religion. Their profession turns on this. And although they do profess to be sincere Christians, you may see by their conduct, on close examination, that they will do nothing that will forfeit this good opinion of men. They will not encounter the odium that they must, if they were to give themselves up to root sin out of the world.

Observe that impenitent sinners are always influenced by one of two things, in all that they do that appears like religion. Either they do them out of regard to mere natural principles as compassion or self-love—principles that are constitutional in them—or from selfishness. They are done either out of regard to their own reputation or happiness, or the gratification of some natural principle in them that has no moral character, and not from the love of God in them. They love "the praise of men more than the praise of God."

I will now mention several things by which you may detect the true character of the class of persons of whom I have been speaking—who make the praise of men their idol, notwithstanding they profess to love God supremely. And they are things by which you can detect your own true characters, if there are any present who properly belong to this class.

1. They do what the Apostle Paul says certain persons did in his day, and for that reason they remained ignorant of the true doctrine; they "measure themselves by themselves, and compare themselves among themselves."

There are a vast many individuals, who, instead of making Jesus Christ their standard of comparison, and the Bible their rule of life, manifestly aim at no such thing. They show that they never seriously dreamed of making the Bible their standard. The great question with them is whether they do about as many things in religion and are about as pious as other people or as the churches around them. Their object is to maintain a respectable profession of religion. Instead of seriously inquiring for themselves what the Bible really requires, and asking how

Jesus Christ would act in such and such cases, they are looking simply at the common run of professing Christians, and are satisfied with doing what is commendable in their estimation. They prove to a demonstration that their object is not so much to do what the Bible lays down as duty, as to do what the great mass of professing Christians do—to do what is respectable, rather than what is right.

2. This class of persons do not trouble themselves about elevating the standard of piety around them.

They are not troubled at the fact that the general standard of piety is so low in the Church, that it is impossible to bring the great mass of sinners to repentance. They think the standard at the present time is high enough. Whatever be the standard at the time, it satisfies them. While the real friends of God and man are complaining of the church because the standard of piety is so low, and trying to wake up the church to elevate the tone of religion, it all seems to this class of persons like censoriousness and a meddlesome, uneasy disposition, and as denoting a bad spirit in them. Just as when Jesus Christ denounced the scribes and Pharisees, and leading professors of his day, they said: "He hath a devil." "Why, he is denouncing our doctors of divinity, and all our best men, and even dares to call the scribes and Pharisees hypocrites, and he tells us that except our righteousness shall exceed theirs, we can in no case enter the Kingdom of Heaven. What a bad spirit he has."

A large part of the church at the present day have the same spirit, and every effort to open the eyes of the church and to make Christians see that they live so low, so worldly, so much like hypocrites that it is impossible the work of the Lord should go on, only excites ill will and occasions reproach. "O," they say, "what a bad spirit he shows, so censorious and so unkind; surely that is anything but the meek and kind and loving spirit of the Son of God." They forget how Jesus Christ poured out his anathemas, enough to make the hills of Judea shake, against those that had the reputation of being the most pious people in that day. Just as if Jesus Christ never said anything severe to anybody, but just fawned over them and soothed them into his kingdom. Who does not know that it was the hypocritical spirit exhibited by professors of religion that roused his soul and moved his indignation and called forth his burning torrents of denunciation? He was always complaining of the very people who were set up as patterns of piety, and called them hypocrites and thundered over their heads the terrible words, "How can ye escape the damnation of hell?"

It is not wonderful, when so many love the praise of men more than the praise of God, that there should be excitement when the truth is told. They are very well satisfied with the standard of piety as it is, and think that while the people are doing so much for Sabbath schools and missions and tracts, that is doing pretty well, and they wonder what the man would have. Alas, alas, for their blindness! They do not seem to know that with all this the lives of the generality of professing Christians are almost as different from the standard of Jesus Christ as light is from darkness.

3. They make a distinction between those requirements of God that are strongly enforced by public sentiment and those that are not thus guarded.

They are very scrupulous in observing such requirements as public sentiment distinctly favors, while they easily set at nought those which public sentiment does not enforce. You have illustrations of this on every side. I might mention the temperance reformation. How many there are who yield to public sentiment in this matter what they never would yield to God or man. At first they waited to see how it would turn. They resisted giving up ardent spirits. But when that became popular, and they found they could do very well with other alcoholic stimulants, they gave it up. But they are determined to yield no farther than public sentiment drives them. They show that it is not their object, in joining the temperance society, to carry out the reform, so as to slay the monster Intemperance; but their object is to maintain a good character. They love "the praise of men more than the praise of God."

See how many individuals there are who keep the Sabbath, not because they love God, but because it is respectable. This is manifest, because they keep it while they are among their acquaintances or where they are known. But when they get where they are not known, or where it will not be a public disgrace, you will find them traveling on the Sabbath.

All those sins that are reprobated by public opinion this class of persons abstains from, but they do other things just as bad which are not thus frowned on. They do those duties which are enforced by public opinion, but not those that are less enforced. They will not stay away from public worship on the Sabbath, because they could not maintain any reputation for religion at all if they did. But they neglect things that are just as peremptorily enjoined in the Word of God. Where an individual habitually disobeys any command of God, knowing it to be such, it is just as certain as his soul lives that the obedience he appears to render is not from a regard to God's authority or love to God, but from other motives. He does not, in fact, obey any command of God. The Apostle has settled this question. "Whosoever," says he, "shall keep the whole law, and offend in one point, is guilty of all"—that is, does not truly keep any one precept of the law. Obedience to God's commands implies an obedient state of heart, and therefore nothing is obedience that does not imply a supreme regard to the authority of God. Now, if a man's heart be right, then whatever God enjoins he regards as of more importance than anything else. And if a man regard anything else of superior weight to God's authority, that is his idol. Whatever we supremely regard—that is our god; whether it be reputation or comfort or riches or honor or whatever it is that we regard supremely, that is the god of our hearts. Whatever a man's reason may be for habitually neglecting anything which he knows to be the command of God, or that he sees to be required to promote the kingdom of Christ, there is demonstration absolute that he regards that as supreme. There is nothing acceptable to God in any of his services. Rest assured, all his religion is the religion of public sentiment. If he neglects anything required by the law of God, because he can pass along in neglect, and public sentiment does not enjoin it; or if he does other things inconsistent with the law of God, merely because public opinion does require it—it is a simple matter of fact that it is public sentiment to which he yields obedience, in all his conduct, and not a regard to the glory of God.

How is it with you, beloved? Do you habitually neglect any requirement of God because it is not sustained and enforced by public sentiment? If you are a professor of religion, it is to be presumed you do not neglect any requirement that is strongly urged by public sentiment. But how is it with others? Do you not habitually neglect some duties? Do you not live in some practices reputable among men, that you know to be contrary to the law of God? If you do, it is demonstration absolute that you regard the opinions of men more than the judgment of God. Write down your name, "hypocrite."

4. This class of professors are apt to indulge in some sins when they are away from home that they would not commit at home.

Many a man who is temperate at home, when he gets to a distance will toss off his glass of brandy and water at the table, or step up to the bar of a steamboat and call for liquor without shame; or if they are in Europe, they will go to the theatre. When I was in the Mediterranean, at Messina, a gentleman asked me if I would go to the theatre with him. "What! I go to the theatre? A minister go to the theatre?" "Why," said he, "you are away from home, and no one would know it." "But would not God know it?" It was plain that he thought, although I was a minister, I could go to the theatre when I was away from home. No matter if God knew it, so long as men did not know it. And how should he get that idea, but by seeing ministers who would do just such things?

5. Another development of the character of these individuals is that they indulge themselves in secret sin.

I am now speaking of something by which you may know yourselves. If you allow yourselves in any sins secretly, when you can get along without having any human being know it, know that God sees it and that he has already written down your name, "hypocrite." You are more afraid of disgrace in the eye of mortals than of disgrace in the eye of God. If you loved God supremely, it would be a small thing to you that any and every body else knew your sins, in comparison with having them known to God. If tempted to any such thing, you would exclaim, "What! shall I commit sin under the eye of God?"

6. They indulge in secret omissions of duty, which they would not dare to have known to others.

They may not practise any secret sins or indulge in those secret pollutions that are spoken of, but they neglect those duties that if they were known to neglect, it would be called disreputable to their Christian character. Such as secret prayer, for instance. They will go to the Communion—yes, to the Communion—and appear to be very pious on the Sabbath; and yet, as to private piety, they know nothing of it. Their closet for prayer is unknown to God or man. It is easy to see that reputation is their idol. They dread to lose their reputation more than to offend God.

How is it with you? Is it a fact that you habitually omit those secret duties, and are more careful to perform your public duties than private ones? Then what is your character? Do you need to be told? "They loved the praise of men more than the praise of God."

7. The conscience of this class of persons seems to be formed on other principles than those of the Gospel.

They seem to have a conscience in those things that are popular, and no conscience at all on those things that are not required by public sentiment. You may preach to them ever so plainly, their duty, and prove it ever so clearly, and even make them confess that it is their duty, and yet so long as public sentiment does not require it, and it is not a matter of reputation, they will continue on in the same way as before. Show them a "Thus saith the Lord," and make them see that their course is palpably inconsistent with Christian perfection and contrary to the interests of the kingdom of Christ, and yet they will not alter. They make it manifest that it is not the requirement of God they regard, but the requirement of public opinion. They love the praise of men more than the praise of God.

8. This class of persons generally dread very much, the thought of being considered fanatical.

They are ignorant, practically, of a first principle in religion, "that all the world is wrong." That the public sentiment of the world is all against God, and that everyone who intends to serve God must in the first instance set his face against the public sentiment of the world. They are to take it for granted that in a world of rebels public sentiment is as certainly wrong as that there is a controversy with God. They have never had their eyes open to this fundamental truth, that the world is wrong, and that God's ways are directly over against their ways. Consequently, it is true, and always has been true, that "all that will live godly in Christ Jesus shall suffer persecution." They shall be called fanatical, superstitious, ultras and the like. They always have been and they always will be, as long as the world is wrong.

But this class of persons will never go further than is consistent with the opinions of worldly men. They say they must do this and that in order to have influence over such men. Right over against this is the course of the true friends of God and man. Their leading aim is to reverse the order of the world and turn the world upside down, to bring all men to obey God and all the opinions of men to conform to the word of God and all the usages and institutions of the world to accord with the spirit of the Gospel.

9. They are very intent on making friends on both sides.

They take the middle course always. They avoid the reputation of being righteous overmuch, on the one hand; and on the other hand, of being lax or irreligious. It has been so for centuries, that a person could maintain a reputable profession of religion without ever being called fanatical. And the standard is still so low that probably the great mass of the Protestant churches are trying to occupy this middle ground. They mean to have friends on both sides. They are not set down as reprobates on the one hand, nor as fanatics or bigots on the other. They are "fashionable Christians!" They may be called fashionable Christians for two reasons. One is that their style of religion is popular and fashionable, and the other is that they generally follow worldly fashions. Their aim in religion is not to do anything that will disgust the world. No matter what God requires, they are determined to be so prudent as not to bring on them the censures of the world nor offend the enemies of God. They have manifestly more regard to men than to God. And if they are ever so circumstanced that they must do that which will displease their friends and neighbors or offend God, they will offend God. If public sentiment clashes with the commands of God, they will yield to public sentiment.

10. They will do more to gain the applause of men than to gain the applause of God.

This is evident from the fact that they will yield obedience only to those requirements of God which are sustained by public opinion. Although they will not exercise self-denial to gain the applause of God, yet they will exercise great self-denial to gain the applause of men. The men that gave up ardent spirits because public sentiment rendered it necessary will give up wine also whenever a public sentiment sufficiently powerful shall demand it, and not till then.

11. They are more anxious to know what are the opinions of men about them than to know what is God's opinion of them.

If one of this class is a minister and preaches a sermon, he is more anxious to know what the people thought of it than to know what God thought of it. And if he make anything like a failure, the disgrace of it with men cuts him ten times more than the thought that he has dishonored God or hindered the salvation of souls. Just so with an elder, or a member of the church, of this class. If he pray in a meeting or exhort, he is more concerned to know what is thought of it than to know how God is pleased.

If such a one has some secret sin found out, he is vastly more distressed about it because he is disgraced than because God is dishonored. Or if he fall into open sin, when he comes to be met with it, he cares as much again about the disgrace as about the sin of it.

They are more anxious about their appearance in the eyes of the world than in the eyes of God. Females of this character are vastly more anxious, when they go to church, how the body shall appear in the eyes of men than how the heart shall appear in the eyes of God. Such a one will be all the week engaged in getting everything in order so as to make her person appear to advantage, and perhaps will not spend half an hour in her closet to prepare her heart to appear before God in his courts. Everybody can see at a glance what this religion is, the moment it is held up to view. Nobody is at a loss to say what that man's or that woman's name is—it is "hypocrite." They will go into the house of God with their hearts dark as midnight, while everything in their external appearance is comely and decent. They must appear well in the eyes of men, no matter how that part is on which God fixes his eye. The heart may be dark and disordered and polluted, and they care not, so long as the eye of man detects no blemish.

12. They refuse to confess their sins in the manner which the law of God requires, lest they should lose their reputation among men.

If they are ever required to make confession of more than they think consistent with their reputation, they are more anxious as to how it will affect their character than to know whether God is satisfied.

Search your hearts, you that have made confessions, and see which most affects your minds—the question what God thought of it, or what men thought of it. Have you refused to confess what you knew God required because it would hurt your reputation among men? Will not God judge your hearts? Only be honest now, and let it be answered.

13. They will yield to custom what they know to be injurious to the cause of religion, and to the welfare of mankind.

A striking instance of this is found in the manner of keeping New Year's Day. Who does not know that the customary manner of keeping New Year's Day—setting out their wine and their rich cake and costly entertainments, and spending the day as they do—is a waste of money, hurtful to health, and injurious to their own souls and to the interests of religion? And yet they do it. Shall we be told that persons who will do this, when they know it is injurious, supremely love God? I care not who attempts to defend such a custom, it is wrong and every Christian must know it to be so. And those who persist in it, when they know better, demonstrate that a supreme regard to God is not their rule of life.

14. They will do things of doubtful character, or things the lawfulness of which they strongly doubt, in obedience to public sentiment.

You will recollect that on the evening of the first day of the year I took up this subject, and showed that those who do things of doubtful character, of the lawfulness of which they are not satisfied, are condemned for it in the sight of God.

15. They are often ashamed to do their duty, and so much ashamed that they will not do it.

Now when a person is so much ashamed to do what God requires as not to do it, it is plain that his own reputation is his idol. How many do you find who are ashamed to acknowledge Jesus Christ, ashamed to reprove sin in high places or low places, and ashamed to speak out when religion is assailed? If they supremely regarded God, could they ever be ashamed of doing their duty? Suppose a man's wife were calumniated, would he be ashamed to defend his wife? By no means. If his children were abused, would he be ashamed to take their part? Not if he loved them, it would not be shame that would deter him from defending his wife or children. If a man was friendly to the administration of the government of his country, and heard it calumniated, would he be ashamed to defend it? He might not think it expedient to speak, for other reasons; but if he was a true friend to the government, he would not be ashamed to speak in its behalf, anywhere.

Now, such persons as I am speaking of will not take decided ground when they are among the enemies of truth, where they would be subject to reproach for doing it. They are very bold for the truth when among its friends, and will make a great display of their courage. But when put to the trial, they will sell the Lord Jesus Christ, or deny him before his enemies and put him to open shame, rather than rebuke wickedness or speak out in his cause among his enemies.

16. They are opposed to all encroachments on their self-indulgence, by advancing light on practical subjects.

They are much disturbed by every new proposal that draws on their purses, or breaks in upon their habitual self-indulgence. And you may talk as much and preach as much in favor of it as you please, there is only one way to reach this kind of people, and that is by creating a new public sentiment. When you have brought over, by the power of benevolence and of conscience, a sufficient number in the community to create a public sentiment in its favor, then they will adopt your new proposals, and not before.

17. They are always distressed at what they call the "ultraism" of the day.

They are much afraid the ultraism of the present day will destroy the church. They say we are carrying things too far, and we shall produce a reaction. Take, for instance, the Temperance Reformation. The true friends of temperance now know that alcohol is the same thing wherever it is found, and that to save the world and banish intemperance, it is necessary to banish alcohol in all its forms. The pinch of the Temperance Reformation has never yet been decided. The mass of the community has never been called to any self-denial in the cause. The place where it will pinch is when it comes to the question whether men will exercise self-denial to crush the evil. If they may continue to drink wine and beer, it is no self-denial to give up ardent spirits. It is only changing the form in which alcohol is taken, and they can drink as freely as before. Many friends of the cause, when they saw what multitudes were rushing into it, were ready to shout a triumph. But the real question is not yet tried. And multitudes will never yield until the friends of God and man can form a public sentiment so strong as to crush the character of every man who will not give it up. You will find many doctors of divinity and pillars of the church, who are able to drink their wine, that will stand their ground; and no command of God, no requirement of benevolence, no desire to save souls, no pity for bleeding humanity, will move such persons, until you can form a public sentiment so powerful as to force them to it, on penalty of loss of reputation. For they love the praise of men.

And it is a query now in my mind, a matter of solemn and anxious doubt, whether in the present low state of piety and decline of revivals of religion in the church, a public sentiment can be formed so powerful as to do this. If not, we shall be driven back. The Temperance Reformation, like a dam of sand, will be swept away, the floodgates will be opened again and the world will go reeling—down to hell. And yet thousands of professors of religion, who want to enjoy public respect and at the same time enjoy themselves in their own way, are crying out as if they were in distress at the ultraism of the times.

18. They are often opposed to men and measures and things while they are unpopular and subject to reproach; and when they become popular, fall in with them.

Let an individual go through the churches in any section, and wake them up to a revival of religion; and while he is little known, these persons are not backward to speak against him. But let him go on and gain influence, and they will fall in and commend him and profess to be his warmest friends. It was just so with Jesus Christ. Before his death, he had a certain degree of popularity. Multitudes would follow him, as he went through the streets, and cry "Hosanna, Hosanna!" But observe, they never would follow him an atom farther than his popularity followed him. As soon as he was arrested as a criminal, they all turned round and began to cry, "Crucify him, crucify him!"

This class of persons, as they set with the tide one way when a man is reproached, so they will set with the tide the other way when he comes to be honored. There is only one exception. And that is, when they have become so far committed to the opposition that they cannot come round without disgrace. And then they will be silent until another opportunity comes up for letting out the burning fires that are rankling within them.

Very often a revival in a church, when it first begins, is opposed by certain members of the church. They do not like to have such things carried on, they are afraid there is too much animal excitement and the like. But the work goes on, and by and by they seem to fall in and go with the multitude. At length the revival is over and the church grows cold again; and before long you will find this class of persons renewing their opposition to the work, and as the church declines they press their opposition, and perhaps, in the end, induce the church itself to take ground against the very revival which they had so much enjoyed. This is the very way in which individuals have acted in regard to revivals in this country. There are many such cases. They were awed by public sentiment and made to bow down to the revival while it was in its power; but by and by, as the revival declines, they begin to let out the opposition that is in their hearts, and which was suppressed for a time because the revival was popular.

It has been just so in regard to the cause of missions, in a degree; if anything should turn up, unfavorable to missions, so as to break the present power of public sentiment in their favor, you would find plenty of these fair-weather supporters turning to the opposition.

19. If any measure is proposed to promote religion, they are very sensitive and scrupulous not to have anything done that is unpopular.

If they live in a city, they ask what will the other churches think of such a measure? And if it is likely to bring reproach on their church or their minister, in view of the ungodly or in view of the other churches, they are distressed about it. No matter how much good it will do or how many souls it will save, they do not want to have anything done to injure the respectability of their church.

20. This class of persons never aims at forming a public sentiment in favor of perfect godliness.

The true friends of God and man are always aiming at forming public sentiment, and correcting public sentiment on all points where it is wrong. They are set, with all their hearts, to search out all the evils in the world and to reform the world and drive out iniquity from the earth. The other class is always following public sentiment as it is, and feeling after the course of the tide, to go that way, shrinking back from everything that goes in the face of public sentiment. And they are ready to brand as imprudent, or rash, any man or anything that goes to stem the tide of public sentiment and turn it the other way.

REMARKS

1. It is easy for persons to take credit for their sins, and make themselves believe certain things are acts of piety, which are in fact only acts of hypocrisy.

They do the things that outwardly pertain to piety and they give themselves credit for being pious, when their motives are all corrupt and hollow, and not one of them drawn from a supreme regard to God's authority. This is manifest from the fact that they do nothing except where God's requirements are backed up by public sentiment. Unless you aim to do *all* your duty and yield obedience in *everything,* the piety for which you claim credit is mere hypocrisy and is in fact sin against God.

2. There is a great deal more apparent piety in the church than there is real piety.

3. There are many things which sinners suppose are good but which are abominable in the sight of God.

4. But for the love of reputation and the fear of disgrace, how many there are in the church who would break out into open apostasy.

How many are there here who know you would break out into open vice, were it not for the restraints of public sentiment, the fear of disgrace and the desire to gain the credit of virtue? Where a person is virtuous from a regard to the authority of God, whether public sentiment favor it or frown upon it, that is true piety. If otherwise, they have their reward. They do it for the sake of gaining credit in the eyes of men, and they gain it. But if they expect any favor at the hand of God, they will assuredly be disappointed. The only reward which he will bestow upon such selfish hypocrites is that they may be damned.

And now I wish to know how many of you will determine to do your duty, and all your duty, according to the will of God, let public sentiment be as it may. Who of you will agree to take the Bible for your rule, Jesus Christ for your pattern, and do what is *right,* in all cases whatever man may say or think? Everyone who is not willing to take this ground must regard himself as a stranger to the grace of God. He is by no means in a state of justification. If he is not resolved upon doing what he knows to be right, let public sentiment be as it may, it is proof positive that he loves the praise of men more than the praise of God.

And let me say to the impenitent sinners present. You see what it is to be a Christian. It is to be governed by the authority of God in all things and not by public sentiment, to live not by hopes and fears but by supreme consecration of yourself unto God. You see that if you mean to be religious, you must count the cost. I will not flatter you. I will never try to coax you to become religious by keeping back the truth. If you mean to be Christians, you must give yourselves wholly up to Christ. You cannot float along to heaven on the waves of public sentiment. I will not deceive you on this point.

Do you ask, sinner, what is to become of all these professors of religion who are conformed to the world and who love the praise of men more than the praise of God? I answer—they will go to hell, with you and with all other hypocrites. Just as certain as that the friendship of the world is enmity with God.

Wherefore, come out from among them, my people, and be ye separate, and I will receive you, saith the Lord; I will be a Father to you, and ye shall be my sons and daughters. And now, who will do it? In the church and among sinners, who will do it? Who? Who is on the Lord's side? Who is willing to say, "We will no longer go with the multitude to do evil, but are determined to do the will of God, in all things whatsoever, and let the world think or say of us as it may"? As many of you as are now willing to do this, will signify it by rising in your places before the congregation, and will then kneel down, while prayer is offered, that God would accept and seal your solemn covenant to obey God henceforth in everything, through evil report and through good report.

Charles Grandison Finney (1792–1875)   *This noted evangelist shook up the Christian world. At twenty-nine he experienced a dramatic and sudden conversion which led to his dynamic success as a revivalist preacher. He established the Broadway Tabernacle in New York in 1834 and later became president of Oberlin College even though his own education had been random and late. He continued with his revival meetings along with his career as educator and was heard by millions in England and America who were swayed by his unconventional methods.*

Dwight Lyman Moody/What Think Ye of Christ?

Saying, What think ye of Christ? whose son is he? They say unto him, The Son of David.

I SUPPOSE there is no one here who has not thought, more or less, about Christ. You have heard about him and read about him and heard men preach about him. For eighteen hundred years men have been talking about him and thinking about him; and some have their minds made up about who he is, and doubtless some have not. And although all these years have rolled away this question comes up, addressed to each of us, today, "What think ye of Christ?"

I do not know why it should not be thought a proper question for one man to put to another. If I were to ask you what you think of any of your prominent men, you would already have your mind made up about him. If I were to ask you what you think of your noble queen, you would speak right out and tell me your opinion in a minute. If I were to ask about your prime minister, you would tell me freely what you had for or against him. And why should not people make up their minds about the Lord Jesus Christ, and take their stand for or against him? If you think well of him, why not speak well of him and range yourselves on his side? And if you think ill of him, and believe him to be an impostor and that he did not die to save the world, why not lift up your voice and say you are against him? It would be a happy day for Christianity if men would just take sides, if we could know positively who was really for him, and who was against him.

It is of very little importance what the world thinks of anyone else. The queen and the statesman, the peers and the princes, must soon be gone. Yes, it matters little, comparatively, what we think of them. Their lives can only interest a few, but every living soul on the face of the earth

What Think Ye of Christ?

is concerned with this Man. The question for the world is, "What think ye of Christ?" I do not ask you what you think of the Episcopal Church or of the Presbyterians or the Baptists or the Roman Catholics. I do not ask you what you think of this minister or that, of this doctrine or that; but I want to ask you what you think of the living person of Christ.

I should like to ask, "Was he really the Son of God—the great God-man?" Did he leave heaven and come down to this world for a purpose? Was it really to seek and to save? I should like to begin with the manger and follow him up through the thirty-three years he was here upon earth. I should ask you what you think of his coming into this world, and being born in a manger when it might have been a palace; why he left the grandeur and the glory of heaven, and the royal retinue of angels; why he passed by palaces and crowns and dominion, and came down here alone.

I should like to ask what you think of him as a *teacher*. He spake as never man spake. I should like to take him up as a preacher. I should like to bring you to that mountainside, that we might listen to the words as they fall from his gentle lips. Talk about the preachers of the present day! I would rather a thousand times be five minutes at the feet of Christ, than listen a lifetime to all the wise men in the world. He used just to hang truth upon anything. Yonder is a sower, a fox, a bird; and he just gathers the truth round them, so that you cannot see a fox, a sower or a bird without thinking what Jesus said. Yonder is a lily of the valley; you cannot see it without thinking of his words, "They toil not, neither do they spin." He makes the little sparrow chirping in the air preach to us. How fresh those wonderful sermons are, how they live today! How we love to tell them to our children, how the children love to hear! "Tell me a story about Jesus,"—how often we hear it; how the little ones love his sermons! No storybook in the world will ever interest them like the stories that he told. And yet how profound he was, how he puzzled the wise men, how the scribes and the Pharisees could never fathom him! Oh, do you not think he was a wonderful preacher?

I should like to ask you what you think of him as a *physician*. A man would soon have a reputation as a doctor if he could cure as Christ did. No case was ever brought to him but what he was a match for. He had but to speak the word, and disease fled before him. Here comes a man covered with leprosy. "Lord, if thou wilt thou canst make me clean," he cries. "I will," says the Great Physician, and in an instant the leprosy is gone. The world has hospitals for incurable diseases, but there were no incurable diseases with him.

Now see him in the little home at Bethany, binding up the wounded hearts of Martha and Mary, and tell me what you think of him as a *comforter*. He is a husband to the widow and a father to the fatherless. The weary may find a resting-place upon that breast, and the friendless may reckon him their friend. He never varies, he never fails, he never dies. His sympathy is ever fresh, his love is ever free. O widow and orphans, O sorrowing and mourning, will you not thank God for Christ the comforter?

But these are not the points I wish to take up. Let us go to those who knew Christ and ask what they thought of him. If you want to find out what a man is nowadays, you inquire about him from those who know him best. I do not wish to be partial; we will go to his enemies, and to his friends. We will ask them, "What think ye of Christ?" We will ask his friends and his enemies. If we only went to those who liked him, you would say, "Oh, he is so blind; he thinks so much of the man that he can't see His faults. You can't get anything out of him, unless it be in His favor; it is a one-sided affair altogether." So we shall go in the first place to his enemies, to those who hated him, persecuted him, cursed and slew him. I shall put you in the jury box, and call upon them to tell us what they think of him.

First, among the witnesses, let us call upon the Pharisees. We know how they hated him. Let us put a few questions to them. Come, Pharisees, tell us what you have against the Son of God. What do *you* think of Christ? Hear what they say, "This man receiveth sinners." What an argument to bring against him! Why, it is the very thing that makes us love him. It is the glory of the Gospel. He receives sinners. If he had not, what would have become of *us*? Have you nothing more to bring against him than *this*? Why, it is one of the greatest compliments that was ever paid him. Once more: when he was hanging on the tree, you had this to say of him, "He saved others, himself he cannot save." And so he did save others, but he could not save himself and save us too. So he laid down his own life for yours and mine. Yes, Pharisees, you have told the truth for once in your lives: *he saved others.* He died for others. He was a ransom for many; so it is quite true what you think of him, *"He saved others, himself he cannot save."*

Now, let us call upon Caiaphas. Let him stand up here in his flowing robes; let us ask him for his evidence. "Caiaphas, you were chief priest when Christ was tried; you were president of the Sanhedrin; you were in the council chamber when they found him guilty; you yourself condemned him. Tell us, what did the witnesses say? On what grounds did you judge him? What testimony was brought against him?"

"He hath spoken blasphemy," says Caiaphas. "He said, 'Hereafter shall ye see the Son of Man sitting on the right hand of power, and coming in the clouds of heaven.' When I heard that, I found him guilty of blasphemy; I rent my mantle and condemned him to death." Yes, all that they had against him was that he was the Son of God; and they slew him for the promise of his coming for his bride.

Now, let us summon Pilate. Let him enter the witness-box. "Pilate, this man was brought before you; you examined him; you talked with him face to face: what think ye of Christ?" "I find no fault in him," says Pilate. "He said he was the King of the Jews [just as he wrote it over the cross], but I find no fault in him." Such is the testimony of the man who examined him. And as he stands there, the center of a Jewish mob, there comes along a man, elbowing his way in haste. He rushes up to Pilate and, thrusting out his hand, gives him a message. He tears it open; his face turns pale as he reads, "Have thou nothing to do with *this just man,* for I have suffered many things this day in a dream because of him." It is from Pilate's wife—her testimony to Christ. You want to know what his enemies thought of him? You want to know what a heathen thought? Well, here it is, "no fault in him"; and the wife of a heathen, "this just man!"

And now, look—in comes Judas. He ought to make a good witness. Let us address him: "Come, tell us, Judas, what think ye of Christ. You knew the Master well; you sold him for thirty pieces of silver; you betrayed him with a kiss; you saw him perform those miracles; you were with him in Jerusalem. In Bethany, when he summoned up Lazarus, you were there. What think ye of him?" I can see him as he comes into the presence of the chief priests; I can hear the money ring as he dashes it upon the table—*"I have betrayed innocent blood!"* Here is the man who betrayed him, and this is what he thinks of him! Yes, my friends, God has made every man who had anything to do with the death of his Son put their testimony on record that he was an innocent man.

Let us take the Centurion, who was present at the execution. He had charge of the Roman soldiers. He had told them to make him carry his cross; he had given orders for the nails to be driven into his feet and hands, for the spear to be thrust in his side. Let the Centurion come forward. "Centurion, you had charge of the executioners; you saw that the order for his death was carried out; you saw him die; you heard him speak upon the cross. Tell us, what think ye of Christ?" Hark! Look at him; he is smiting his breast as he cries, *"Truly, this was the Son of God!"*

I might go to the thief upon the cross, and ask what he thought of Him. At first he railed upon Him and reviled Him. But then he thought better of it. "This man hath done nothing amiss," he says. I might go further. I might summon the very devils themselves and ask them for their testimony. Have *they* anything to say of him? Why, the very devils called him the Son of God! In Mark we have the unclean spirit crying, "Jesus, thou Son of the most High God." Men say, "Oh, I believe Christ to be the Son of God, and because I believe it intellectually, I shall be saved." I tell you the devils did that. And they did more than that, *they trembled.*

Let us bring in his friends. We want you to hear their evidence. Let us call that prince of preachers. Let us hear the forerunner, the wilderness preacher, John. Save the Master himself, none ever preached like this man—this man who drew all Jerusalem and all Judea into the wilderness to hear him; this man who burst upon the nations like the flash of a meteor. Let John the Baptist come with his leathern girdle and his hairy coat, and let him tell us what he thinks of Christ. His words, though they were echoed in the wilderness of Palestine, are written in the Book forever, "Behold the Lamb of God which taketh away the sin of the world." This is what John the Baptist thought of him. "I bare record that he is the Son of God." No wonder he drew all Jerusalem and Judea to him, because he preached Christ. And whenever men preach Christ, they are sure to have plenty of followers.

Let us bring in Peter, who was with him on the mount of transfiguration, who was with him the night he was betrayed. "Come, Peter, tell us what you think of Christ. Stand in this witness-box and testify of him. You denied him once. You said, with a curse, you did not know him. Was it true, Peter? Don't you know him?" "Know him!" I can imagine Peter saying, "It was a lie I told them. I *did* know him." Afterwards I can hear him charging home their guilt upon these Jerusalem sinners. He calls him "both Lord and Christ." Such was the testimony on the day of Pentecost, "God hath made that same Jesus both Lord and Christ." And tradition tells us that when they came to execute Peter, he felt he was not worthy to die in the way his Master died, and he requested to be crucified with his head downward. So much did Peter think of him!

Now let us hear from the beloved disciple John. He knew more about Christ than any other man. He had laid his head on his Saviour's bosom. He had heard the throbbing of that loving heart. Look into his Gospel if you wish to know what he thought of Him.

Matthew writes of him as the Royal King come from his throne. Mark writes of him as the servant, and Luke as the Son of Man. John takes up his pen and, with one stroke, forever settles the question of Unitarianism. He goes right back before the time of Adam. "In the beginning was the Word, and the Word was with God, and the Word was God." Look into Revelation. He calls him "the bright and the Morning Star." So John thought well of him—because he knew him well.

We might bring in Thomas, the doubting disciple. "You doubted him,Thomas? You would not believe he had risen, and you put your fingers into the wound in his side. What do you think of him?" *"My Lord and my God!"* says Thomas.

Then go over to Decapolis and you will find Christ has been there casting out devils. Let us call the men of that country and ask what they think of him. "He hath done all things well," they say.

But we have other witnesses to bring in. Take the persecuting Saul, once one of the worst of his enemies. Breathing out threatenings, he meets him. "Saul, Saul, why persecutest thou me?" says Christ; and he might have added, "What have I done to you? Have I injured you in any way? Did I not come to bless you? Why do you treat me thus, Saul?" And then Saul asks, "Who art thou, Lord?" "I am Jesus of Nazareth, whom thou persecutest." You see, he was not ashamed of his name, although he had been in heaven—"I am *Jesus of Nazareth.*" What a change did that one interview make to Paul! A few years after we hear him say, "I have suffered the loss of all things, and do count them but dross that I may win Christ." Such a testimony to the Saviour!

But I shall go still further. I shall go away from earth into the other world. I shall summon the angels and ask what they think of Christ. They saw him in the bosom of the Father before the world was. Before the dawn of creation, before the morning stars sang together, he was there. They saw him leave the throne and come down to the manger. What a scene for them to witness. Ask these heavenly beings what they thought of him then. For once they are permitted to speak; for once the silence of heaven is broken. Listen to their song on the plains of Bethlehem, "Behold, I bring you good tidings of great joy which shall be to all people. For unto you is born this day, in the city of David, a Saviour, which is Christ the Lord." He leaves the throne to save the world. Is it a wonder the angels thought well of him?

Then there are the redeemed saints—they that see him face to face. Here on earth he was never known; no one seemed really to be acquainted with him; but he was known in that world where he had been from the foundation. What do they think of him there? If we could hear from heaven, we should hear a shout which would glorify and magnify his name. We are told that when John was in the Spirit on the Lord's day, and being caught up, he heard a shout around him, ten thousand times ten thousand, and thousands and thousands of voices, "Worthy is the Lamb that was slain to receive power, and riches, and wisdom, and strength, and honor, and glory, and blessing." Yes, he is worthy of all this. Heaven cannot speak too well of him. Oh, that earth would take up the echo, and join with heaven in singing, "Worthy to receive power, and riches, and wisdom, and strength, and honor, and glory, and blessing!"

But there is yet another witness, a higher still. Some think that the God of the Old Testament is the Christ of the New. But when Jesus came out of Jordan, baptized by John, there came a voice from heaven. God the Father spoke. It was his testimony to Christ: "This is my beloved Son, in whom I am well pleased." Ah, yes! God the Father thinks well of the Son. And if God is well pleased with him, so ought we. If the sinner and God are well pleased with Christ, then the sinner and God can meet. The moment you say as the Father said, "I am well pleased with him," and accept him, you are wedded to God. Will you not believe the testimony? Will you not believe this witness, this last of all, the Lord of hosts, the King of kings himself? Once more he repeats it, so that all may know it. With Peter and James and John, on the mount of transfiguration, he cries again, "This is my beloved Son; hear him." And that voice went echoing and re-echoing through Palestine, through all the earth from sea to sea; yes, that voice is echoing still, "hear him; hear him."

My friend, will you hear him today? Hark! what is he saying to you? "Come unto me, all ye that labor and are heavy laden, and I will give you rest. Take my yoke upon you and learn of me, for I am meek and lowly in heart, and ye shall find rest unto your souls. For my yoke is easy, and my burden is light." Will you not think well of such a Saviour? Will you not believe in him? Will you not trust in him with all your heart and mind? Will you not live for him? If he laid down his life for us, is it not the least we can do to lay down ours for him? If he bore the Cross and died on it for me, ought I not to be willing to take it up for him? Oh, have we not reason to think well of him. Do you think it is right and noble to lift up your voice against such a Saviour? Do you think it is just to cry, "Crucify him! Crucify him!" Oh, may God help all of us to glorify the Father, by thinking well of his only-begotten Son.

Dwight Lyman Moody (1837–1899) *Although Dwight L. Moody had little formal education, he established Bible schools in his home town, Northfield, Massachusetts, as well as the Moody Institute in Chicago. He drew thousands into the Christian fold through his preaching here and in Great Britain during his tours with Ira D. Sankey, a song leader. Moody influenced hundreds of thousands of people by his message of conversion and salvation, and his effect on the organization of young people within the Congregational Church is incalculable.*

Thomas DeWitt Talmage/Old Wells Dug Out

And Isaac digged again the wells of water, which they had digged in the days of Abraham his father; for the Philistines had stopped them after the death of Abraham; and he called their names after the names by which his father had called them.

GENESIS 26:18

IN Oriental lands a well of water is a fortune. If a king dug one, he became as famous as though he had built a pyramid or conquered a province. Great battles were fought for the conquest or defense of wells of water; castles and towers were erected to secure permanent possession of them. The traveler today finds the well of Jacob dug one hundred feet through a solid rock of limestone. These ancient wells of water were surrounded by walls of rock. This wall of rock was covered up with a great slab. In the center of the slab there was a hole through which the leathern bottle or earthen jar was let down. This opening was covered by a stone. When Jacob, a young man of seventy years, was courting Rachel, he won her favor, the Bible says, by removing the stone from the opening of the well. He liked *her* because she was industrious enough to come down and water the camels. She liked *him* because he was clever enough to lay hold and give a lift to one who needed it.

It was considered one of the greatest calamities that could happen to a nation when these wells of water were stopped. Isaac, you see in the text, found out that the wells of water, that had been dug out by his father Abraham at great expense and care, had been filled up by the spiteful Philistines. Immediately Isaac orders them all opened again. I see the spades plunging, and the earth tossing and the water starting, until the old wells are entirely restored; and the cattle come down to the trough and thrust their nostrils in the water, their bodies quaking at every swallow, until they lift up their heads and look around and take a long breath, the water from the sides of their mouths dripping in sparkles down into the trough. I never tasted such water in my life as in my boyhood I drank out of the moss-covered bucket that swung up on the chains of the old well sweep; and I think when Isaac leaned over the curb of these restored wells, he felt within himself that it was a beverage worthy of God's brewing. He was very careful to call all the wells by the same names which his father had called them by; and if this well was called "The Well in the Valley" or "The Well by the Rock" or "The Well of Bubbles," Isaac baptized it with the same nomenclature.

You have noticed, my Christian friends, that many of the old Gospel wells that our fathers dug have been filled up by the modern Philistines. They have thrown in their skepticisms and their philosophies until the well is almost filled up and it is nigh impossible to get one drop of the clear water. These men tell us that you ought to put the Bible on the same shelf with the Koran and the old Persion manuscripts, and to read it with the same spirit; and there is not a day but somebody comes along and drops a brick or a stone or a carcass in this old Gospel well. We are told that all the world wants is development, forgetful of the fact that without the Gospel the world always develops downward, and that if you should take the religion of Christ out of this world, in one hundred years it would develop into the "Five Points" of the universe. Yet there are a great many men and there are a great many rostrums whose whole work it is to fill up these Christian wells.

You will not think it strange, then, if the Isaac who speaks to you this morning tries to dig open some of the old wells made by Abraham, his father, nor will you be surprised if he calls them by the same old names.

Bring your shovel and pickaxe and crowbar, and the first well we will open is the glorious "Well of the Atonement." It is nearly filled up with the chips and debris of old philosophies that were worn-out in the time of Confucius and Zeno, but which smart men in our day unwrap from their mummy bandages and try to make us believe are original with themselves. I plunge the shovel to the very bottom of the well, and I find the clear water starting. Glorious " Well of the Atonement!" Perhaps there are people here who do not know what "atonement" means, it is so long since you have heard the definition. The word itself, if you give it a peculiar pronunciation, will show you the meaning—at-one-ment.

Man is a sinner, and deserves to die. Jesus comes in and bears his punishments and weeps his griefs. I was lost once, but now I am found. I deserved to die, but Jesus took the lances into his own heart, until his face grew pale and his chin dropped on his chest and he had strength only to say, "It is finished." The boat swung round into the trough of the sea and would have been swamped, but Jesus took hold of the oar. I was set in the battle, and must have been cut to pieces had not, at nightfall, he who rideth on the white horse come into the fray. That which must have been the Waterloo of my defeat now becomes the Waterloo of my triumph, because Blucher has come up to save. Expiation! expiation! The law tried me for high treason against God, and found me guilty. The angels of God were the jurors impaneled in the case, and they found me guilty. I was asked what I had to say why sentence of eternal death should not be pronounced upon me, and I had nothing to say. I stood on the scaffold of God's justice; the black cap of eternal death was about to be drawn over my eyes, when from the hill of Calvary One came. He dashed through the ranks of earth and heaven and hell. He rode swiftly. His garments were dyed with blood, his face was bleeding, his feet were dabbled with gore and he cried out, "Save that man from going down to the pit. I am the ransom." And he threw back the coat from his heart, and that heart burst into a crimson fountain and he dropped dead at my feet. And I felt of his hands and they were stiff, and I felt of his feet and they were cold, and I felt of his heart and it was pulseless, and I cried, "Dead!" And angels with excited wings flew upward, amidst the thrones, crying, "Dead!" and spirits lost in black brood wheeled down amidst the caverns, crying, "Dead!" Expiation! Expiation!

Cowper, overborne with his sin, threw himself into a chair by the window, picked up a New Testament, and his eye lighted upon this, "Whom God hath set forth as a propitiation through faith in his blood"; and instantly he was free! Unless Christ pays our debt, we go to eternal jail. Unless our Joseph opens the king's corncrib, we die of famine. One sacrifice for all.

A heathen got worried about his sins, and came to a priest and asked how he might be cured. The priest said, "If you will drive spikes in your shoes and walk five hundred miles, you will get over it." So he drove spikes in his shoes and began the pilgrimage, trembling, tottering, agonizing on the way, until he came about twenty miles and sat down under a tree, exhausted. Near by a missionary was preaching Christ, the Saviour of all men. When the heathen heard it, he pulled off his sandals, threw them as far as he could, and cried, "That's what I want; give me Jesus! give me Jesus!" Oh, ye who have been convicted and worn of sin, trudging on all your days to reap eternal woe, will you not, this morning, at the announcement of a full and glorious atonement, throw your torturing transgressions to the winds? "The blood of Jesus Christ cleanseth from all sin"—that was the very passage that came to the tent of Hedley Vicars, the brave English soldier, and changed him into a hero for the Lord.

Around this great "Well of the Atonement" the chief battles of Christianity are to be fought. Ye Bedouins of infidelity, take the other wells but do not touch this. I call it by the same name that our father Abraham gave it—"the Atonement." Here is where he stood, his staff against the well-curb. Here is where he walked, the track of his feet all around about the well. This is the very water that with trembling hand, in his dying moment, he put to his lips. Oh, ye sun-struck, desert-worn pilgrims, drive up your camels and dismount. A pitcher of water for each one of you, and I will fill the trough for the camels. See the bucket tumble and fish into the depths; but I bring it up again, hand over hand, crying, "Ho, everyone that thirsteth, come ye to the waters!"

Now, bring your shovels and your pickaxes, and we will try to open another well. I call it "The Well of Christian Comfort." You have noticed that there are a good many new ways of comforting. Your father dies. Your neighbor comes in, and he says, "It is only a natural law that your father should die. The machinery is merely worn out"; and before he leaves you, he makes some other excellent remarks about the coagulation of blood, and the difference between respiratory and nitrogenized food. Your child dies, and your philosophic neighbor comes, and for your soothing tells you that it was impossible the child should live with such a state of mucous membrane. Out! with your chemistry and physiology when I have trouble, and give me a plain New Testament! I would rather have an illiterate man from the backwoods who knows Christ, talk with me when I am in trouble, than the profoundest worldling who does not know him. The Gospel, without telling you anything about mucous membrane or gastric juice or hydrochloric acid, comes and says, "All things together work for good to those who love God," and that if your child is gone it is only because Jesus has folded it in his arms, and that the Judgment Day will explain things that are now inexplicable. Oh, let us dig out this Gospel well of comfort. Take away the stoicism and fatality with which you have been trying to fill it. Drive up the great herd of your cares and anxieties, and stop their bleating in this cool fountain! To this well David came when he lost Absalom; and Paul, when his back was red and raw with the scourge; and Dr. Young, when his daughter died; and Latimer, when the flames of martyrdom leaped on his track; and M'Kail, when he heard the knife sharpening for his beheading; and all God's sheep in all the ages.

After one of Napoleon's battles, it was found that the fight had been so terrific that, when the muster roll was called of one regiment, there were only three privates and one drummer boy that answered. An awful fight that! Oh, that Christ today might come so mightily for the slaying of your troubles and sorrows that when you go home and call the muster roll of the terrible troop, not one—not one—shall answer, Christ having quelched every annoyance and salved every gash and wiped every tear and made complete extermination.

Now bring your shovels and pickaxes and we will dig out another well—a well opened by our father Abraham, but which the Philistines have filled up. It is "The Well of Gospel Invitation." I suppose you have noticed that religious address in this day, for the most part, has gone into the abstract and essayic. You know the word "sinner" is almost dropped out of the Christian vocabulary; it is not thought polite to use that word now. It is methodistic or old-fashioned. If you want to tell men that they are sinners, you must say they are spiritually erratic or have moral deficits or they have not had a proper spiritual development; and I have not heard in twenty years that old hymn,

Come, ye sinners, poor and needy.

In the first place, they are not sinners; and in the second place, they are neither poor nor needy. I have heard Christian men in prayer meetings and elsewhere talk as though there were no very great radical change before a man becomes a Christian. All he has got to do is to stop swearing, clear his throat a few times, take a good wash, and he is ready for heaven. My friends, if every man has not gone astray, and if the whole race is not plunged in sin and ruin, then that Bible is the greatest fraud ever enacted; for, from beginning to end, it sets forth that they are. Now, my brothers and sisters, if a man must be born again in order to see the kingdom of God, and if a man is absolutely ruined unless Christ check his course, why not proclaim it? There must be an infinite and radical change in every man's heart, or he cannot come within ten thousand miles of heaven. There must be an earthquake in his soul, shaking down his sins; and there must be the trumpet blast of Christ's resurrection bringing him up from the depths of sin and darkness into the glorious life of the Gospel. Do you know why more men do not come to Christ? It is because men are not invited that they do not come. You get a general invitation from your friend, "Come round sometime to my house and dine with me." You do not go. But he says, "Come around today at four o'clock, and bring your family, and we'll dine together." And you say, "I don't know as I have any engagement; I will come." "I expect you at four o'clock." And you go. The world feels it is a general invitation to come around sometime and sit at the great Gospel feast, and men do not come because they are not specially invited. It is because you do not take hold of them and say, "My brother, come to Christ; come now—come now." How was it that in the days of Daniel Baker and Truman Osborne and Nettleton, so many thousands came to Jesus? Because those men did nothing else but invite them to come. They spent their lifetime uttering invitations, and they did not mince matters either. Where did John Bunyan's pilgrim start from? Did he start from some easy, quiet, cozy place? No; if you have read John Bunyan's *Pilgrim's Progress,* you know where he started from, and that was the *City of Destruction*, where every sinner starts from. Do you know what Livingstone, the Scotch minister, was preaching about in Scotland when three hundred souls under one sermon came to Christ? He was preaching about the human heart as unclean and hard and stony. Do you know what George Whitefield was preaching about in his first sermon, when fifteen souls saw the salvation of God? It was this: "Ye must be born again." Do you know what is the last subject he ever preached upon? "Flee the wrath to come." Oh, that the Lord God would come into our pulpits and prayer meetings and Christian circles, and bring us from our fine rhetoric and profound metaphysics and our elegant hair-splitting, to the old-fashioned "Well of Gospel Invitation." There are enough sinners in this house this morning, if they should come to God, to make joy enough in heaven to keep jubilee a thousand years. Why not come? Have you never had a special invitation to come? If not, I give it now: you, you, you, come now to Jesus! Why do you try to cover up that cancer with a piece of court plaster when Christ the surgeon, with his scalpel, would take it all away and it would never come again? Do you know that your nature is all wrong unless it has been changed by the grace of God? Do you not know that God can not be pleased with you, my dear brother, in your present state? Do you know that your sinful condition excites the wrath of God? "God is angry with the wicked every day." Do you not know that you have made war upon God? Do you not know that you have plunged your spear into the Saviour's side, and that you have punctured his temples and spiked his feet, and that you have broken his heart?

Oh, is this what he deserves, you blood-bought soul? Is this the price you pay him for his long earthly tramp and his shelterless nights and his dying prayer and the groan that made creation shiver? Do you want to drive another nail into him? Do you want to stick him with another thorn? Do you want to join the mob that with bloody hands smote him on the cheek, crying, "His blood be on us and our children forever." Oh, your sins! And when I say that, I do not pick out some man who may not have been in a house of worship for forty years, but I pick out any man you choose whose heart has not been changed by the grace of God. Oh, your sins! I press them on your attention—the sins of your lifetime. What a record for a death pillow. What data for the Judgment Day. What a cup of gall for your lips. Look at all the sins of your childhood and riper years, with their forked tongues and adder stings and deathless poignancy, unless Jesus with his heel shall crush the serpents. You have sinned against your God; you have sinned against your Jesus; you have sinned against your grave—ay, you have sinned against the little resting place of your darling child, for you will never see her again unless you repent. How can you go to the good place, the pure place where she is, your heart unpardoned? You have sinned against a Christian father's counsel and a dying mother's prayer.

If we are this morning on the wrong side, let us cross over—let us cross over now. Blessed Jesus, we come, bruised with sin, and throw ourselves in the arms of thy compassion! None ever wanted thee more than we. Oh, turn on us thy benediction! Whatever else we lose or get, we must win heaven. "Lord, save us—we perish!"

Thomas DeWitt Talmage (1832–1901)   *Dr. Talmage was born in Bound Brook, New Jersey. His gift for publishing brought him to the Christian Herald. His sermons appeared in more than six hundred newspapers, with Brooklyn Tabernacle the outlet for his preaching skills.*

Russell Herman Conwell/
Nothing but Slag

IN the thirteenth chapter of Nehemiah, the second verse, the last clause of the verse, are these words, "Howbeit our God turned the curse into a blessing."

Slag was all there was left; nothing but slag—ashes, remnants, broken pieces and heaps of rubbish, remains of what had once been a furnace—slag. There are lives that are nothing but slag; there are men who hear me speak now—and it is why I speak—who regard their lives as failures, who look upon the past burning experience with only a sense of present loss, who feel that they are like slag, upon which nothing will grow, which contains nothing apparently of any value, nothing but slag. That is the life, that is the result, that is the sum total of the years wasted—lives nothing but slag. It is to bring a measure of the love which Jesus brought into the world, and to present the godly side of his character that we may in some measure imitate it, that I endeavor to speak tonight of how our God turned this curse into a blessing.

When Balaam went to curse the people of Israel from Moab, and looked down on the encampment of the Israelites, God compelled him to bless them.

It is well for many of us when we wake up and find that our lives are wasted, nothing but slag.

The slag a mine of values
Up in Bethlehem, Pennsylvania, some years ago, a young man inherited an iron furnace. He endeavored to carry it on as best he could, but being a young man, with inherited wealth, he was not acquainted with the present work, his muscles were not fitted for it, his brain was not adapted to it, his education had led him aside into literary affairs rather than into iron and steel. He endeavored as best he could to manage the furnace but it continually ran down; and as the rates of freight went up

and the expense of getting coal was greater and the difficulty of mining
the iron ore in the Superior regions increased his difficulty, he was
almost in despair, and one night unexpectedly, and when he was fearing
the oncoming of his creditors, the last of the crisis fell—the furnace
burned to the ground, burst forth from its bonds of heat and destroyed
the whole plant.

All he could do the next morning was to go out and look over the pile
of slag. A few pieces of molten iron were left and parts of the brickwork
remained, but it was nothing but an advertisement of ruin, a useless
wreck of human life. He had no money and he had no furnace—nothing
that his father had left him—so his position looked wretched indeed. He
had nothing but a long ridge of slag along the river at Bethlehem. He
went out in the gloom and showed his friends and his creditors around
over the place, and said, "My grandfather began here, and my father has
been piling up this slag here for fifty years, and I have been piling it here
for ten years; I have wasted all my father's fortune, and all there is, is
slag."

But there are times when, if we imitate the godly example set for us,
we shall find that slag is not the most worthless material to have after all.
We shall find that dust and ashes is not the most wretched condition,
and that out of a wasted life, that seems utterly wasted, broken forever,
there may be found much after all which is a blessing. That man said,
"This is all I own, this is all I own."

As he gazed over the wretched heaps of heated bricks, where the
furnace itself had fallen through, with one side upon the slag heap, he
found a little creeping rivulet of iron, that had been melted into the slag
heap and had trickled down, chilled, like icicles, through the ends of the
slag heap. A friend said to him, "You must have wasted a good deal of
iron here, because here it is all melted over by this accident." He caught
at the thought, "That is true, we have wasted a good deal of iron, we
have been very careless about it, we will now examine it and see if there
is anything left worth remelting."

He called the attention of a scientific man to it, who said, "With
improved methods you would get out of that slag heap nearly as much
value for steel as you formerly got out of it for iron." Another man said,
"Don't be discouraged; don't you know they make cement of slag? They
make it in England, not in this country, but there the best cement is made
out of slag." He then wrote for particulars, and with the advertisement
came the directions showing him how he could make the most beautiful
crown glass out of that heap. It began to seem to be an altogether new
mine to him, and then at last, as though the resources of the slag heap
could never be exhausted, a man came and offered him a considerable
sum for it, which he refused, but they finally went into partnership and
used the slag heap to make this patent stone for building purposes.

You can go to Bethlehem now, and they will tell you that you cannot
find a trace of that slag heap, it has been turned into iron, turned into
cement, turned into patent stone, and the man, not having the fortune
that was left to him, lives in this city; one of our most esteemed citizens,

and one of his intimate friends told me the story of his life. It was a slag heap, nothing but ashes and dust and slag, a life that seemed to be ruined and wasted, and yet to him the curse became a blessing, and in God's way, he turned that which was useless to that which was very, very useful.

I remember after a great fire in Boston, which swept away a whole block of valuable property, I, as a newspaper man, went over the ruins for the purpose of making a report to my paper concerning it. I had been up the whole night, as the fire was a large one and had carried away millions of dollars worth of property, but I came around in the morning and stood upon the corner of Franklin and Pearl streets, and there was a sign put on a rough board, "Cast down, but not destroyed." Everything was in ruins; there was nothing but ashes, nothing there except the lot itself, and there it was, that quotation from Second Corinthians: "Cast down, but not destroyed."

He had lost everything apparently, but yet, in the corner of the cellar, in the corner next to Pearl street, there were some drugs stored, and the fire had produced many great changes, changes to such an extent that a professor from Harvard University ordered that the police should guard that cellar in order that the institution to which he belonged might make an examination of the great results that had been accomplished on these drugs contained in the cellar, by the awful and continuous heat of so many hours' duration. Out of that examination came—a relative of mine was interested in the chemical examination, so I know it in detail—out of that examination came to that man who owned the block—and he owns it still—a far greater wealth than he ever had before. Out of the known combinations which heat will make of chemicals and minerals so deposited as they were at the time of this fire, there came an almost complete scientific revolution. In the *Scientific Weekly* and in *The Popular Scientific Monthly* there was, the second month after that fire, a long list of improvements which that fire revealed in the management and discoveries of chemistry.

The schoolmaster failure

"Cast down, but not destroyed." Clear down to the bottom, seemingly to have nothing. "Persecuted, but not forsaken; cast down, but not destroyed." This text expresses all through the spirit of Christ, and one of the sides of his character that is worth your consideration and mine, my friend, for I know you are discouraged, but God sent me here to speak to you because you are discouraged, because no man is exempt from these experiences. We are born into this world imperfect, sinful beings, inclined to do wrong; and the only education we can ever get is from the education of our failures, for "we rise by stepping-stones upon our own dead selves." Never can you find it any different. No man has ever made a great success that should be a credit to him or others unless it has come from his wise calculations of previous failures.

Education is that. If you take a child to school, it fails in its work; if it does not, it does not need to go to school. It is going to school to learn from failures. You give him a problem, and he tries to work it out, but he fails. That shows him his ignorance, his imperfections; that shows that he is unrighteous; he has learned that he is a sinner, that he is not in accordance with God, he has made a failure. He then works it over again, and makes another failure; he tries it again and makes another failure, learning all the time from his failures, until he is able to work out the problem. That is progress, that is education. No kind of education in life is any different; we are born into these imperfections, and when we do learn anything, we learn it from previous failures. All of you have learned to make a dress, though you failed many times; some are able to make a beautiful painting, though they failed again and again before they were able to do it. Who ever accomplished anything worth accomplishing without being obliged to lift themselves forward by the failures of the past, without stepping upward from their failures?

The spirit of the learner

I saw a little child, as you see them again and again, in the cars one day, near the steam-heating pipe; and he went near to it, and made an awful face and began to whistle with an expression of fear, not that he was really afraid, but he knew that that iron was hot—he knew it was hot. The day was when that child did not know that iron was hot, and when he could not put his hands on that hot piece of iron as if it was cold; but he learned by failures, by the experience of touching his little fingers to it, and by feeling the burn that it was dangerous to approach too near. None of us learn except in that way.

A young man who was here the other day wrote to me from a distant city, saying that he had made up his mind that he was not fitted for a place to which I had recommended him to go. He had this godly spirit, because he wisely did what many a young man failed to do, and determined to learn from his lack of sense. He had been in a place and had been discharged, and instead of getting angry and saying "The world owes me a living," instead of dressing himself up in his best and going out after he had been discharged and saying, "I knew altogether too much for that place," or "They wanted to put some intimate friend in my place," or "I needed political influence," he wisely learned from his lack of sense and sat down, and, as he wrote to me, he began to examine himself and to say, "Why did I fail to keep that place, why did I fail?" And the more he thought of it and the more he studied over it, he concluded that he had not been the friend that he ought to have been to the proprietor, that he did not understand his business as well as other people understood it, and that he was not so faithful in his hours as he ought to have been—until at last he made up his mind that it was his own fault that he lost the place.

He was a wise man. That man is a fool who makes up his mind that it was the other man's fault when he was discharged. It is your own fault if you are discharged. Take it home and learn this valuable lesson as this young man learned it. The world wants men, the world wants you and it wants you to be useful to it; and if you have been discharged, it is your own fault. I do not mean necessarily that it is because of a wickedness, but it is because of your own lack of ability or lack of faithfulness. Go back, young man, and old man, and examine yourself, and say, "I will now see why I failed, and out of my failure I will get wisdom that will prevent failure." Don't be like the little idiot baby; nothing but an idiot baby puts its finger on the range a second time. Find out why you lose your place. Find out what you could have done that would have made you of more use to your employer, and find out where your weakness is; and determine the next time that you will learn from your failures, and make a resource of it. The slag is full of valuable material, but you cannot see it. What can a man do with his ruined life?

Glory out of ashes

How strange this thought came to me when I was at Atlanta, Georgia. I looked out from the hotel cupola, on the distant Kenesaw Mountains, the Chattahoochee River, and could not persuade myself that there were no guns under clouds of smoke, no shufflings and tramping of armed men, no beating of drums, no call of the trumpet and bugle. I could not persuade myself. It seemed to me as though I was not in the natural place, because all those things had been so indelibly fastened on my memory on those days, when from the banks of the Chattahoochee River we were ordered to shell Atlanta. I remember seeing the spire of a church, half-hidden by the trees, and I said to the gunners, "Now take that steeple and make that your corner and aim at that, the city must lie somewhere around that steeple. A city always rises around the church steeple." We could not see the city, but we could see this spire, and I knew it marked the place where the inhabitants were. That was the only part of the city that was visible at all, yet we fired at it, and by firing at it we fired at the city itself.

Then there was the rushing of troops and the hurrying of cavalry, and we rushed on to Atlanta. It so impressed itself upon my young mind that when I went back to Atlanta, Georgia, again, I could not realize there were no guns there, no army there, no tents there. I still remember that day when General McPherson went down in that thicket near Atlanta—one of the truest friends to the soldiers of the Army of the West, the noblest and truest patriot of all that army—and so when I went to Atlanta, Georgia, and looked at the landscape and saw the Kenesaw Mountains, where I had been wounded years before, I saw no remains of the army. It was not there, and I looked and looked about, and strange wonder filled my heart.

What a city, what a growth, what grand buildings, what large enterprises, what manufacturing, what magnificent dwellings! Great Atlanta, the Chicago of the South, the very heart of the South country, containing so much enterprise, so much of business push, that America is proud of the great city, teeming with honor and love, with all its enterprising spirit, a help of the Southern lands, a blessing to the nation. Great and mighty city of Atlanta, I am proud of you today; but the last time, years before, we fired our shot into that same city, and we fired our shot into the very church which invited me to preach in it while I was there. Oh, what a change! What was the difference between that and another Southern city which I visited not long after that? Oh, the difference! When the people of Atlanta found that the war was over and that the South had really been driven back to itself, and that the slaves were freed, they came under the guidance of some of those brave generals of the South.

The people of Atlanta said, "Let us consider it settled; the God of battles has decided the thing; let us go back to our lodges and our work, and let us take hold of the ashes of the city and built up a new city." They did that with the spirit with which they had defended it, like men in desperation, and at last everything was completed. They determined to raise up from the ashes that which should be new and glorious, and the united spirit of the people made the magnificent city of Atlanta—built out of slag that which never would have been had it not been shelled by the Union troops as I have described. It would have been nothing but a weak, mean city with small, narrow streets, had it not been for the disaster which came upon it—which ought not to have come, the result of previous sin, but having learned the lesson of the past, they said, "Let us now begin anew," and out of that ruin and confusion arose a new and grand city.

The other city to which I refer said, "We will stand by the lost cause; we believe we ought to succeed, and perhaps some day we shall succeed." And several of their great leaders took that position. They never would vote in the land, they would move out of the country; and some of its inhabitants did move out of the country, even to Mexico; and when I visited it, the grass grew in the streets, and the people, discouraged, are wondering when the boom of redemption shall ever come to them as it did to Atlanta. They speak in disparaging terms of the boom that the people of Atlanta enjoy. It was not a boom, but the people of Atlanta had this spirit of godliness, this spirit of Christliness, that out of the curse they compelled to come a blessing.

I met a gentleman on the train in Florida who was performing some curious tricks with his left hand. I found out that he could do almost anything with his left hand. He could chop wood and play the violin and perform various tricks of sleight of hand with it. His left hand was worth both of mine. I asked him if he had always had that ability with his left hand. He said no, but when he had both hands he did not appreciate either of them, and when he lost his right hand he was compelled to educate his left hand. After he had lost his right hand, he availed himself of the other remaining hand, and at last he became so wonderfully expert.

There comes to me now a voice of a woman who some years ago called me to her house. She had laid aside all her children in the cemetery, and there was not one child left in that once busy household. It was the saddest I had entered for years. The blinds were kept close, and there were shadows everywhere. That mother sat there, and as she can well testify—though I would not advertise her, God will let me use this illustration and not do harm to her—she complained to me of herself, "I might have saved my children if I had only administered the medicine differently and only brought them up differently, and only taken the warning friends offered about their health and did as people advised me." Oh, wretched mother! She has lost all her children, but she feels that she might have saved them and kept them alive still. Is there a wretchedness greater than that?

You may go there now, and there are three lovely children there. Three more have been sent of God, and they are growing up in the strength and beauty of holiness. That mother learned from the deaths of the past how to care for them. They are now in their happy home—a sweeter home, I may say, is not in this great city. She learned out of the grievous past as Job learned out of his. So there has come a blessing to that home. Of all those sins of omission—and there were many—it is now too late to take one back. We cannot help the past, but let us take the future and build it into something that is better. The cry of every life is, "I might have done better."

I look back on my schooldays, and if there is anything that I am thankful for it is for the whippings I got. I well remember that long switch that had been run through the ashes that it might not break over the backs of the disobedient children. Well I remember punishment after punishment, and I am more thankful for that than for the geography which I forgot or the geometry that I did not learn. Yes, I am more thankful for that than even the kisses that some of them gave me, because out of the pain and failure of it, out of the disgrace of it, there came the determination to do better in the future, to try at least to do something more.

Down in Havana a man had the yellow fever, and was obliged to be set aside by his people, separated, in a sort of retirement, though he was not very sick with the yellow fever. He told me that while he was there a physician came to attend him who also caught the yellow fever, and they were both together in the same room. The physician was one of those wise men, and he said, "Now I am sick and cannot do anything else, I will study this disease on this man and myself, and when I get through I will know all about the yellow fever." When he got over his sickness and his friend had recovered, he became the chief physician, the head physician of the city of Havana. He had learned all about the disease while he was sick with it himself, that he might use his own sickness for other people's health.

It was like that man who was wrecked on a bar on the coast of Florida, and after having been there several days and finally rescued, he thought there ought to be a lighthouse there. He devoted his lifetime to obtaining it, and he finally got the government to aid him in putting a lighthouse there, and it now sends out its light over the waters to save others from danger.

In partnership with Christ's spirit
When General Grant was a young man he was in such disgrace because

of his drinking that he was sent out of the army, sent home, a great disgrace was upon him, and the people said, "That is the end of Ulysses; he will never do anything of any account anymore." It is a blessing for people to get into a disgrace; it is the result of sin. To Grant came this great disgrace. It settled upon him like a pall, with the chill of an icicle— Ulysses S. Grant expelled from the army!

Then he went back to his home, and he was glad to do anything, glad to chop wood. He would do anything. He had no hope or expectation of promotion anymore. Humility had come to him. He had learned that a man can be a sinner, and a man needs to learn that if he wants to succeed. Having had a full understanding of his disgrace, he went out into the world feeling its gloom everywhere. He was willing to do the humblest things, and when the war broke out he was willing to enlist as a common soldier. But someone said, "We need West Point men—we need you to drill the soldiers." He said, "I do not think I will get any command. I am willing to enlist as a common soldier." That led them to believe that he was fit to be a lieutenant, and when he was willing to take that they thought he was fit to be a captain, and when he was willing to take that they thought he ought to be a major, and then they thought he ought to be a colonel, and at last they thought he ought to be a brigadier-general, and General Grant's life, up to the day of his death, was quiet and retired and left no shadow of the previous bitter experience. That same kind of thing that could so teach the lesson to General Grant, that same kind of disgrace that could make him humble, made his life successful as it could not have been without it—just as out of the slag heap came iron, cement and glass. Christ gives this disposition to men, and it is he only who can give it.

If a man would have the spirit of God to recover from a wasted life that which will mean the highest success, he needs the very spirit of our Lord Jesus Christ, and I urge upon you that the first step toward your recovery, toward using the wasted life, is that you go into partnership at once with the spirit of the Lord Jesus Christ.

Russell Herman Conwell (1843–1925) *Russell Conwell gave the world Temple University, Baptist Temple and "Acres of Diamonds." After this master of pulpit and platform was ordained in 1879, millions listened to his famous lecture and responded to his eloquence and style.*

Horace Bushnell/**Christ Regenerates Even the Desires**

And James and John, the sons of Zebedee, came unto him, saying, Master, we would that thou shouldest do for us whatsoever we shall desire.

MARK 10:35

HAD Christ ever been willing to indulge in satire, I think he would have done it here. These young gentlemen make a request so large, and withal so very absurd, that we at least can scarcely restrain a smile at their expense. "Whatsoever we desire"—what power in the creation could give it? And then it would be strange, above all, if they themselves could endure the gift. Still the Saviour hears them kindly and considerately, only showing them, when they come to state the particular thing they want, that even that thing—the sitting on his right and left—means perhaps a good deal more than they imagine; namely, that they drink of his bitter cup and be baptized with his fiery baptism. And when he finds them eager enough to answer still that they can do even that, he only turns them off in the gentlest manner, as children that he sees are looking after a toy which it would cost them a tragedy of suffering to accept. I think we can see, too, in his manner, that he regards them with a pity so considerate, simply because the absurdity they are in is nothing but the common absurdity of the whole living world. For what are we all saying, young and old, the young more eagerly, the old more indivertibly, but exactly what amounts to the same thing, under one form of language or another—"Let us have this, that, the other, anything and everything we desire." Sometimes, if we could see it, we are really saying it in our prayers; though if we should pause long enough upon the matter to let our apprehension run a little way, I think we should almost anyone of us begin to suspect that, having his particular desire, he might sometimes have more than he could bear, and might perfectly know that, if all of us could have it, we should make the world a bedlam of confusion without even a chance of order and harmony left. The first and most forward point accordingly which meets us in the consideration of this subject, is that—

Our human desire, in the common plane of nature and the world, is blind, or unintelligent—out of all keeping with our real wants and possibilities.

I mean by this that we are commonly desiring just what would be the greatest damage to us or the misery worst to be suffered and do not know it; that our tamest desires are often most untamed as regards the order of reason; and that we are all desiring unwittingly what is exactly contrary to God's counsel, what is possible never to be, and if it might, would set us in general repugnance with each other, and society itself.

We are apt to imagine that since we are consciously beings of intelligence, our desires must of course be included, and be themselves intelligent as we are. But we are not intelligent beings, it happens, in the sense here supposed. We are only a little intelligent, in a very few things; and we do not mean by claiming this title, if we understand ourselves, much more than that we are of another grade in comparison with the animals—able that is to be intelligent if we get the opportunity, as they are not. We get room thus, large enough for the fact of a general state of unreason in our desires. After all they may be about as far from intelligence as they can be—possibly not more intelligent than our passions, appetites and bodily secretions are.

In one view still, they are motive forces of endowment for intelligent action, instigators of energy, purpose and character. If we knew them only as they move in their law, bound up in the original sweet harmony of an upright state, we should doubtless see them working instinctively on as co-factors with intelligence, if not intelligent themselves. But, in their present wild way, we see them plainly loosed from their law by transgression—heavings all and foamings of the inward tumult—aspiration, soul-hunger, hate, ambition, pride, passion, lust of gain, lust of power. And what do they signify more visibly than that all right harmony and proportion are gone, as far as they are concerned? Nothing has its natural value before them, because they are reeking themselves in all kinds of disorder bodily and mental. They are phantoms without perception. Even smoke is scarcely less intelligent.

That we may better conceive this general truth, revert, first of all, to the grounds out of which they get their spring. They do not come after reason commonly, asking permission of reason, but they begin their instigations from a fund of raw lustings in the nature clean back of intelligence; rushing out as troops in a certain wildness and confused, blind huddle, that allows us to think of them with no great respect. Understanding well their disorder and confusion, we have it as a common way of speaking that reason must govern them—which supposes, clearly, that reason is not in them. And what do we better know than that only a very partial government of them is possible; that they swarm so fast and fly so far and wildly, that no queen bee of reason can possibly control the hive.

The next thing to be noted is that they have no respect to possibilities and causes, and terms of moral award. Thus one man desires dry weather, and another rain; one, office, and another the same office; one to own a house, another the same house; some to be honorable without character; some to be useful without industry; some to be learned without study. We desire also to own what we mortgage, keep what we sell and get what nobody can have. We cipher out gains against the terms of arithmetic, and even pray God squarely against each other. We run riot in this manner all the while, even against possibilities themselves. A child crying after the moon is in the same scale of intelligence.

Causes again we as little respect. Having it as a clear test of insanity to be reaching after what every body knows eternal causes forbid, we are yet all the while doing it. We want our clocks to move a great deal faster in the playtimes appointed for childhood, and a great deal slower in the payment times appointed in the engagements of manhood. We want poor soils to bear great crops, indolence to be thrifty, intemperance to be healthy, and to have all good supplies come in, doing nothing to earn or provide them.

Against all terms and conditions of morality, also, we want to be confided in, having neither truth nor honesty. We desire to be honored, not having worth enough even to be respected. We want the comforts of religion without religion, asking for rewards to come without duties, and that evils fly away which are fastened by our bad deserts. Of course our judgment goes not with the nonsense there may be in such desires, but they nonetheless make haste, scorning all detentions of judgment.

We get also another kind of proof in this matter, by discovering afterward how absurd our desires have been—that the marriage we sought would have kept us from a good one, and would have been itself a bitter woe; that the bad weather of yesterday, so much against our patience, kept us from the car that was wrecked, or the steamer that was sunk by an explosion; that the treachery of a friend, so much deplored, saved us from the whirlpool of temptation into which we were plunging; that the failure of an adventure we were prosecuting with high expectation, was the only thing that could have sobered our feeling, and prepared us to a penitent life. Sitting down thus, after many years, and looking back on the desires that have instigated our feeling, we discover what a smoke of delusion was in them, and how nearly absurd they were. How often has their crossing been our benefit, and how many thousand times over have we seen it proved by experiment that they were blind instigations thrusting us onward, had they not been mercifully defeated, on results of unspeakable disaster.

There is yet another fact concerning them which has only been adverted to, and requires to be more formally stated; namely, that they are not only blind or wild, as I have been saying, but are also a great part of them morally bad, or wicked—reeking with selfishness, fouled by lust, bittered and soured by envies, jealousies, resentments, revenges, wounded pride, mortified littleness. Thus it was that even Goethe, no very staunch confessor of orthodoxy, was constrained to say, "There is something in every man's heart, which if we could know, would make us hate him." And why not also make him hate himself? Hateful is the only fit epithet for this murky-looking crew that are always breaking into the mind, and hovering in among its best thoughts. Who that is not insane can think it possible to set them in right order, and tame them by his mere will?

What then, is there no possibility but to be driven wild and hag-ridden always by these phantoms? I think there is, and I shall now undertake, for a second stage in my subject, to show—

That Christ new-molds the desires in their spring, and configures them inwardly to God, regenerating the soul at this deepest and most hidden point of character.

We commonly speak of a new-creating grace for souls in the matter of principle, will, the affections; and we magnify our Gospel in the fact that it can undertake a work so nearly central. I think it can do more—that it can even go through into what is background, down into substructure, where the impulsions of desire begin to move unasked, and, by their own self-instigation, stir on all the disorders of the will and the heart; that it can go through, I say, and down among them, reducing them to law, and setting them in harmony with God as they rise.

I do not mean by this that we are put on this work of reduction ourselves, under the divine helps given us. Thus it may be conceived that we are only now to undertake, ourselves, more hopefully the government of our desires. But this matter of government begins too late; for it supposes that the desires to be governed at any given time are already broken loose in their rampages, so that if, by due campaigning, we should get them under, there will always be new ones, not less wild, coming after. Besides, we do not see far enough to govern them understandingly, or in any but a certain coarse way. Such as are most plainly wild, vaulting as it were above the moon, we can well enough distinguish and repress. We can know something, and can see a little way; but if we could see just one inch farther, how often should we stand back from a desire that seems to be quite wise, even as from a precipice. You would see, for example, that the horse you are desiring and bargaining for today will kick you into eternity tomorrow. And so a single stage farther of perception would, almost every hour, set you back in recoil from some other and still other desired object. We can do something, of course, by self-government in this matter, ought to do what we can or what God will help us do wisely; but we want most visibly some other more competent and less partial kind of remedy.

Sometimes a different kind of work is undertaken, that is supposed to be more adequate. A certain class of devotees, meaning to be eminently Christian, set themselves to the task of extirpating their desires, counting it the very essence of perfection to have no desires. It is not as if they were merely in a ferment of misrule, but as if they were properties of nature inherently bad. Hence the attempt is by abnegations, penances, macerations, poverties, mortifications, vows of solitude and complete withdrawment from the world to kill them off; expecting that when they are dead sin itself will be dead, and all the goings on of the soul will be in purity, whereupon the vision of God will follow. Alas, it is not seen that when these impulsive forces of the soul are extirpated, the corrosive will be left in as much greater activity. And the result is that the imagination, goaded by remorse, breaks into riot; and the poor anchorite—how often has it been the fact—begins to see devils and falls into a kind of saintly delirium tremens which is real insanity.

Our Gospel, as I now proceed to show, has a better way. It is never jealous of the desires, puts us to no task of repression or extirpation. It proposes to keep them still on hand, as integral and even necessary parts of our great moral nature. In them it beholds the grand impulsions of activity, the robustness of health, the spiritual momentum of all noblest energies, including even the energies of prayer itself. It even undertakes to intensify the desires, in the highest degree possible, only turning them away from what is selfish and low to what is worthy and good; giving promises for arguments, and saying, "ask what ye will," "open thy mouth wide, and I will fill it."

And it is most refreshing to see how these two young men, James and John, who came to Jesus in their most absurd request, had afterward got on, and had learned to have not smaller desires, but larger and more free, because now trained to be in God's own order. They write books of Scripture under their names, and one of them says, "Whatsoever we ask, we know that we have the petitions that we desired of him"; "whatsoever we ask we receive of him, because we keep his commandments, and do those things that are pleasing in his sight." He was in God's order, and now his desires went all to their mark. The other in his book is yet closer to the point, saying, "If any of you lack wisdom, let him ask of God that giveth to all men liberally, and upbraideth not. But let him ask in faith, nothing wavering." And again he lectures more at large—"From whence come wars and fightings among you? Come they not hence even of your lusts, that war in your members? Ye lust and have not; ye kill and desire to have, and cannot obtain; ye fight and war, yet ye have not, because ye ask not. Ye ask and receive not, because ye ask amiss, that ye may consume it upon your lusts. Do ye think that the Scripture saith in vain the spirit that dwelleth in us lusteth to envy? But he giveth more grace."

Yes, more grace, all the grace that is wanted to set the soul in God's harmony, and give it such desires as he can fitly grant. So these two greedy ones of the former day, we can see, had now made great progress. Living for so long a time in Christ, they had learned to have all their wild lustings put in accord with him, and so to have them liberally filled without upbraiding.

Let us now see how this grace, which is called "more grace," draws the desires, in this manner, into their true cast of relationship with God.

It is done partly, we shall see, by prayer itself; that is, by prayer helped as it is and wrought in by the Spirit of God. For how grand a fact is it, and how full of hope, that the Spirit of God has presence in us so pervasively, being at the very spring point of all most hidden movement in us, even back of all that we can reach by our consciousness. And there by his subtle, most silent, really infinite power, he works configuring the desires, before they are born into consciousness, to the reigning order and will of God. So that when we know not what we should pray for, he helpeth our informities and, so to speak, maketh intercession for us, heaving out our groanings of desire, otherwise impossible to be uttered, into prayers that are molded according to the will of God. And so all prayer is encouraged, by promises that make an institute of it, for the schooling and training of our desires, and drawing them into conformity with God and the everlasting reason of things.

In this way of prayer we obtain our request, because we have been drawn closely enough to be in true chime with his will, and so to make an authorized pull on his favor, by our right-deserving; even as the bowline from a boat, pulling on some object to which it is fastened, draws not so much the shore to it, as it to the shore. In this way it comes to pass that souls which are much in prayer, and get skill in it, obtain their desires in great part by learning how to have good ones moderated in the will of God, being drawn so closely to him by their prayers that bad ones fall away more and more completely, and leave them petitioning out of purity. In passing through which process the Spirit helps them on, preparing them to prayer by the restored quality of their desires.

Again, there is a power in the new love Christ begets in the soul, to remold or recast the desires in terms of harmony with each other and with God. When the supreme love is changed, being itself an imperial and naturally regnant principle, all the powers of misrule, including the desires, fall into chime with it. The love also is luminous and pure, so that no base underling, that would kennel back of knowledge in the mind, can hide from it. Besides, it does not have to govern or keep down, for it bathes and tinges all through, so to speak, even the desiring substance, with a color from itself. And then it follows that, as the love is, so the desires will be. Loving my enemy, I shall desire only his good. Loving God, I shall desire all that belongs to his will and the advance of his Kingdom. And so, indirectly and by association, all the wild ferment of the corrupted nature, all the desires that belong to a sensual, earthly, selfish habit will be gradually changed; and the whole order, and scale and scheme of desire will be replaced by another. In this love even the drunkard's appetite will be silent, for he will have only to abide in this love to be free almost without a struggle. For it is a tide so full that every basest longing is submerged by it. "Breadth, length, depth, height, and to know the love of God that passeth knowledge," says an apostle, "that ye might be filled with all the fullness of God." And when the soul is full in this manner, it wants nothing more; because it can hold nothing more, least of all anything contrary. All the wild wishes and vagrant longings settle now into rest when the fullness of God is come. Unruly desires will of course begin to have their liberty again when the love abates; but abiding long enough in God as we may, they will even die.

I know not how it is that the religious teachers have so little to say of the desires, when the Gospel grace moves on them in so great stress of attention. Perhaps it is because they class them with the merely instinctive motions, calling them irresponsible, and letting them be so ruled out of the account. Whereas they are at the very bottom, in one view, of all responsibility cast off; and the soul must be hampered, and galled and fouled everlastingly by their misdoing unless they are rectified. They are in fact the hell of the mind, and nothing is salvation which does not restore them. Clearly enough, we cannot purge them or set them in order by any course of training. We educate the intellect so as to harmonize it largely with nature, and law and truth; we educate the taste, the sentiment and, to a certain extent, the affections; also form, color, music; also the hand, the eye, the muscular force. Schools on schools, colleges on colleges we organize for these and other such kinds of training. But we have no colleges for the desires, and see not how we could have if we would.

For where shall such kind of training begin, and by what course go on? Where are the diagrams? Where is the logic? What objectivities are there to work by? Diogenes, I believe, was the only professor in this line; and he undertook to moderate the desires by his gibes, much as he might still a tempest by whistling it down. And yet it is but fair to say that he did what he could. Should he soberly reprove them, they would only laugh at him. Should he reason with them, what care have they for reason? Inventing a gauge for them, where is the gauge? Who shall keep it? When shall it be applied? No discipline requiring eyes can enter intelligence into these blind factors. Not amenable to reason, or capable of it; able, on the other hand, to obfuscate all reason; able to be a robber talent as against the strength and fair success and peace of all the others; able, in short, as was just now intimated, to make a hell of the mind. Where is the heaven? Here in Christ Jesus, have I not shown you? In him, coming forth to die, have you not, after all, the needed university, the sufficient and complete discipline? Drawing near to him, as he to you, and finding how to walk with him, will not even your desire be learning tenderly to say, "Whom have I in heaven but thee, and there is none upon earth that I desire besides thee'? In this most difficult matter, come and see what he will do for you; or rather, what he will not do. Indeed I know not any other change in mind that can abate so many frictions, quell so many distractions, invigorate so great concentration of thought in such evenness of repose—nothing, in short, that will so much advance the possibilities of a good and great life.

And saying this, I cannot forget or keep out of mind the example of a once dear classmate and friend who not long ago took his reward on high. He was not a brilliant man as we commonly speak, but there was a massive equipoise and justness in the harmonized action of his powers that was remarkable to us all. The robust life he had in body and mind and moral habit, required him never to be gathering up his equilibrium,

for it was never lost. He was not in his own opinion at that time a
Christian, but he scarcely could have been a more sound integer, if he
had been, to others. A few months after his graduation, he wrote me that
he was a good deal tossed by the question to what he should turn
himself, as the engagement of his life. We had supposed that he would of
course take his place in the law. But "the law," said he, "is for money,
and money I do not want. I have enough of that already (he belonged to
an immensely rich family); therefore I am questioning whether I can do
better than to put in my life with the best, even with Christ and his
cause. I think I shall there be satisfied, and I do not see anything else
where I can be." The result was that his whole desire fell into this
current and grew large upon him, getting volume to fill his great nature
full; and he went into his clearly divine call as a preacher of Christ with
such energy and such visible devotion that he was pushed forward
shortly into a high church-leadership that widely signalized his life, and
made his name, in his death and before it, a name of great public honor.
And I think of him now as probably the happiest, best harmonized,
noblest-keyed man of all my acquaintance here. Would to God, my
friends, that in such high example he might quicken you to follow.

And if he should, let me tell you, in this short catalogue of specifica-
tions, what the result will be.

You will be wishing less and doing more.

Your momentum will be heavier and your impulse stronger.

You will have a more piercing intellectual perception.

Your inspirations will range higher because your desires do.

Your serenity will be more perfect as the sky of your mind is more
pure.

Your enjoyments will be larger and less invaded by distractions.

You will have a more condensed vigor of will.

You will have a great deal less need of success and a great deal more of
it.

You will die less missing life, and more missed by it.

All which may God in his mercy grant.

Horace Bushnell (1802–1876)   *Born near Litchfield, Connecticut, Bushnell's life
nearly paralleled that of Henry Beecher—both were Congregational pastors,
preachers and scholars. Bushnell's sermons were widely read here and overseas, and his original work* Christian Nurture *(1847) is actively used in
seminaries today.*

Martin Luther
(1483-1546)

John Calvin
(1509-1564)

John Wesley
(1703-1791)

Henry Ward Beecher
(1813-1877)

Phillips Brooks
(1835-1893)

Dwight Lyman Moody
(1837-1899)

Charles Haddon Spurgeon
(1834-1892)

Henry Drummond
(1851-1897)

Rodney (Gipsy) Smith
(1860-1947)

Billy Sunday
(1862-1935)

Henry Sloane Coffin
(1877-1954)

Joseph Fort Newton
(1880-1950)

Halford E. Luccock
(1885-1960)

Leslie D. Weatherhead
(1893-1976)

Bishop Fulton J. Sheen
(1899-   )

Frederick William Robertson/
The Message of the Church to Men of Wealth

*And Nabal answered David's servants, and said, Who is David?
and who is the son of Jesse? There be many servants nowadays that
break away every man from his master. Shall I then take my bread,
and my water, and my flesh that I have killed for my shearers, and
give it unto men, whom I know not whence they be?*

SAMUEL 25:10, 11

I HAVE selected this passage for our subject this evening because it is one of the earliest cases recorded in the Bible in which the interests of the employer and the employed, the man of wealth and the man of work, stood, or seemed to stand, in antagonism to each other.

It was a period in which an old system of things was breaking up, and the new one was not yet established. The patriarchal relationship of tutelage and dependence was gone, and monarchy was not yet in firm existence. Saul was on the throne, but his rule was irregular and disputed. Many things were slowly growing up into custom which had not yet the force of law; and the first steps by which custom passes into law from precedent to precedent are often steps at every one of which struggle and resistance must take place.

The history of the chapter is briefly this: Nabal, the wealthy sheepmaster, fed his flocks in the pastures of Carmel. David was leader of a band of men who got their living by the sword on the same hills— outlaws, whose excesses he in some degree restrained, and over whom he retained a leader's influence. A rude irregular honor was not unknown among those fierce men. They honorably abstained from injuring Nabal's flocks. They did more: they protected them from all harm against the marauders of the neighborhood. By the confession of Nabal's own herdsmen, "they were a wall unto them both by night and day, all the time they were with them keeping their flocks."

And thus a kind of right grew up, irregular enough but sufficient to establish a claim on Nabal for remuneration of these services. A new claim, not admitted by him; reckoned by him an exaction which could be enforced by no law; enforced only by that law which is above all statute-law, deciding according to emergencies—an indefinable, instinctive sense of fairness and justice. But as there was no law, and each man was to himself a law and the sole arbiter of his own rights, what help was there but that disputes should rise between the wealthy proprietors and their self-constituted champions, with exaction and tyranny on the one side, churlishness and parsimony on the other? Hence a fruitful and ever-fresh source of struggle—the one class struggling to take as much, and the other to give as little, as possible. In modern language, the Rights of Labor were in conflict with the Rights of Property.

The story proceeds thus: David presented a demand, moderate and courteous enough (I Samuel 25:6-8). It was refused by Nabal, and added to the refusal were those insulting taunts of low birth and outcast condition which are worse than injury, and sting, making men's blood run fire. One court of appeal was left. There remained nothing but the trial by force. "Gird ye on," said David, "every man his sword."

Now observe the fearful, hopeless character of this struggle. The question had come to this: whether David, with his ferocious and needy six hundred mountaineers, united by the sense of wrong, or Nabal, with his well-fed and trained hirelings, bound by interest and not by love to his cause, were stronger. Which was the more powerful—want whetted by insult or selfishness pampered by abundance? They who wished to keep by force or they who wished to take? An awful and uncertain spectacle, but the spectacle which is exhibited in every country where rights are keenly felt and duties lightly regarded, where insolent demand is met by insulting defiance. Wherever classes are held apart by rivalry and selfishness instead of drawn together by the law of love, wherever there has not been established a kingdom of heaven, but only a kingdom of the world—there exist the forces of inevitable collision.

A cause of this false social state: the false basis on
which social superiority was held to rest
Throughout, Nabal's conduct was built upon the assumption of his own superiority. He was a man of wealth. David was dependent on his own daily efforts. Was not that enough to settle the question of superiority and inferiority? It was enough on both sides for a long time, till the falsehood of the assumption became palpable and intolerable. But palpable and intolerable it did become at last.

A social falsehood will be borne long, even with considerable inconvenience, until it forces itself obtrusively on men's attention and can be endured no longer. The exact point at which this social falsehood—that wealth constitutes superiority and has a right to the subordination of inferiors—becomes intolerable, varies according to several circumstances.

The evils of poverty are comparative—they depend on climate. In warm climates, where little food, no fuel and scanty shelter are required, the sting is scarcely felt till poverty becomes starvation. They depend on contrast. Far above the point where poverty becomes actual famine, it may become unbearable if contrasted strongly with the unnecessary luxury and abundance enjoyed by the classes above. Where all suffer equally, as men and officers suffer in an Arctic voyage, men bear hardship with cheerfulness; but where the suffering weighs heavily on some and the luxury of enjoyment is out of all proportion monopolized by a few, the point of reaction is reached long before penury has become actual want. Or again, when wealth or rank assumes an insulting, domineering character—when contemptuous names for the poor are invented, and become current among the more unfeeling of a wealthy class—then the falsehood of superiority can be tolerated no longer. We do not envy honors which are meekly borne, nor wealth which is unostentatious.

Now it was this which brought matters to a crisis. David had borne poverty long—nay, he and his men had long endured the contrast between their own cavern-homes and beds upon the rock, and Nabal's comforts. But when Nabal added to this those pungent, biting sneers which sink into poor men's hearts and rankle—which are not forgotten but come out fresh in the day of retribution—"Who is David? and who is the son of Jesse? There be many servants nowadays that break away every man from his master"; then David began to measure himself with Nabal—not a wiser man, nor a better, nor even a stronger. Who is this Nabal? Intellectually, a fool; morally, a profligate, drowning reason in excess of wine at the annual sheep shearing; a tyrant over his slaves, overbearing to men who only ask of him their rights. Then rose the question which Nabal had better not have forced men to answer for themselves. By what right does this possessor of wealth lord it over men who are inferior in no one particular?

Now observe two things.

1. An apparent inconsistency in David's conduct. David had received injury after injury from Saul, and had only forgiven. One injury from Nabal, and David is striding over the hills to revenge his wrong with naked steel. How came this reverence and irreverence to mix together?

We reply. Saul had a claim of authority on David's allegiance; Nabal, only one of rank. Between these the Bible makes a vast difference. It says, the powers which be are ordained of God. But "upper" and "lower," as belonging to difference in property, are fictitious terms— true, if character corresponds with titular superiority; false, if it does not. And such was the difference manifested in the life of the Son of God. To lawful authority, whether Roman, Jewish, or even priestly, he paid deference; but to the titled mark of conventional distinction, none. Rabbi, rabbi, was no divine authority. It was not power, a delegated attribute of God—it was only a name. In Saul, therefore, David reverenced one his superior in authority; but in Nabal he only had before him one surpassing him in wealth. And David refused, somewhat too rudely, to acknowledge the bad, great man as his superior—would pay him no reverence, respect or allegiance whatever. Let us mark that distinction well, so often confused; kings, masters, parents—here is a power ordained of God. Honor it. But wealth, name, title, distinctions—always fictitious, often false and vicious; if you can claim homage for these separate from worth, you confound two things essentially different. Try that by the test of his life. Name the text where Christ claimed reverence for wealth or rank. On the Mount did the Son of Man bow the knee to the majesty of wealth and wrong, or was his Sonship shown in this, that he would not bow down to that as if of God?

2. This great falsehood respecting superior and inferior rested on a truth. There had been a superiority in the wealthy class once. In the patriarchal system wealth and rule had gone together. The father of the family and tribe was the one in whom proprietorship was centered, but the patriarchal system had passed away. Men like Nabal succeeded to the patriarch's wealth, and expected the subordination which had been yielded to patriarchal character and position; and this when every particular of relationship was altered. Once the patriarch was the protector of his dependents. Now David's class was independent, and the protectors rather than the protected—at all events, able to defend themselves. Once the rich man was ruler in virtue of paternal relationship. Now wealth was severed from rule and relationship; a man might be rich, yet neither a ruler nor a protector nor a kinsman. And the fallacy of Nabal's expectation consisted in this, that he demanded for wealth that reverence which had once been due to men who happened to be wealthy.

It is a fallacy in which we are perpetually entangled. We expect reverence for that which was once a symbol of what was reverenced, but is reverenced no longer. Here in England it is common to complain that there is no longer any respect of inferiors towards superiors—that servants were once devoted and grateful, tenants submissive, subjects enthusiastically loyal. But we forget that servants were once protected by their masters, and tenants safe from wrong only through the guardianship of their powerful lords; that thence a personal gratitude grew up; that now they are protected by the law from wrong by a different social system altogether; and that the individual bond of gratitude subsists no longer. We expect that to masters and employers the same reverence and devotedness shall be rendered which were due to them under other circumstances, and for different reasons—as if wealth and rank had ever been the claim to reverence, and not merely the accidents and accompaniments of the claim; as if anything less sacred than holy ties could purchase sacred feelings; as if the homage of free manhood could be due to gold and name; as if to the mere Nabal-fool who is labeled as worth so much, and whose signature carries with it so much coin, the holiest and most ennobling sensations of the soul, reverence and loyalty, were due by God's appointment.

No. That patriarchal system has passed forever. No sentimental wailings for the past, no fond regrets for the virtues of a bygone age, no melancholy, poetical, retrospective antiquarianism can restore it. In

Church and State the past is past; and you can no more bring back the blind reverence than the rude virtues of those days. The day has come in which, if feudal loyalty or patriarchal reverence are to be commanded, they must be won by patriarchal virtues or feudal real superiorities.

A cause of this unhealthy social state:
a false conception respecting rights
It would be unjust to Nabal to represent this as an act of willful oppression and conscious injustice. He did what appeared to him fair between man and man. He paid his laborers. Why should he pay anything beyond stipulated wages?

David's demand appeared an extravagant and insolent one, provoking unfeigned astonishment and indignation. It was an invasion of his rights. It was a dictation with respect to the employment of that which was his own. "Shall I then take my bread, and my water, and my flesh that I have killed for my shearers, and give it unto men whom I know not whence they be?"

Recollect, too, there was something to be said for Nabal. This view of the irresponsible right of property was not his invention. It was the view probably entertained by all his class. It had descended to him from his parents. They were prescriptive and admitted rights on which he stood. And however false or unjust a prescriptive right may be, however baseless when examined, there is much excuse for those who have inherited and not invented it; for it is hard to see through the falsehood of any system by which we profit, and which is upheld by general consent, especially when good men too uphold it. Rare indeed is that pure-heartedness which sees with eagle glance through conventionalisms. This is a wrong, and I and my own class are the doers of it.

On the other hand, David and his needy followers were not slow to perceive that they had their rights over that property of Nabal's.

Men on whom wrongs press are the first to feel them, and their cries of pain and indignation are the appointed means of God to direct to their wrongs the attention of society. Very often the fierce and maddened shriek of suffering is the first intimation that a wrong exists at all.

There was no law in Israel to establish David's claims. This guardianship of Nabal's flocks was partly a self-constituted thing. No bargain had been made, no sum of reward expressly stipulated. But there is a law besides and above all written law, which gives to written laws their authority, and from which so often as they diverge, it is woe to the framers of the law; for their law must perish, and the Eternal Law unseen will get itself acknowledged as a truth from heaven or a truth from hell—a truth begirt with fire and sword, if they will not read it except so.

In point of fact, David had a right to a share of Nabal's profits. The harvest was in part David's harvest, for without David it never could have been reaped. The sheep were in part David's sheep, for without David not a sheep would have been spared by the marauders of the hills. Not a sheaf of corn was carried to Nabal's barn, nor a night passed in repose by Nabal's shepherds, but what told of the share of David in the saving of that sheaf and the procurement of that repose (not the less real because it was past and unseen). The right which the soldier has by law to his pay, was the right which David had by unwritten law—a right resting on the fact that his services were indispensable for the harvest.

Here, then, is one of the earliest instances of the Rights of Labor coming into collision with the Rights of Property—rights shadowy, undefined, perpetually shifting their boundaries, varying with every case, altering with every age, incapable of being adjusted except rudely by law, and leaving always something which the most subtle and elaborate law cannot define, and which in any moment may grow up into a wrong.

Now when it comes to this, Rights against Rights, there is no determination of the question but by overwhelming numbers or blood. David's remedy was a short, sharp, decisive one. "Gird ye on every man his sword." And it is difficult, for the sake of humanity, to say to which side in such a quarrel we should wish well. If the rich man succeed in civil war, he will bind the chain of degradation more severely and more surely for years, or ages, on the crushed serf. If the champions of popular rights succeed by the sword, you may then await in awe the reign of tyranny, licentiousness and lawlessness. For the victory of the lawless, with the memory of past wrongs to avenge, is almost more sanguinary than the victory of those who have had power long, and whose power had been defied.

We find another cause in circumstances. Want and unjust exclusion precipitated David and his men into this rebellion. It is common enough to lay too much weight on circumstances. Nothing can be more false than the popular theory that ameliorated outward condition is the panacea for the evils of society. The Gospel principle begins from within, and works outward.

The world's principle begins with the outward condition, and expects to influence inwardly. To expect that by changing the world without, in order to suit the world within, by taking away all difficulties and removing all temptations, instead of hardening the man within against the force of outward temptation—to adapt the lot to the man, instead of molding the spirit to the lot, is to reverse the Gospel method of procedure. Nevertheless, even that favorite speculation of theorists, that perfect circumstances will produce perfect character, contains a truth. Circumstances of outward condition are not the sole efficients in the production of of character, but they are efficients which must not be ignored. Favorable condition will not produce excellence, but the want of it often hinders excellence. It is true that vice leads to poverty. All the moralizers tell us that, but it is also true that poverty leads to vice.

There are some in this world to whom, speaking humanly, social injustice and social inequalities have made goodness impossible. Take, for instance, the case of these bandits on Mount Carmel. Some of them were outlawed by their own crimes, but others doubtless by debts not willfully contracted—one at least, David, by a most unjust and unrighteous persecution. And these men, excluded, needy, exasperated by a sense of wrong, untaught outcasts, could you gravely expect from them obedience, patience, meekness, religious resignation? Yes, my brethren, that is exactly the marvelous impossibility people do most inconsistently expect; and there are no bounds to their astonishment if they do not get what they expect. Superhuman honesty from starving men, to whom life by hopelessness has become a gambler's desperate chance; chivalrous loyalty and high forbearance from creatures to whom the order of society has presented itself only as an unjust system of partiality. We forget that forbearance and obedience are the very last and highest lessons learned by the spirit in its most careful training. By those unhallowed conventionalisms through which we, like heathens and not like Christians, crush the small offender and court the great one; that damnable cowardice by which we banish the seduced and half admire the seducer; by which, in defiance of all manliness and all generosity, we punish the weak and tempted, and let the tempter go free—by all these we make men and women outcasts, and then expect from them the sublimest graces of reverence and resignation

The message of the Church to the man of wealth
The message of the Church contains those principles of life which, carried out, would, and hereafter will, realize the Divine Order of Society. The revealed Message does not create the facts of our human-ity—it simply makes them known. The Gospel did not make God our Father; it authoritatively reveals that he is so. It did not create a new duty of loving one another; it revealed the old duty which existed from eternity, and must exist as long as humanity is humanity. It was no new commandment, but an old commandment which had been heard from the beginning.

The Church of God is that living body of men who are called by him out of the world, not to be the inventors of a new social system, but to exhibit in the world by word and life, chiefly by life, what humanity is, was and will be, in the idea of God. Now so far as the social economy is concerned, the revelations of the Church will coincide with the discov-eries of a Scientific Political Economy. Political Economy discovers slowly the facts of the immutable laws of social well-being. But the living principles of those laws, which cause them to be obeyed, Christianity has revealed to loving hearts long before. The Spirit discovers them to the spirit. For instance, Political Economy, gazing on such a fact as this of civil war, would arrive at the same principles which the Church arrives at. She too would say, "Not selfishness, but love." Only that she arrives at these principles by experience, not intuition; by terrible lessons, not revelation; by revolutions, wars and famines, not by spiritual impulses of charity.

And so because these principles were eternally true in humanity, we find in the conduct of Abigail toward David in this early age, not explicitly, but implicitly, the very principles which the Church of Christ has given to the world; and more, the very principles which a sound political economy would sanction. In her reply to David we have the anticipation by a loving heart of those duties which selfish prudence must have taught at last.

1. The spiritual dignity of man as man. Recollect David was the poor man, but Abigail, the highborn lady, admits his worth, "The Lord will certainly make my lord a sure house; because my lord fighteth the battles of the Lord, and evil 'hath not been found in thee all thy days." Here is a truth revealed to that age. Nabal's day, and the day of such as Nabal, is past; another power is rising above the horizon. David's cause is God's cause. Worth does not mean what a man is worth—you must find some better definition than that.

Now this is the very truth revealed in the Incarnation. David, Israel's model king, the king by the grace of God, not by the conventional rules of human choice, is a shepherd's son. Christ, the King who is to reign over our regenerated humanity, is humbly born, the poor woman's Son. That is the Church's message to the man of wealth, and a message which it seems has to be learned afresh in every age. It was new to Nabal. It was new to the men of the age of Christ. In his day they were offended in him because he was humbly born. "Is not this the carpenter's son?" It is the offense now. They who retain those superstitious ideas of the eternal superiority of rank and wealth have the first principles of the Gospel yet to learn. How can they believe in the Son of Mary? They may honor him with the lip, they deny him in his brenthren. Whoever helps to keep alive that ancient lie of upper and lower, resting the distinction not on official authority or personal worth, but on wealth and title, is doing his part to hinder the establishment of the Redeemer's kingdom.

Now the Church of Christ proclaims that truth in baptism. She speaks of a kingdom here in which all are, as spirits, equal. She reveals a fact. She does not affect to create the fact. She says, not hypothetically, "This child may be the child of God if prevenient grace has taken place, or if hereafter he shall have certain feelings and experiences"; nor, "Hereby I create this child magically by supernatural power in one moment what it was not a moment before"; but she says, authoritatively, "I pronounce this child the child of God, the brother of Christ the First-born, the Son of him who has taught us by his Son to call him our Father, not my Father. Whatever that child may become hereafter in fact, he is now, by right of creation and redemption. the child of God. Rich or poor, titled or untitled, he shares the spiritual nature of the second Adam, the Lord from heaven."

2. The second truth expressed by Abigail was the law of sacrifice. She did not heal the grievance with smooth words. Starving men are not to be pacified by professions of good will. She brought her two hundred loaves, and her two skins of wine, her five sheep ready dressed, etc. A princely provision.

You might have said this was waste—half would have been enough. But the truth is, liberality is a most real economy. She could not stand there calculating the smallest possible expense at which the affront might be wiped out. True economy is to pay liberally and fairly for

faithful service. The largest charity is the best economy. Nabal had had
a faithful servant. He should have counted no expense too great to retain
his services, instead of cheapening and depreciating them. But we
wrong Abigail if we call this economy or calculation. In fact, had it been
done on economical principles, it would have failed. Ten times this sum
from Nabal would not have arrested revenge. For Nabal it was too late.
Concessions extracted by fear only provoke exaction further. The poor
know well what is given because it must be given, and what is conceded
from a sense of justice. They feel only what is real. David's men and
David felt that these were not the gifts of a sordid calculation, but the
offerings of a generous heart. And it won them—their gratitude, their
enthusiasm, their unfeigned homage.

This is the attractive power of that great law whose highest expression was the cross. "I, if I be lifted up, will draw all men unto me." Say
what you will, it is not interest, but the sight of noble qualities and true
sacrifice which commands the devotion of the world. Yea, even the
bandit and the outcast will bend before that as before a divine thing. In
one form or another, it draws all men, it commands all men.

Now this the Church proclaims as part of its special message to the
rich. It says that the Divine Death was a sacrifice. It declares that death
to be the law of every life which is to be like his. It says that the law,
which alone can interpret the mystery of life, is the self-sacrifice of
Christ. It proclaims the law of his life to have been this, "For their sakes I
devote [sanctify] Myself, that they also may be devoted through the
truth."

In other words, the self-sacrifice of the Redeemer was to be the living
principle and law of the self-devotion of his people. It asserts that to be
the principle which alone can make any human life a true life. "I fill up
that which is behind of the afflictions of Christ in my flesh, for his body's
sake, which is the Church." We have petrified *that* sacrifice into a dead
theological dogma, about the exact efficacy of which we dispute
metaphysically and charge each other with heresy. That atonement will
become a living fact only when we humbly recognize in it the eternal
fact that sacrifice is the law of life. The very mockers at the crucifixion
unwittingly declared the principle, "He saved others; himself he cannot
save." Of course, how could he save himself who had to save others?
You can only save others when you have ceased to think of saving your
own soul; you can only truly bless when you have done with the pursuit
of personal happiness. Did you ever hear of a soldier who saved his
country by making it his chief work to secure himself? And was the
Captain of our salvation to become the Saviour by contravening that
universal law of sacrifice, or by obeying it?

Brother men, the early Church gave expression to that principle of
sacrifice in a very touching way. They had all things in common.
"Neither said any of them that aught of the things which he possessed
was his own." They failed, not because they declared that, but because
men began to think that the duty of sharing was compulsory. They
proclaimed principles which were unnatural, inasmuch as they set aside

all personal feelings, which are part of our nature too. They virtually compelled private property to cease, because he who retained private property when all were giving up was degraded, and hence became a hypocrite and liar like Ananias.

But let us not lose the truth which they expressed in an exaggerated way, "Neither said any of them that aught of the things which he possessed was his own." Property is sacred. It is *private* property; if it were not, it could not be sacrificed. If it were to be shared equally by the idle and the industrious, there could be no love in giving. Property is the rich man's own. Nabal is right in saying, "my bread, my water, my flesh." But there is a higher right which says, "It is not yours." And that voice speaks to every rich man in one way or another, according as he is selfish or unselfish, coming as a voice of terror or a voice of blessing. It came to Nabal with a double curse, turning his heart into stone with the vision of the danger and the armed ranks of David's avengers, and laying on David's soul the sin of intended murder. It came to the heart of Abigail with a double blessing, blessing her who gave and him who took.

To the spirit of the Cross alone we look as the remedy for social evils. When the people of this great country, especially the rich, shall have been touched with the spirit of the cross to a largeness of sacrifice of which they have not dreamed as yet, there will be an atonement between the Rights of Labor and the Rights of Property.

3. The last part of the church's message to the man of wealth touches the matter of rightful influence.

Very remarkable is the demeanor of David toward Nabal, as contrasted with his demeanor toward Abigail. In the one case, defiance and a haughty self-assertion of equality; in the other, deference, respect and the most eloquent benediction. It was not therefore against the wealthy class, but against individuals of the class, that the wrath of these men burned.

See, then, the folly and the falsehood of the sentimental regret that there is no longer any reverence felt toward superiors. There is reverence to superiors, if only it can be shown that they are superiors. Reverence is deeply rooted in the heart of humanity—you cannot tear it out. Civilization, science and progress only change its direction; they do not weaken its force. If it no longer bows before crucifixes and candles, priests and relics, it is not extinguished toward what is truly sacred and what is priestly in man. The fiercest revolt against false authority is only a step toward submission to rightful authority. Emancipation from false lords only sets the heart free to honor true ones. The freeborn David will not do homage to Nabal. Well, now go and mourn over the degenerate age which no longer feels respect for that which is above it. But behold, David has found a something nobler than himself. Feminine charity, sacrifice and justice—and in gratitude and profoundest respect he bows to that. The state of society which is coming is not one of protection and dependence, nor one of mysterious authority and blind obedience to it, nor one in which any class shall be privileged by Divine right and another remain in perpetual tutelage; but it is one in which unselfish

services and personal qualities will command, by Divine right, gratitude
and admiration, and secure a true and spiritual leadership.

Oh, let not the rich misread the signs of the times, or mistake their
brethren. They have less and less respect for titles and riches, for
vestments and ecclesiastical pretensions; but they have a real respect for
superior knowledge and superior goodness. They listen like children to
those whom they believe to know a subject better than themselves. Let
those who know it say whether there is not something inexpressibly
touching and even humbling in the large, hearty, manly, English
reverence and love which the workingmen show toward those who love
and serve them truly, and save them from themselves and from doing
wrong. See how David's feelings gush forth, "Blessed be the Lord God of
Israel which sent thee this day to meet me; and blessed be thy advice,
and blessed be thou which hast kept me this day from coming to shed
blood, and from avenging myself with mine own hand."

The rich and the great may have that love if they will.

To conclude. Doubtless David was wrong; he had no right even to
redress wrongs thus. Patience was his divinely appointed duty, and
doubtless in such circumstances we should be very ready to preach
submission and to blame David. Alas, we, the clergy of the Church of
England, have been only too ready to do this. For three long centuries we
have taught submission to the powers that be, as if that were the only
text in Scripture bearing on the relations between the ruler and the
ruled. Rarely have we dared to demand of the powers that be, justice; of
the wealthy man and the titled, duties. We have produced folios of
slavish flattery upon the Divine Right of Power. Shame on us, we have
not denounced the wrongs done to weakness. And yet for one text in the
Bible which requires submission and patience from the poor, you will
find a hundred which denounce the vices of the rich. In the writings of
the noble old Jewish prophets, that, and almost that only, in the Old
Testament, with a deep roll of words that sound like Sinai thunders; and
that in the New Testament in words less impassioned and more calmly
terrible from the apostles and their Master. And woe to us in the great
day of God if we have been the sycophants of the rich instead of the
redressers of the poor man's wrongs. Woe to us if we have been tutoring
David into respect to his superior, Nabal, and forgotten that David's
cause, not Nabal's, is the cause of God.

Frederick William Robertson (1816–1853) *This London-born preacher
achieved enduring fame with the posthumous publication of his sermons which
remain especially rewarding to the student minister. Robertson's brief, brilliant
career was particularly shining in his Brighton sermons.*

John Henry Jowett/
Blinding the Mind

T HERE is a phrase of the Apostle Paul which contains a warning peculiarly relevant to the times through which we are passing. It is this, "The god of this world hath blinded the minds." What is the significance of the phrase, "The god of this world"? Here is a certain evil influence personified. A certain immoral energy or contagion is conceived and presented as an active, aggressive, personal force, which deliberately seeks to dwarf and bruise and lame the richly-dowered souls of men. He is elsewhere depicted as of princely line, with imposing retinues and armies, moving stealthily amid human affairs, and inciting men to rebellion against the holy sovereignty of God. He is represented as "the prince of the powers of the air," subtle and persuasive as an atmosphere, insinuating himself into the most sacred privacies and invading even the most holy place. He is "the god of this world," receiving homage and worship, the god to whom countless thousands offer ceaseless sacrifice, while the holy Lord of grace and glory is neglected or defied. I am not now concerned with this personification, whether it be literalistic or merely figurative; but I am concerned with the reality of the power itself, whose seductive energy corrupts our holiest treasures, and blunts and spoils the finest perceptions of the soul.

Now, everybody is familiar with the characteristics of this destructive ministry. There is no need of abstruse or hair-splitting analysis. The issues are obtrusive; we have only to examine our own souls and their besetments, and the peril is revealed. We may have dropped the personification, but we recognize the energy which is personified. We may have abandoned the figure, but we are familiar with the thing. We may no longer speak of "the god of this world," but "worldliness" itself is palpable and rampant. This is our modern phraseology. We speak of "the worldly" and "the unworldly," but unfortunately the terms are very loosely and indefinitely used, or used with a quite perverse significance. The "unworldly" is too often identified with the "other worldly," and is interpreted as an austere isolation from all festivity, and from the hard, hand-soiling concerns of practical life. And on the other hand, "worldliness" is too often identified with gaiety, or levity or prodigality, with drink and pride, with theatrical glamor and vulgar sheen. But these interpretations do not touch the heart of the matter. What, then, is worldliness? Worldliness is life without ideals, life without moral vistas, life devoid of poetic vision. It is life without the halo, life without the mystic nimbus which invests it with venerable and awful sanctity. It is imprisonment within the material, no windows opening out upon ethereal, moral or altruistic ends. It is the five senses without the moral sense. It is quickness to appetite and dullness to conscience. It is engrossment in sensations; it is heedlessness to God's "awful rose of dawn." It is rank materialism.

Now this powerful contagion operates in the deprivation of sight. Materialism and moral blindness stand in the relation of cause and effect. "The god of this world hath blinded the minds." That is to say, a practical materialism destroys the eyes of the soul. The materialistic life deadens the conscience, and in the long run puts it to death. The materialistic life stupefies the imagination, and in the long run makes it inoperative. The materialistic life defiles the affections, and converts their crystalline lens into a minister of darkness and night. The materialistic life coarsens the spiritual instincts, and renders them nonappreciative of things unseen. And so it is with all the vision-powers of life; a practical materialism plugs or scales them and makes the spirit blind.

But I will still further narrow the interpretation, and confine this [sermon] to that aspect of worldliness which is concerned with the bare pursuit of material gain. If "the god of this world" must be given a single name, let the name be Mammon, and let the love of money be the worship which is offered at his shrine. And does the god of money blind the mind? Let it get into the pulpit, and everybody knows the result. The spiritual heavens become opaque, and there is no awe-inspiring discernment of "things unseen." Everybody recognizes its destructiveness in the ministry, but everybody does not equally recognize the destructiveness in other lives and other professions. But the moral issues are one and the same; always and everywhere the god of money blinds the mind.

Let me give a scriptural illustration of its nefarious work. A woman, who had been spiritually enfranchised by the Lord, and who had been led out of the dreary, wan land of sin into the fair, bright lily-land of God's eternal peace, brought an alabaster box of ointment, very precious, and anointed her Deliverer's feet. And there was one standing by, who looked upon it with uninspired and unillumined eyes, and said, "To what purpose is this waste?" ... "This he said ... because he was a thief, and carried the bag." He was the victim of the god of money, and he was blind; and he could see no beauty or grace in this passionate love-offering of an emancipated child of God. There was nothing winsome about the woman that he should commend her; and, more than that, when he looked upon the woman's Lord there was "no beauty" that he should desire him. "What will ye give me, and I will deliver him unto you? And they covenanted with him for thirty pieces of silver." And for that "thirty pieces of silver" he sold his Lord! May we not add, "the god of this world" had blinded his mind?

But there is no need for us to go back to those remote days for illustration of the truth. Every succeeding century has abounded in confirmation of its truth. Let me confine myself to witnesses from modern history. I know of no more shameful page in the history of our country than the page which tells the story of our early demeanor in the American Civil War. The North was valorously intent upon lifting the tyranny of the South, and letting the bondslave free. And vast multitudes of our people sympathized with the callous and slave-holding South, and ranged themselves in bitter antagonism to the chivalrous North. And what was the explanation? Just this—they were unable to see the interests of humanity because of their interests in cotton. They couldn't see the slave for the dollar, or they saw him only as a chattel to be despised. Henry Ward Beecher came over to expostulate with our countrymen, and to seek to open their eyes. He came here to plead for the slaves, those slaves unveiled to us in the bleeding pages of *Uncle Tom's Cabin*. He came to Liverpool. Now listen to a contemporary document and you will think you are reading the Press of the past few weeks. "It would be impossible for tongue or pen adequately to describe the scenes at the meeting. The great hall was packed to the crushing point. The mob was out in force. The interruptions were incessant: catcalls, groans and hisses." And at what part of the meeting did the disorder culminate? It was when Beecher, bit by bit, got these sentences and rammed them home: "When I was twelve years old, my father hired Charles Smith, a man as black as lampblack, to work on his farm. I slept with him in the same room. [Oh! oh!] Ah, that don't suit you. [Uproar.] I ate with him at the same table; I sang with him out of the same hymnbook; I cried when he prayed over me at night; and if I had serious impressions of religion early in life, they were due to the fidelity and example of that poor, humble farm-laborer, black Charles Smith. [Tremendous uproar.]" What think you of the significance of that uproar? They saw no moral dignity in Charles Smith that they should desire him. That Liverpool mob could not see the slave because they were so intent upon the dollar.

Read the chivalrous history of the good Lord Shaftesbury. In his early manhood, when he began his noble crusade of emancipation, women and girls were employed in coal mines, as beasts of burden. Their condition haunted him, and became a nightmare which possessed him day and night, and he set about to ameliorate their lot. He sought to prohibit their employment. With what result? The mine owners were up and in arms, "It spells ruin to our trade!" They could not see the degradation for the gold. They feared a shrinking purse more than a shrunken womanhood. They could not see the woman for the bank. But Lord Shaftesbury disregarded their cries, and at length he had the supreme happiness of putting a stop to this infamous sort of labor by an act which declared that, after a certain limited period, no woman or girl should ever again be employed in our collieries and mines.

When Queen Victoria came to the throne, a dispute with China was developing into a very ugly menace. Soon after, it broke out into open war. And what did we fight about? We fought for the right of Great Britain to force a destructive trade upon a people who did not want it, in spite of the protestations of its government, and in spite of all such national opinion as could find a public expression. There was money in it for Britian, there was revenue in it for India, and therefore China had got to have it. It is China's burden, China's curse, China's appalling woe, and still we force it on her. And the explanation is clear. We cannot see the evil for the revenue. We cannot see the wasting victim for the swelling exchequer. Some day Britain will get the gold dust out of her eyes, and then she will see; she will see the reeking opium dens, and the emaciated manhood, and the devastated families, and the blighted race, and in her shame she will wash her hands of the traffic, and decree the emancipation of a people. At present, money plugs the eyes.

And there is very great need that in our own day we deliver ourselves from the servitude of this mammon. In our day, when the Spirit of God is at work in our midst, inciting dissatisfaction and unrest, and creating a ferment among the peoples, our vision and our sympathy can be dulled and checked by the common love of money. The peril is insidious, and it invades even the most holy place. The spirit of greed dwells not alone among the wealthy and the well-to-do; it can make its home with people of slender means. What we need, above all things, is to have our eyes anointed with the eye-salve of grace, that so our vision may be single and simple, and we may have the mind of Christ. What we need is unscaled sight, and with unscaled sight there will come fresh and healthy sympathies, and an eager participation in every chivalrous crusade.

John Henry Jowett (1864–1923)   *Dr. Jowett's preaching ministry spanned two centuries and two continents. Born in England, he held distinguished pulpits in New York City and London. A Congregationalist by ordination, he gave the Beecher Lectures at Yale in 1912. His published sermons have been read throughout the Christian world.*

George Campbell Morgan/
Work

My Father worketh even until now, and I work.
JOHN 5:17

Working together with him.
II CORINTHIANS 6:1

T HIS is now the fourth of this series of discourses on the simple things of the Christian life. Life, health, growth, work: that is the true order. It is impossible intelligently to speak of Christian work save as we have first considered the subjects mentioned. As in the material world, so also in the spiritual, death accomplishes nothing, disease weakens effort, dwarfhood is incompetent. To state that threefold principle from the positive side, life is always expressed in toil, health is the condition for victorious effort and growth is increasing capacity for work.

We must tarry by way of introduction to emphasise the importance of these preliminary matters, for a great deal of the weakness and inefficiency of Christian service is due to the fact of their neglect. First, there can be no real work with God or for God unless there be in the soul the life of God. This may be stated in other ways, which perhaps to some will be more forceful. How can I persuade men to crown him King, while I am still in rebellion against him? How can it ever be possible for me to cooperate with him in his work of bringing purity into human life, while I cherish impurity in my own heart? Or, to go back again to the figure which we are following in this series, how can a man who is dead cooperate with the living Lord?

That principle has been accepted and acted upon in certain departments of Christian activity, and neglected in others. For instance, I presume no one would think that any man was really fit to preach the Gospel of the Son of God who had not himself obeyed it. We should all be prepared to safeguard the pulpits of the Christian Church against the man who did not in his own heart and soul know the life of God. Here there is no difference of opinion; but we have not been quite so particular in other departments. We have not always been sufficiently careful in the matter of those appointed to teach in our Sunday Schools. The great essential in the instruction of children in the things of God is that their spiritual welfare should never be entrusted to one who knows nothing of spiritual life. Again, no persons should be put to lead the singing in a Christian church simply because they are musical. No man should touch the sacred work of the Christian faith at any point, save as he has received the life of God by the communication of the Spirit of God. To attempt Christian service in order to obtain life is utterly unreasonable and useless. Yet how often is this being done. How continually people come to those of us who are entrusted with over-sight, and say they wish to take up some Christian work. And the first inquiry is, or ought to be, whether they belong to Christ. Sometimes the answer is given in the negative, and the hope is expressed that they will become his by working for him. That can never be. In the name of God do not take up that work until you are born of God. For your own sake, for the sake of the work, for the sake of God, let none ever lay hands to Christian toil who is not a sharer of the Christ-life. Death, I repeat, can accomplish nothing.

To take the second point for emphasis. Our Christian service is always weakened when our spirituality is atrophied at any point. If there be no holiness of life, then service is always feeble. If I regard iniquity in my heart, even though I be a child of God, the Lord will not hear me; for if I thus put myself out of loving touch and fellowship with God, how can my service be accepted by him, or be acceptable to him? Herein is the heinousness of sin in the believer—sin permitted, excused, condoned—not merely that it injures the life of that particular soul, but that it paralyses the power of service. Every child of God is more than a treasure won for the heart of God. In his economy every child received is another soldier added to the ranks, another builder to help in rearing the great building. For battle and for building the Master came; and I can neither help him in his fight, nor in his building, if my spiritual forces are weakened by the presence of anything in my life which is unholy, whether things of the flesh or of the mind, yea, even of the spirit. Does not this self-same apostle in this very connection urge us to "cleanse ourselves from all defilement of flesh and spirit, perfecting holiness in the fear of the Lord"? If there be an arrest in the spiritual development, there is also an arrest in the power for service.

This truth is so self-evident that it scarcely needs demonstrating. Here is a person who joined the Christian Church, shall we say, ten years ago. In those early days of Christian experience the vision was clear, and the love was intense and warm and passionate—"first love," as Jesus calls it. But gradually, through some evil thing permitted, the fire of enthusiasm has cooled, until hardly a spark is burning on the altar, and the old compassion has gone, until there is hardly any pitying love for the lost and undone. What is the inevitable result for the backslider as to his Christian service? He will either withdraw from it altogether, ceasing to offer the gift which he knows cannot be accepted, or he will maintain its outward form, observe its routine and obey its ritual; but the constraining love, the personal devotion to his Lord and his interests, the peace and joy and blessing that he used to experience, are all wanting, and the service is lifeless and worthless. The arrest of development was at the same time arrest in the power of service. Consequently, I repeat, we can never intelligently speak of service save as we bear in mind the fact that there must first be life and health and growth.

If these things be granted, let me ask you to notice the Scriptures at the beginning of this study, as revealing the nature and power of Christian activity. Let us first take them separately and look at them in their relation to the context.

"My Father worketh even until now, and I work." These words occur in connection with the story of the healing of the man who had been in the grip of infirmity for thirty-eight years. When Jesus had healed him, the rulers met and challenged him, demanding how he dared carry his bed on the Sabbath day. And the man, who did not know Jesus, did not know who he was, answered, with splendid artlessness and simplicity, "He that made me whole, the same said unto me, take up thy bed and walk." Presently the rulers found Jesus, and sought to persecute him, and to slay him, because he had violated the Sabbath. It was in answer to that charge that our Lord thus spoke. To these critics of his action who were carping about the external, and had no sympathy with the deep, underlying meaning of love, he said, "My Father worketh until now, and I work." Will you let me put the inner meaning of that answer of Jesus into quite other words? It is as though he had said, God has no Sabbath, he has no rest. "My Father worketh even until now, and I work." It is as though he told them how man by his sin broke Sabbath for God, and how God can never find his rest until he has dealt with sin and put it away. "My Father worketh." There is fine irony in the answer, and splendid satire upon the pettiness of men who will let a crippled man lie unhealed in the porches rather than have the externality of the Sabbath violated. In effect, Jesus said to them as they criticised his action: I healed this man; it is my work, and my work is God's work and we are both at work on the Sabbath because of sin. That man lying there in his infirmity is one of the evidences of the presence of sin in the world, and God cannot rest while man suffers as a result of his own sin. "My Father worketh even until now, and I work."

Thus we may deduce from this answer of Christ these meanings. It is his great declaration of the fact—and I pause for words, for to me it is one of the deepest and sublimest facts, and I hardly know how to express it—

of God's restlessness in the presence of man's unrest. It is a sublime unveiling of the fact that God in his heaven cannot be at rest while the man he has made in his own image and likeness, the man who is his offspring by creation, is restless on account of sin. "My Father worketh even until now, and I work."

It is moreover, and therefore, a declaration of God's ceaseless activity toward the removal of the cause of man's unrest. What had Jesus done on that Sabbath day? Had he really broken the Sabbath? No, he had made Sabbath-keeping possible for a man. He had not broken in upon rest. He had created the opportunity for rest. He had not violated the great law that demands that man shall find opportunity for quietness and peace. Supposing Jesus had not passed that way on that Sabbath day, or, passing, had passed on, and had left that man in his limitation, there would have been added to his tale of years another Sabbath without rest. How many he had had! Thirty-eight years, and perhaps in all of them no real Sabbath, nothing but pain and weariness, nothing but restlessness, nothing but the sickness of heart that comes from hope deferred; a poor, lone, bruised, broken man, without Sabbath. Jesus stands out as the revelation of God, as he says in effect, to give that man rest I lose my rest. To restore to him the living beauty of one golden Sabbath day I will heal him now and let him carry home his bed. He kept Sabbath that day. Every man knows that the activity of Jesus was activity toward the removal of the cause of human unrest. In Christ's activity I have a revelation of God's activity. Working, ever working, through processes which to our hurried, transient life seem very slow, but always working, restless in the presence of man's unrest, and forevermore striving toward the removal of the cause of man's unrest. That is God's work.

Then notice that Jesus brings himself, in the simple affirmation of the text, and more wonderfully in the discourse which follows, into union with God in that work. "My Father worketh even until now, and I work." Jesus did not speak of a work which God had done, and which he then took up and carried on. He did not affirm that he continued God's work at a point where God left it. That would be misinterpretation of the words of Jesus. What he does affirm is his perfect unity with God. "My Father worketh even until now, and I work." We are both working. We are working in perfect cooperation. There is a splendid suggestion in that present tense of Jesus. He who said of himself, "I am," said of himself, "I work." Not, I worked, or I will work, or I am working for the moment, but "I work." He declares his harmony with God. It is the coordination of toil which is here declared. God and Christ are one in their restlessness in the presence of human unrest. They are one in their ceaseless activity to remove its cause.

Let us now turn to the phrase in the Corinthian epistle. I am not often given to taking words out of their context, neither do I intend to do so now in spirit. This phrase is very suggestive: "Working together with him." The apostle has been defending and explaining the Christian ministry; and incidentally and inferentially he gathers into his great argument the thought of all such as are in fellowship with God in life and service. If you go back to the verses preceding, you will find that the apostle declares what God's work is. "God was in Christ, reconciling the world unto himself." He then proceeds, "We are ambassadors, therefore, on behalf of Christ, as though God were entreating by us; we beseech you on behalf of Christ, be ye reconciled to God." "Working together with him." It is only a phrase, but it is lit with glory and charged with power. It declares this man's realization that he also is in the holy partnership, that he also has a share to take in the work of God. "My Father worketh even until now, and I work." "Working together with him."

The work of the Christian man in the world begins with unceasing restlessness because of man's unrest. You are a Christian. Are you content in the world with the world as you see it? Tell me what you say when you look at evil, and I will tell you whether you are a Christ-man or not. Is there a Divine discontent burning in your heart, that drives you out into active service? Then you are working together with him. Can you be perfectly at rest in this great city, with all its sin and sorrow and sighing and restlessness? Then you know nothing of his life in your soul. God cannot rest while men are restless. Can you?

This unrest expresses itself in unceasing conflict with sin. I thank God that he has never made peace with sin. I thank God that he has never signed a truce with it in this poor heart of mine. How I have tried to persuade him to. How, ever and anon in the years that have gone, I have tried to excuse some darling sin, but he has never made peace with it. I have known it, and have hidden it. I have had to say with the Psalmist, "When I kept silence, my bones waxed old through my roaring all the day long; for day and night thy hand was heavy upon me." Thank God for his heavy hand wherever sin abides in the life. And so the man of God is filled with anger in the presence of sin. It is told of Hannibal that when he came in utter amazement and grief into the presence of his father, crucified by the Romans, he lifted his hand in the presence of that Roman cross, and swore by all his gods that he would fight to the death the power that had crucified his father. The Christian man is a man who has been to the Cross, and he has seen what sin has wrought for his God, and he lifts his hand in the presence of that Cross, and swears to fight sin to the death, in his own heart, in his home, in his city, in the world. My Father worketh against sin in ceaseless activity, and I work. We also are the sworn foes of sin, even as God is. Why is God the foe of sin? In order that he may save the sinner. I love that word "save." Do not let us drop it out of our speech in these days. It is not a narrow word, shallow and meaningless. It is a great word. God is the foe of sin in order that he may save men. Why does God hate sin in me? Why has he never made peace with it? Because he knows that it harms me, and all the fiery fierceness of his wrath is fed by the fuel of his infinite love for the sinner. So, if we are workers together with him, the purpose of our conflict with sin is that we may make Sabbath for the man who has none, that we may lead the restless into rest, the wounded into healing, the wearied home and the lost back again to the heart of God.

George Campell Morgan (1863–1945)   *Most Americans believed Campbell Morgan to be a United States citizen, since his ministry was so constant and popular in North America. Born in Gloucestershire, he was to cross the Atlantic at least fifty times in response to preaching invitations across America. He was the author of nearly twenty books of sermons.*

Rodney (Gipsy) Smith/As Jesus Passed by; or, Follow Me

And as Jesus passed by, he saw a man called Matthew, sitting at the place of toll: and he saith unto him, follow me. And he arose and followed him.

MATTHEW 9:9

THIS is Matthew's modest way of telling all generations how he was converted. Matthew could have made a great deal more of that epoch-making moment in his life. Sometimes I think when he wrote just as much as my text he would not write any more that day. Can you not see between the lines what a story is there untold? He does not even tell you that he lived in a big house. He does not tell you that he made a big feast. He does not tell you that he invited all his old friends to come and meet with Jesus at the feast. He leaves others to tell you that little bit of the story. He simply says there was a feast. Very modest is Matthew. He says Jesus saw a man, and said to that man, "Follow me," and the man followed; that is all.

Some of us at certain moments of our lives cannot trust ourselves to tell all the story. We keep something back; we cannot trust ourselves to put the story into words. There are pages in every life that will never be written. There are stories untold to mortal ear over which the angels rejoice. There are moments when only the sky and the sun, the moon and the stars, the birds and the flowers, and the heaven eternal can hear all we have to say of his wonderful grace and mercy. We can only tell a bit of it, just a little bit of it. I want you to think of this wonderful moment—and it was a wonderful moment, a moment when gospels were born, a moment in which history began to breathe, a moment when in his soul there was placed the germ-joy that will make heaven pulsate with hallelujahs. It was a wonderful moment in his life when he saw Jesus standing there calling him by name, speaking to him as a man would to his friend, appealing to him.

Why should Jesus go to this man? Because this man needed Jesus. I believe deep down in this man's heart he was longing for Christ. I am not so sure that he had not heard John the Baptist preach. I am not so sure that he was not already a convicted sinner. I am not so sure that he had not heard John say, "Behold the Lamb of God!" There were moments in his life when he longed to get a look at that dear face, to hear the music of that voice, and catch some inspiration from his life-giving message, and to feel the touch that healed. And I can imagine that even that day he could not see his books for his tears. He was at his business, you remember; he sat at the place of toll, everything in front of him, and while he was thinking of the inward longings, while the soul-hunger was gnawing, while the man within the man was talking to him and setting in motion thoughts and feelings that were eternal, I can imagine him saying, "Oh, shall I ever see him?" And maybe he laid his head on his hands in his grief, and at that moment Jesus said, "Matthew, Matthew, follow me."

You know Matthew was ready to do it. He did it instantly, without asking a question, without any hesitation. He acted as though he had made his plans as to what he would do if he had the chance. He left all. He does not tell you that, he leaves the others to add that bit to the story; and his all was the possibility of becoming very rich. He left it all: he left his books, he left his business, he left his office, he left his position, he left his friends, he left *all* to follow Jesus. Matthew had counted the cost, and knew what he would do if the chance came. Jesus knew it too. He knew where Matthew sat, just as he knew where Nathanael prayed under the fig tree. He knows where you are, Matthew at the place of toll or Nathanael under the fig tree or Zaccheus in the tree. He knows, he sees. There is no look heavenward, there is no desire heavenward, there is no aspiration after goodness, there is not an honest struggle for a nobler life in your heart, in your home, anywhere, everywhere, but what God sees and God knows. And, listen to me, there never is a good desire, there never is a noble thought, there never will be an aspiration for a holier life, but what is God-given and God-inspired. He knows. And he knows where you sit, my brother.

Here is a man handicapped, a jewel in an unlikely place; here is a man that nobody wanted, ostracized by his very profession, separated from decent folk by his calling, unpopular and hated. There he was; he never had had a chance. The church did not want him, and Jesus Christ took the trouble to save him. The church of his day did not want him, and I am afraid there are some churches in England who would not thank you to fill them with the harlots, the publicans, the gamblers, the drunkards and the sinners. And yet they are the sort that heaven opens its doors to. Don't forget that. They are the people for whom Christ died—not the righteous, but sinners. And there are people who would sit in committee and dictate to the Son of God as to who he is to save. They did it in Matthew's day. There are people who would sit in judgment on the Christ of God. They would question the authority of Omnipotence to save the sinner. "This man eateth with sinners." It shows how much they knew of this man and his mission to the world.

What does this story mean? It means this: that for every man there is a chance. The Christ I have to preach gives a chance to the worst, to the most unlikely, to the most degraded, to the most hated, to the most sinful, to the most despised, to the people who were born into the world with the devil in their blood, the blood of the gambler in their veins, the blood of the harlot in their veins. And when I think of it all and look at some people, the wonder to me is that they are not worse than they are. God have pity on the little boys and girls in the world who are made drunk before they are a year old. God have pity on the childlife of today! For such Jesus came.

And he chooses to find out about these people, the people that nobody wants, and he says, "I want you; I am after you." It is a new way of treating sinners. Did you ever think of it? A new way of treating sinners, wrongdoers. Prison for wrongdoers, the law courts for wrongdoers; the whole fabric of society is built up to keep off wrongdoers, to keep away wrongdoers, to keep out wrongdoers, to shut up and shut off wrongdoers; and Jesus Christ comes and opens his arms to them, and says, "Come to me; I will receive you." That is the Christ for me! To set the prisoner free, to break the chains of them that are bound, to open the prison doors and say, "March out; I will make you free by my mighty power." It means a chance for every man. And Jesus sees far more in these people that are far from him than we have seen yet.

If you and I had the eyes of Christ we should see in the filthiest wretch that walks the street something worth saving. If you and I only had the vision of Calvary we should never weary, we should never tire, we should never lose heart and we should never lose hope. We should believe that for the worst there is a throne, a song, an anthem. May God help us to believe our Gospel!

Why did Jesus go to Matthew? Because Jesus knew that Matthew needed him. Nobody could do for Matthew what Jesus could. Don't forget that. Matthew had never had a chance. Nobody but Jesus could give him one. He was in a bad setting; his whole life was a tangle, his whole life was knots. Nobody wanted him. And you know people like that. There are some connected with you that you would rather not see. You tremble when you see them, and when their name is mentioned. There are some names you do not talk about to others; you try to forget; you won't talk about them. There is a skeleton in every cupboard. The most of us here have somebody connected with us that we do not like to mention; we try to forget; and yet, God knows, the agony of it eats the life out of us. They are the people who need him.

It is no good to say to some people, "Believe, believe." They need somebody's fingers to unravel the knots, to untie and straighten things out; and who is to do it? Those whose whole life has been cursed from their very birth, they are handicapped in their very blood—and who is to deliver them? Can anybody do it? Is there no God who can do it? Listen—the fingers that weaved the rainbow into a scarf and wrapped it around the shoulders of the dying storm, the fingers that painted the lily-bell and threw out the planets, the fingers that were dipped in the mighty sea of eternity and shook out on this old planet, making the ocean to drop and the rivers to stream—the same fingers can take hold on these tangled lives and can make them whole again, for he came to make the crooked straight, and the rough places plain. Blessed be God, Jesus can do for Matthew what nobody else can; and he can do for you, my brother, what your friends cannot do. He can take the desire for drink out of you; he can cure the love of gambling that is eating the soul out of you; he can put out the fires of lust that are burning in your being and consuming you by inches; he can take the devil of lying out of you, the devil of cheating out of you, of fraud out of you, of hypocrisy out of you. Jesus can do what nobody else can; the preacher cannot, the Church cannot, but the Lord Jesus, who loves you, is mighty to save.

Let me go another step. There was something that Matthew could do for Jesus that nobody else could—and I say that reverently. Jesus needed Matthew. Ay, and he needs you. They looked at him and said, "He is a sinner." "Yes," said Jesus, "and he will write my first Gospel." Only give him a chance; you do not know what there is hidden in the drunkard. There may be a preacher, there may be an evangelist, there may be a gospel. You do not know. Give them a chance; give them all a chance. "A sinner." They were fond of using these words. "He is a sinner." They used them about the man in the tree. "Yes," said Jesus, "he is a sinner, and he is a son of Abraham." And it was Jesus who spoke on both occasions. You would not have gone for a scribe for the Son of God to a publican. No! But Jesus has a wonderful way of showing what he can do with unlikely material. A little child cried just now. Its little voice in coming days may startle the nation. The waving of its little hand may marshal the hosts of God. Who can tell? That little boy at your side may become a Spurgeon, a McLaren, a Whitefield, a Wesley. Who can tell the possibilities of a child? That little girl may be a Mrs. Fletcher, a Florence Nightingale, a Catherine Booth. Who can tell? And God wants them all. There are gospels hidden away, untold yet, but they will shine out and flash in letters, golden capitals, and make the world glad with a great gladness.

You saw the sinner; Jesus saw the man. He saw the sinner too, and he knew what the sinner would be when grace had had a chance. The world sees the face and the clothes and the house, the street you live in, where you work, and reckons you up by how much your salary is. Jesus does not reckon that way. See that sailor—drunken, filthy, vile of lip and impure in soul—a drunken sailor. Nobody wanted him; nobody cared for him. God looked at him and saved him; and his name was John Newton, the poet, the preacher, but God could see the theologian, the preacher, in the drunken sailor.

See that man, a swearing tinker; so swearing, he says of himself, that when he began to swear his neighbors shuddered. Nobody wanted that tinker. But God looked at him and saved him; and his name was John Bunyan, the immortal dreamer. You would not have looked for *The Pilgrim's Progress* in that swearing tinker.

God looked at that man, a publican—and you know what a publican is—helping his brother to sell beer in Gloucester. God looked at him and saved him; and his name was George Whitefield, the mighty preacher. Look at that man selling boots and shoes in a shoe store in Chicago. God looked at him and saved him, and when he took the trouble to save him and that young fellow offered himself to a Congregational church as a church member, they saw so little in him that they put him back on trial for twelve months; and his name was Moody. And Moody has put one hand on America and another hand on Britain, and they moved toward the Cross.

See that man, the plaything of the village, full of devilry, mischief, roguery, fond of pleasure and sin. Nobody cared for him except his mates, and God saved him; and his name was Peter Mackenzie, a sunbeam in the lives of thousands. Look at this picture—a gipsy tent; there is a father and five little motherless children, without a Bible, without school. Nobody wanted them—who does want a gipsy? Nobody—outsider, ostracized, despised and rejected. But God looked on that poor father and those five motherless little things and saw them, in their ignorance and heathenism, hungry for God. And he looked again, and he said, "There are six preachers in that tent." And he put those arms that were nailed to the tree round the father and the children and saved them all; and I am one of them. It takes love to see. Love saw more in Matthew than anybody; and sees more in you, my brother, than anybody else; and if no one wants you, he does, and if no one loves you, he does. If no one cares, he cares; and if you think there is not a friend in the world, you have more friends than you think, and they are closer to you than you dream. God is here, and he says, "Come to me, follow me, and I will save you; I will give you a chance for this world and the next. Only follow me."

Matthew never did a wiser or nobler thing than when he took Christ home. Everybody there had a chance of blessing that day. Think of what it would mean for your home if you, my brother, took Christ home with you. Your wife and children would have a chance they have never had before. If both of you—husband and wife—bow at his dear feet together, what joy there will be in heaven and on earth. It would mean your home for Jesus. You will give Christ a chance with every child in your home by taking him there. Matthew took Jesus home with him; and he will go home with you if you will ask him, and he will go with you this night. God help you!

I can believe there are scores and hundreds who mean to follow Jesus. Who will leave all to follow Jesus? Who will sacrifice everything for Jesus' sake? Who will take their stand for Jesus, and who will go home and say to their friends, "I have come to tell you what great things the Lord hath done for me"? Jesus calls to you. Will you follow?

Rodney (Gipsy) Smith (1860–1947) *Gipsy Smith was indeed the son of gipsies. A native of England, he became a famous evangelist, first serving with General Booth during the early beginnings of the Salvation Army. He was much beloved by American audiences.*

Joseph Fort Newton/
The Immortal Life

Jesus said unto her, I am the resurrection, and the life; he that believeth in me, though he were dead, yet shall he live; and whosoever liveth and believeth in me shall never die. Believest thou this?

JOHN 11:25, 26

A GAIN the tide of eternity, by men called "Time," has brought us to the day of all days the best, the crest and crown of the Christian year: the Day of Eternal Life. The sweet order of Easter Day is blended with a beautiful confusion, in which the mysteries of religion are mixed with the mysteries of nature; and that is as it should be, because it is the day of the cosmic Christ—the mighty Lord of life and death and all that lies between and beyond.

Out of a red sunset an Oriental poet once saw a friend riding over the desert toward his tent, wrapped in glory like a heavenly halo, and the poet exclaimed, "Glory to the Almighty, the sun has risen in the west!" Out of the crimson sunset on Good Friday, its horror and its heroism, the risen Christ comes riding in majesty today, the best friend of the human heart, and we cry out, "Glory to the Almighty, the sun has risen in the west!"

Out of death comes life; out of agony comes joy; out of defeat, victory; out of sunset, dawn. Where we had least hope of sunrise, "the Son of righteousness arises with healing in his wings," in fulfillment of his own tremendous words:

I am the resurrection, and the life: he that believeth in me, though he were dead, yet shall he live; and whosoever liveth and believeth in me, shall never die. Believest thou this?

How often, alas, we have heard those words as a part of the Office of the

Burial of the Dead; and it was so I first heard them as a tiny lad when my father was buried. Clinging to the hand of my little mother, on that snowy day I looked for the first time into an open grave, and it seemed that everything was lost—as if the bottom had dropped out of life. Then the kindly old country preacher began the service: "I am the resurrection, and the life"—never shall I forget the thrill of those words! It was as if a great, gentle hand, stronger than the hand of man and more tender than the hand of woman, had been put forth from the unseen to help and heal—from that day to this I have loved Jesus to distraction. Forty-six years later I stood on the same spot, when the little mother whose hand I held in days that come not back was laid away; and again the words, "I am the resurrection, and the life," spoke to me out of the depth of death—nay, out of the heart of God—and there was sunrise in the west!

Of all expositions of those words the noblest is the picture, by Browning, of the death of St. John the Evangelist of Love, the last of the glorious company of the apostles, and the only one to die a natural death. The little knot of disciples stood round watching the great head sinking lower and yet lower, until at last the flame of life flickered and, as it seemed, went out. Loneliness, like a cold, crawling sea-mist, filled their hearts; for there was no one left who had seen the face of Jesus, no one who could say, "I heard his voice"—and how much had been left untold! Desperately the little group tried to coax back a tiny spark of life, but in vain, till a lad ran for a copy of the Gospel, found the page, and read, "I am the resurrection, and the life." Hearing the voice of his Lord, the seemingly dead man sat up and poured out his soul in one last luminous talk.

What stupendous words, "I am the resurrection, and the life," and how utterly empty and unreal, if not wildly insane, upon the lips of the gentle, winsome humanitarian Christ who, however heroic and fascinating, is only one of ourselves—purer, braver, more unearthly—yet guessing at the riddle of life as we have to do, knowing nothing certainly of his own destiny or ours, himself a victim of muddy, all-devouring death, which seems to divide divinity with God. No! No! Here speaks the Master of life and death, the Lord of worlds other than this orb of dust, the revealer of the meaning of life, a voice out of the heart of things—a voice not simply of comfort, but of command. Here shines a light that never was on sea or land, fairer than the prophet-vision, brighter than the poet-dream. Nevertheless, this being who towers so far above us is still so close to our humanity, his whole life so entwined with our piteous, passionate, and pathetic life on earth, that we somehow feel that what is true of him is in some degree true, potentially, of ourselves. How these two truths can be united may be hard to know—save in a paradox profounder than thought—but they are equally vivid, equally valid and equally blessed in our historic Christian faith; and to lose either truth is to lose the other. Here, to say it once more, is the highest reach of holiness in man answered by a voice older than the earth and deeper than death:

Before Abraham was, I am—life endless at both ends, moving with a higher rhythm, stretching away into unfathomable depths and distances; one vast life that lives and cannot die, gathering all our broken lights into its eternal radiance.

I am the Light of the World—the sun is up; shadows of death and dark fatality flee away; blind thoughts we know not nor can name are forgotten like fear in the night. It is daybreak; life everywhere is radiant, earth is a valley with a lark-song over it.

I am the Way—the path marked out for the soul; the way without which there is no going, to lose which is to wander in a wilderness, or end in a blind alley; the way which, if we follow it faithfully, shineth more and more unto the perfect day.

I am the Truth—the truth about life and death, which breaks through language and escapes; the truth that makes all other truth true; nay, more, the truth that can never be uttered, but must be acted, incarnated; the truth that sets life to music.

I am the Life—the life that interprets life; no mere story of life, but life itself—intense, creative, palpitating, prophetic; life in a new dimension, with a new radiance, overflowing, sweeping dim death away as in a flood of light and power and joy.

I am the Good Shepherd—the shepherd of ages and journeying generations, whose heart aches with compassion for the multitudes who wander afar, seeking without finding; the mighty shepherd in whose bosom the lambs find a haven and a home.

I am the Door—the door out of night into dawn; the door into another room in the house not made with hands, "our dwelling place in all generations"; the sheltering home of all souls, however far-wandering, where we shall see "that one face" and be satisfied. "Behold, I have set before you an open door, and no man can shut it."

I am the Resurrection, and the Life—death is abolished, as the radio abolishes distance; it no longer exists, save as a cloud-shadow wandering across the human valley. "Let not your heart be troubled, neither let it be afraid"—death is other than we think or fear.

Behold, I am alive for evermore—the word of one who has death behind him, never to face it again—a thing left below, defeated and outsped—having passed through its shadow, making a path of light "which shineth more and more unto the perfect day."

Now, consider. No one else has ever spoken such words to humanity; no one can do it. Never once does Jesus say, "I believe," as we must needs do, praying help for our unbelief. No. "I *am* the resurrection and the life"—it is not merely an anthem of affirmation; it is a revelation of another order, rhythm and cadence of life. He does not argue; he unveils the truth. He does not promise immortality in some dim, far time beyond; he illumines it, bringing both "life and immortality to light." It is not only a prophecy but a possession—such a reversal of faith, such a transvaluation of values as baffles thought and bewilders imagination. "I *am* the resurrection": God is here, eternity is now, death is nothing to the soul; it is a staggering truth, so vast that our minds seem unable to grasp and hold it. Once we do grasp it, once we do lay it to heart and know its power, then we know the meaning of the words, "Behold, I make all things new." Life everyway is infinite; the sky begins at the top of the ground. O my soul, remember, consider and rejoice in God thy Saviour!

Here is the song of the immortal life, breaking in upon our broken days and years, gathering our fugitive and fragmentary lives into its sovereign harmony, if we have ears to hear and hearts to heed and understand. Slowly, upon our dim eyes, blinded by dusty death, there dawns the vision of a spiritual order in which all the holy things of life—its higher values, its haunting prophecies—have their source, sanction, security and satisfaction. To the reality of that realm all the noblest creative life of humanity bears witness, dimly or clearly, and from it the purest souls of the race have drawn inward sustaining. Of that order, "the Lord of all Good Life" was and is a citizen; its laws were revealed in his life; its meaning spoke in his words, pitched not in the past nor in the future but in "the mystic tense"; its light became incandescent in his personality. By its serene power he was Master of disease, discord and dark fatality—nay, more, of life and time and death; in its fellowship he still lives and serves humanity, a thousand times more alive than in the days of his flesh. By the power of Spirit his swift and gentle years moved with the lilt of a lyric, and even the tragedy of his death—in which he faced the worst and found the best—became the epic of the life everlasting.

As Dante said, Jesus taught us "how to make our lives eternal," and if we learn his secret we shall know neither fret nor fear. In prayer, in glad obedience, in high adventure—giving all, daring all—he drew the fullness of God into his life, fulfilling what others had dreamed. By the wonder of his personality he released a new power in human life—"the power of an endless life"—power over sin, over sorrow, over brute matter and black despair. Here lies the secret of social stability and nobility, no less than of triumphant character. Half a life ago Dostoevski foretold the orgy of modern Russia—anarchy running mad and running red—when, in *The Possessed*, one of his characters cries out, prophetically:

> Listen, I've reckoned them all up: a teacher who laughs with children at their God is on our side. The juries who acquit every criminal are ours. Among officials and literary men we have lots, lots, and they don't know it themselves. Do you know how many we shall catch with little, ready-made ideas? The Russian God has already been vanquished by cheap vodka. The peasants are drunk, the churches are empty. Oh, this generation has only to grow up. Ah, what a pity there is no proletariat. But there will be, there will be; we are going that way.

What happened in Russia will happen among us, when we let the altar fires of our fathers go out and our faith fail. All the dear interests and institutions of humanity have their basis in the eternal life, else they cannot abide. Our human world is kept in place and urged along its orbit by unseen forces. Thence come those impulses to progress, those insights and aspirations, which impel man to vaster issues—they are the pressure upon him of the endless life. Liberty, justice, love, truth are things of the eternal life, without which customs are cobwebs and laws are ropes of sand. Toward the end of his life Dostoevski divided the race into two classes, those who know the eternal life and those who do not; and the fate of civilization, he said, will rest with those who are citizens of eternity. The power of an endless life is thus the creative and constructive force of humanity, and when it is lost society becomes a pigsty.

Here, no less, is the secret of spiritual character and personality, the two loveliest flowers grown in these short days of sun and frost. Only recently a great physician said that subconscious health cannot be obtained in one who has lost faith in immortality. Without it the noblest powers of the soul are inhibited; its finest instincts are frustrated, having no happy release and no promise of fulfillment. When we know the eternal life, all doors are open and the great aspirations of the heart take wings. The impingement of eternity upon us gives to the moral sense an august authority, and makes religion not a dogma, but an eternal communion. Life everywhere grows in dignity, meaning, worth and grace when it is lived in the fellowship of eternal things. The power of an endless life—it is the life of faith, of love, of fellowship, of joy. It makes a man stand up like a tower, foursquare to all the winds of the world, a defense to the weak or the weary. It is one with all dear friendships, with every tender tie which unites us with those nearest to us, with every bond of sympathy binding us to humanity—aye, with those whom we have loved and lost awhile.

What life really is, what it prophesies, what it may actually become even here on earth—transfiguring all "our fleshly dress with bright shoots of everlastingness"—is shown us in the life of Jesus, by the truth he taught and still more by his personality. He was so aglow with the power and joy of life, so in tune with its vivid, creative urge and insight, that his words seem to have a life of their own, and grow. He was a spiritual biologist who thought of religion in terms of life—not of life in terms of religion—and he hardly used the word "death" at all, since death is not an event but a tendency, and true life is the death of death. By his death Jesus gave life to his religion, and by his resurrection he made religion a life, even the eternal life in time, free, radiant, abundant, creative, victorious—a quest, a conquest, a consecration.

In literature there is an exalted zone of song wherein if a man step his footfall echoes forever, defying time and change and death; and thus the echo of an hour of prayer among the Judean hills, or a lyric sung at a Greek festival, becomes a part of the eternal speech of mankind. Just so, there is in the life of the spirit a level of loyalty, of luminous lucidity, of immaculate perception, of all-giving love, which joins the mortal to the immortal, and death is seen to be only the shadow of life as it spreads its wings for flight; only a dark room in which life changes its robe and marches on. Others enter that realm, briefly, in rare hours of insight and understanding, when the mood is pure and the vision is clear; but Jesus lived in it, obeyed its laws, unveiled its reality, and revealed its emancipating truth. Hence the strange, searching, haunting, healing quality of his words, which seem like birds let loose from a region above our reach of which we are dimly aware, and toward which both wisdom and faith point. Hence, too, the refrain that echoes through his teaching: "He that hath ears to hear, let him hear."

From that radiant realm, in the rhythm of its profound and transcendent experience of God, Jesus spoke the words, *I am the resurrection, and the life.* Such words are notes in an eternal world-song, a divine symphony which began when the morning stars sang together over a newborn earth, and which runs through all things. It is the song of life itself, underflowing all the tumult and tragedy of time, upbearing the life and death of humanity—its sins and woes, its griefs and heartaches—and lifting all at last into the rhythm and cadence of an eternal life; an august undertone prophetic of a final harmony of all things with God. All religions, all philosophies are but broken echoes of one everlasting music, prose versions of a divine poetry singing even "in the mud and scum of things," an all-sustaining, undefeatable melody:

> *It singeth low in every heart,*
> *We hear it each and all.*

At last, rising above all discord and seeming defeat, it will break in triumphant anthems of adoration upon the throne of God, proclaiming that "life is ever lord of death and love can never lose its own." Believest thou this?

By the same token, if we would know the power of an endless life, defeating death and dull dismay, it must be by contact and fellowship with the Lord of life. Ever the path lies at our feet, if we follow on to realize the life that is triumphant, and the road mounts steadily: "And this is life eternal, to know thee the only true God, and Jesus Christ, whom thou hast sent." For thou, O God, art life, thou art reality, and thou art our Father.

> *Safe in the care of heavenly powers,*
> *The good we dreamed but might not do,*
> *Lost beauty magically new,*
> *Shall spring as surely as the flowers*
> *When, 'mid the sobbing of the rain,*
> *The heart of April beats again.*

> *Celestial spirit that doth roll*
> *The heart's sepulchral stone away,*
> *Be this our resurrection day,*
> *The singing Easter of the Soul:*
> *O gentle Master of the Wise,*
> *Teach me to say, "I will arise!"*

Joseph Fort Newton (1880–1950)   *Ordained as a Southern Baptist, Dr. Newton served eight major pulpits in this country and City Temple in London. He later became an Episcopalian, author of a dozen books, and an important liaison between Christians of all persuasions.*

Henry Sloane Coffin/The Claims of the Church upon Christians

Said Jesus to them, as my Father hath sent me, even so send I you. And when he had said this, he breathed on them, and saith unto them, Receive ye the Holy Spirit.

JOHN 20:1, 22

I N Jesus' commission to his first disciples we get a clear definition of the Christian church. It is the company of those who share the purpose of Jesus and possess his Father's Spirit for its accomplishment.

Protestantism has so emphasized the individual's personal fellowship with God that it has often lost sight of his necessary fellowship with the church, the communion of those of like purpose organized for collective service. We need to remind ourselves that, unique as was Jesus' relation to God, he was a loyal churchman.

He was born into the Jewish church, and the first recorded incidents of his childhood—his circumcision and presentation in the temple—were his public recognition as a church member. The earliest expression of his own religious experience was his saying to his parents that he must be in his Father's house. That church was the heir of patriarchs, prophets, lawgivers, psalmists, sages, and of generations of lowly and earnest, believing men and women. Two of the evangelists give us genealogies, which interest us today not so much as lines of physical descent but as the ancestry of Jesus' faith. The heritage of the Jewish church was Jesus' birthright. He expressed his respect for the official leaders of the body which had preserved the choicest religious experiences of the past in its Scriptures, kept alive devotion to the God of Israel in the world, and was holding up, however imperfectly, the ideal of his kingdom, when he said, "The scribes and Pharisees sit on Moses' seat: all things, therefore, whatsoever they bid you, these observe and do." In that church's trust his faith was born; in its worship and teaching his soul was shaped and nourished; in its consecration the flame of his own sacrifice was kindled. To it he owed a debt which he never repudiated.

A Christian today is under no less obligation to the church. Those who stand aloof from it and coolly criticize it, as though they sustained no personal relation to it, are as unfilial as the man who would "peep and botanize upon his mother's grave." There are doubtless some things about the church with which we cannot sympathize. Its beliefs may appear to us crude at a number of points, and its official creeds phrased in obsolete forms; its standards of conduct may seem deficient in social obligation; its outlook may be narrow, prejudiced and exclusive of much that is not alien to the purpose of the Son of man; its methods may impress us as pathetically ineffective with large sections of our population. The Jewish church in Jesus' day was lacking in his eyes in all these respects; but the fact remained that it had been his spiritual mother, and this kinship gave him a responsibility he could not disown.

Again, its fellowship seemed to him indispensable for his own religious inspiration. The life in which all succeeding generations have seen the fullness of the Godhead was not self-sufficient. Jesus' originality consisted in his discriminating appropriation of the best he found in existing institutions, ideals, beliefs, and transforming it for his own purpose. He went regularly to the services of the synagogue and kept the appointed festivals at Jerusalem. There must have been many phrases in the prayers of the liturgy which he found imperfect and even objectionable. There were portions of the church's recognized Scriptures which he considered outworn and inadequate representations of God. He must often have been bored by dull and unenlightened sermons. Some of the church's leaders did not command his respect, and many of his fellow worshippers must have seemed insincere and uninspiring. But he did not depend upon his own Bible reading and private communion with God for the development of his spirit. The fellowship of kindred souls and the stimulus of social worship were to him essential for his religious vitality.

Many high-principled Christians do not attend church services and have no formal connection with the organization today. It is undeniable that there are many religious stimuli besides those that come from public worship and fellowship with the church—stimuli in literature, in education, in social service; but if the Son of God could not do without inspirations which came to him from the Jewish church, it is surely not likely that a modern Christian can maintain his spiritual life at its utmost vigor without constant contact with the Christian church, which, however faulty, is certainly no faultier than the church Jesus knew.

And again, Jesus found in the church the largest opportunity for the investment of his personal religious life. According to Luke's narrative, as soon as he became aware of his special spiritual endowment and had gone through the testing in the wilderness, he returned to the synagogue in which he had been reared, and announced that the Spirit of the Lord was upon him. It is in a religious society that a man can find his largest usefulness for the kingdom. In an organization others will supplement him, catch his zeal, receive his new ideas, spread his influence where he cannot personally go and carry on the impetus of his life long after he has ceased to be. The Jewish church offered Jesus pulpits from which to speak his message, a theology in which to clothe his thoughts, a heritage of spiritual force with which he could ally himself, a membership of believing people from which he drew his first adherents. He seemed to feel that if he could capture this organization, and get it to adopt his purpose, he would have an incalculable reinforcement. He was disappointed; but whatever success he attained, he won through it.

Where can a man with the purpose of Christ today find a larger opportunity than in the Christian church? Here is the impetus of the past to forward him; here are lives with kindred faith and devotion to be his partners; here is a wealth of sentiment to which he can appeal; here is conveniently arranged machinery to multiply his effectiveness; here is a body into which he can infuse his spirit, and which will conserve the results of his work long after he has passed away. If he disagrees with its official creeds, let him seek to revise and improve them, as Jesus sought to teach the church of his age. If he thinks that it is wasting its energies on trifles, let him recall it to its divine commission, as Jesus set forth to the congregation at Nazareth the purpose of God. If he considers its methods ineffective, let him show it a more excellent way; and the church, with all its traditionalism, is sincerely eager to be made more efficient. Let him inspire it, by his thought and consecration and sacrifice, with a new spirit, with more of its own spirit—the Eternal Spirit of the God and Father of Jesus Christ. A Christian can do most, not in isolation, but in fellowship with the company of like-purposing believers. And wherever the church is, lives that are not in direct touch with it are richer in ideals, fairer in character and more fruitful in service for its inspiring presence in their neighborhood. There are, doubtless, showers of divine blessing that refresh God's earth everywhere, and dews of mercy that form nightly over the most parched and barren soil; but the church is the channel through which the central stream of divine life is flowing to fructify the earth with fruits of righteousness akin to those of Jesus.

In every age the church has felt that the flow of divine life and power in it was a mere trickle; and this is true today. We recognize the church's mission—to cleanse every sphere of our social life and permeate a whole world with the Spirit of God in Christ. And how titanic the task is! The church looks expectantly and trustfully to its sons and daughters in the schools and colleges of the land, pleading with them to acknowledge their spiritual debt, to avail themselves of its stores of garnered and living inspiration, and to bring the wealth of their endowment and energy to augment its forces and fulfill its worldwide mission. And shall it look in vain?

Henry Sloane Coffin (1877–1954)   *A member of a famous New York family, in church and in business, Dr. Coffin served the Madison Avenue Presbyterian Church for nearly four decades. Always popular on university campuses, Dr. Coffin spoke to the needs and hopes of thousands of students.*

Martin Luther King, Jr./Loving Your Enemies

Ye have heard that it hath been said, Thou shalt love thy neighbour, and hate thine enemy. But I say unto you, Love your enemies, bless them that curse you, do good to them that hate you, and pray for them which despitefully use you, and persecute you; that ye may be the children of your Father which is in heaven.

MATTHEW 5:43–45

PROBABLY no admonition of Jesus has been more difficult to follow than the command to "love your enemies." Some men have sincerely felt that its actual practice is not possible. It is easy, they say, to love those who love you, but how can one love those who openly and insidiously seek to defeat you? Others, like the philosopher Nietzsche, contend that Jesus' exhortation to love one's enemies is testimony to the fact that the Christian ethic is designed for the weak and cowardly, and not for the strong and courageous. Jesus, they say, was an impractical idealist.

In spite of these insistent questions and persistent objections, this command of Jesus challenges us with new urgency. Upheaval after upheaval has reminded us that modern man is traveling along a road called hate, in a journey that will bring us to destruction and damnation. Far from being the pious injunction of a utopian dreamer, the command to love one's enemy is an absolute necessity for our survival. Love even for enemies is the key to the solution of the problems of our world. Jesus is not an impractical idealist; he is the practical realist.

I am certain that Jesus understood the difficulty inherent in the act of loving one's enemy. He never joined the ranks of those who talk glibly about the easiness of the moral life. He realized that every genuine expression of love grows out of a consistent and total surrender to God. So when Jesus said "Love your enemy," he was not unmindful of its stringent qualities. Yet he meant every word of it. Our responsibility as Christians is to discover the meaning of this command and seek passionately to live it out in our daily lives.

Let us be practical and ask the question, "How do we love our enemies?"

First, we must develop and maintain the capacity to forgive. He who is devoid of the power to forgive is devoid of the power to love. It is impossible even to begin the act of loving one's enemies without the prior acceptance of the necessity, over and over again, of forgiving those who inflict evil and injury upon us. It is also necessary to realize that the forgiving act must always be initiated by the person who has been wronged, the victim of some great hurt, the recipient of some tortuous injustice, the absorber of some terrible act of oppression. The wrong-doer may request forgiveness. He may come to himself, and, like the prodigal son, move up some dusty road, his heart palpitating with the desire for forgiveness. But only the injured neighbor, the loving father back home, can really pour out the warm waters of forgiveness.

Forgiveness does not mean ignoring what has been done or putting a false label on an evil act. It means, rather, that the evil act no longer remains as a barrier to the relationship. Forgiveness is a catalyst creating the atmosphere necessary for a fresh start and a new beginning. It is the lifting of a burden or the canceling of a debt. The words "I will forgive you, but I'll never forget what you've done" never explain the real nature of forgiveness. Certainly one can never forget, if that means erasing it totally from his mind. But when we forgive, we forget in the sense that the evil deed is no longer a mental block impeding a new relationship. Likewise, we can never say, "I will forgive you, but I won't have anything further to do with you." Forgiveness means reconciliation, a coming together again. Without this, no man can love his enemies. The degree to which we are able to forgive determines the degree to which we are able to love our enemies.

Second, we must recognize that the evil deed of the enemy-neighbor, the thing that hurts, never quite expresses all that he is. An element of goodness may be found even in our worst enemy. Each of us is something of a schizophrenic personality, tragically divided against ourselves. A persistent civil war rages within all of our lives. Something within us causes us to lament with Ovid, the Latin poet, "I see and approve the better things, but follow worse," or to agree with Plato that human personality is like a charioteer having two headstrong horses, each wanting to go in a different direction, or to repeat with the Apostle Paul, "The good that I would I do not; but the evil which I would not, that I do."

This simply means that there is some good in the worst of us and some evil in the best of us. When we discover this, we are less prone to hate our enemies. When we look beneath the surface, beneath the impulsive evil deed, we see within our enemy-neighbor a measure of goodness and know that the viciousness and evilness of his acts are not quite representative of all that he is. We see him in a new light. We recognize that his hate grows out of fear, pride, ignorance, prejudice and misunderstanding; but in spite of this, we know God's image is ineffably etched in his being. Then we love our enemies by realizing that they are not totally bad and that they are not beyond the reach of God's redemptive love.

Third, we must not seek to defeat or humiliate the enemy but to win his friendship and understanding. At times we are able to humiliate our worst enemy. Inevitably, his weak moments come and we are able to thrust in his side the spear of defeat. But this we must not do. Every word and deed must contribute to an understanding with the enemy and release those vast reservoirs of goodwill which have been blocked by impenetrable walls of hate.

The meaning of love is not to be confused with some sentimental outpouring. Love is something much deeper than emotional bosh. Perhaps the Greek language can clear our confusion at this point. In the Greek New Testament are three words for love. The word *eros* is a sort of aesthetic or romantic love. In the Platonic dialogues *eros* is a yearning of the soul for the realm of the divine. The second word is *philia,* a reciprocal love and the intimate affection and friendship between friends. We love those whom we like, and we love because we are loved. The third word is *agape,* understanding and creative, redemptive goodwill for all men. An overflowing love which seeks nothing in return, *agape* is the love of God operating in the human heart. At this level, we love men not because we like them, nor because their ways appeal to us, nor even because they possess some type of divine spark; we love every man because God loves him. At this level, we love the person who does an evil deed, although we hate the deed that he does.

Now we can see what Jesus meant when he said, "Love your enemies." We should be happy that he did not say, "Like your enemies." It is almost impossible to like some people. "Like" is a sentimental and affectionate word. How can we be affectionate toward a person whose avowed aim is to crush our very being and place innumerable stumbling blocks in our path? How can we like a person who is threatening our children and bombing our homes? This is impossible. But Jesus recognized that *love* is greater than *like.* When Jesus bids us to love our enemies, he is speaking neither of *eros* nor *philia;* he is speaking of *agape,* understanding and creative, redemptive goodwill for all men. Only by following this way and responding with this type of love are we able to be children of our Father who is in heaven.

Let us move now from the practical *how* to the theoretical *why:* "Why should we love our enemies?" The first reason is fairly obvious. Returning hate for hate multiplies hate, adding deeper darkness to a night already devoid of stars. Darkness cannot drive out darkness; only light can do that. Hate cannot drive out hate; only love can do that. Hate multiplies hate, violence multiplies violence, and toughness multiplies toughness in a descending spiral of destruction. So when Jesus says "Love your enemies," he is setting forth a profound and ultimately inescapable admonition. Have we not come to such an impasse in the modern world that we must love our enemies—or else? The chain reaction of evil—hate begetting hate, wars producing more wars—must be broken, or we shall be plunged into the dark abyss of annihilation.

Another reason why we must love our enemies is that hate scars the soul and distorts the personality. Mindful that hate is an evil and dangerous force, we too often think of what it does to the person hated. This is understandable, for hate brings irreparable damage to its victims. We have seen its ugly consequences in the ignominious deaths brought to six million Jews by a hate-obsessed madman named Hitler, in the unspeakable violence inflicted upon Negroes by blood-thirsty mobs, in the dark horrors of war, and in the terrible indignities and injustices perpetrated against millions of God's children by unconscionable oppressors.

But there is another side which we must never overlook. Hate is just as injurious to the person who hates. Like an unchecked cancer, hate corrodes the personality and eats away its vital unity. Hate destroys a man's sense of values and his objectivity. It causes him to describe the beautiful as ugly and the ugly as beautiful, and to confuse the true with the false and the false with the true.

Dr. E. Franklin Frazier, in an interesting essay entitled "The Pathology of Race Prejudice," included several examples of white persons who were normal, amiable and congenial in their day-to-day relationships with other white persons, but when they were challenged to think of Negroes as equals or even to discuss the question of racial injustice, they reacted with unbelievable irrationality and an abnormal unbalance. This happens when hate lingers in our minds. Psychiatrists report that many of the strange things that happen in the subconscious, many of our inner conflicts, are rooted in hate. They say, "Love or perish." Modern psychology recognizes what Jesus taught centuries ago: hate divides the personality, and love in an amazing and inexorable way unites it.

A third reason why we should love our enemies is that love is the only force capable of transforming an enemy into a friend. We never get rid of an enemy by meeting hate with hate; we get rid of an enemy by getting rid of enmity. By its very nature, hate destroys and tears down; by its very nature, love creates and builds up. Love transforms with redemptive power.

Lincoln tried love and left for all history a magnificent drama of reconciliation. When he was campaigning for the presidency one of his archenemies was a man named Stanton. For some reason Stanton hated Lincoln. He used every ounce of his energy to degrade him in the eyes of the public. So deep-rooted was Stanton's hate for Lincoln that he uttered unkind words about his physical appearance, and sought to embarrass him at every point with the bitterest diatribes. But in spite of this Lincoln was elected president of the United States. Then came the period when he had to select his cabinet, which would consist of the persons who would be his most intimate associates in implementing his program. He started choosing men here and there for the various secretaryships. The day finally came for Lincoln to select a man to fill the all-important post of Secretary of War. Can you imagine whom Lincoln chose to fill this post? None other than the man named Stanton. There was an immediate uproar in the inner circle when the news began to spread. Adviser after adviser was heard saying, "Mr. President, you are making a mistake. Do you know this man Stanton? Are you familiar with all of the ugly things he said about you? He is your enemy. He will seek to sabotage your program. Have you thought this through, Mr. President?" Mr. Lincoln's answer was terse and to the point: "Yes, I know Mr. Stanton. I am aware of all the terrible things he has said about me. But after looking over the nation, I find that he is the best man for the job." So Stanton became Abraham Lincoln's Secretary of War and rendered an invaluable service to his nation and his President. Not many years later Lincoln was assassinated. Many laudable things were said about him. Even today millions of people still adore him as the greatest of all Americans. H. G. Wells selected him as one of the six great men of history. But of all the great statements made about Abraham Lincoln, the words of Stanton remain among the greatest. Standing near the dead body of the man he once hated, Stanton referred to him as one of the greatest men that ever lived and said, "He now belongs to the ages." If Lincoln had hated Stanton, both men would have gone to their graves as bitter enemies. But through the power of love Lincoln transformed an enemy into a friend. It was this same attitude that made it possible for Lincoln to speak a kind word about the South during the Civil War when feeling was most bitter. Asked by a shocked bystander how he could do this, Lincoln said, "Madam, do I not destroy my enemies when I make them my friends?" This is the power of redemptive love.

We must hasten to say that these are not the ultimate reasons why we should love our enemies. An even more basic reason why we are commanded to love is expressed explicitly in Jesus' words, "Love your enemies . . . that ye may be the children of your Father which is in heaven." We are called to this difficult task in order to realize a unique relationship with God. We are potential sons of God. Through love that potentiality becomes actuality. We must love our enemies, because only by loving them can we know God and experience the beauty of his holiness.

The relevance of what I have said to the crisis in race relations should be readily apparent. There will be no permanent solution to the race problem until oppressed men develop the capacity to love their enemies. The darkness of racial injustice will be dispelled only by the light of forgiving love. For more than three centuries American Negroes have been battered by the iron rod of oppression, frustrated by day and bewildered by night by unbearable injustice, and burdened with the ugly weight of discrimination. Forced to live with these shameful conditions, we are tempted to become bitter and to retaliate with a corresponding hate. But if this happens, the new order we seek will be little more than a duplicate of the old order. We must in strength and humility meet hate with love.

Of course, this is not *practical*. Life is a matter of getting even, of hitting back, of dog eat dog. Am I saying that Jesus commands us to love those who hurt and oppress us? Do I sound like most preachers—idealistic and impractical? Maybe in some distant Utopia, you say, that idea will work, but not in the hard, cold world in which we live.

My friends, we have followed the so-called practical way for too long a time now, and it has led inexorably to deeper confusion and chaos. Time is cluttered with the wreckage of communities which surrendered to hatred and violence. For the salvation of our nation and the salvation of mankind, we must follow another way. This does not mean that we abandon our righteous efforts. With every ounce of our energy we must continue to rid this nation of the incubus of segregation. But we shall not in the process relinquish our privilege and our obligation to love. While abhorring segregation, we shall love the segregationist. This is the only way to create the beloved community.

To our most bitter opponents we say: "We shall match your capacity to inflict suffering by our capacity to endure suffering. We shall meet your physical force with soul force. Do to us what you will, and we shall continue to love you. We cannot in all good conscience obey your unjust laws, because noncooperation with evil is as much a moral obligation as is cooperation with good. Throw us in jail, and we shall still love you. Bomb out homes and threaten our children, and we shall still love you. Send your hooded perpetrators of violence into our community at the midnight hour and beat us and leave us half dead, and we shall still love you. But be ye assured that we will wear you down by our capacity to suffer. One day we shall win freedom, but not only for ourselves. We shall so appeal to your heart and conscience that we shall win you in the process, and our victory will be a double victory."

Love is the most durable power in the world. This creative force, so beautifully exemplified in the life of our Christ, is the most potent instrument available in mankind's quest for peace and security. Napoleon Bonaparte, the great military genius, looking back over his years of conquest, is reported to have said: "Alexander, Caesar, Charlemagne and I have built great empires. But upon what did they depend? They depended on force. But centuries ago Jesus started an empire that was built on love, and even to this day millions will die for him." Who can doubt the veracity of these words? The great military leaders of the past have gone, and their empires have crumbled and burned to ashes. But the empire of Jesus, built solidly and majestically on the foundation of love, is still growing. It started with a small group of dedicated men, who, through the inspiration of their Lord, were able to shake the hinges from the gates of the Roman Empire, and carry the gospel into all the world. Today the vast earthly kingdom of Christ numbers more than 900,000,000 and covers every land and tribe. Today we hear again the promise of victory:

Jesus shall reign where'er the sun
Does his successive journeys run;

His kingdom stretch from shore to shore,
Till moon shall wax and wane no more.

Another choir joyously responds:

In Christ there is no East or West,
In Him no South or North,
But one great Fellowship of Love
Throughout the whole wide earth.

Jesus is eternally right. History is replete with the bleached bones of nations that refused to listen to him. May we in the twentieth century hear and follow his words—before it is too late. May we solemnly realize that we shall never be true sons of our heavenly Father until we love our enemies and pray for those who persecute us.

Martin Luther King, Jr. (1929–1968) *Before his assassination in 1968, Martin Luther King, Jr., was the leading exponent of civil rights in North America. Through his preaching and speaking, Dr. King gathered the forces for justice for the American black community. Educated in Boston, he became pastor, preacher, author and leader.*

Karl Barth/Unto You Is Born This Day a Saviour

Dear heavenly Father! As we are gathered here to rejoice in thy dear Son who became man and a brother for our sake, we beseech thee most heartily—show us how great is the mercy, loving-kindness and help that thou hast prepared in him for us all!

Open our hearts and our understanding and we shall grasp that in him is forgiveness of all our sins, is seed and growth for a new life, is comfort and counsel in life and death, is hope for the whole world!

Create in us a true spirit of freedom to go out humbly and courageously, and meet thy Son who comes to us!

Grant today to the whole Christian church and to the world as well that many may break through the glitter and vanity of the holiday season and truly celebrate Christmas with us. Amen.

And it came to pass in those days, that there went out a decree from Caesar Augustus, that all the world should be taxed.

And all went to be taxed, every one into his own city.

And Joseph also went up from Galilee, out of the city of Nazareth, into Judea, unto the city of David, which is called Bethlehem; (because he was of the house and lineage of David;)

To be taxed with Mary his espoused wife, being great with child.

And so it was, that, while they were there, the days were accomplished that she should be delivered.

And she brought forth her first-born son and wrapped him in swaddling clothes, and laid him in a manger; because there was no room for them in the inn.

And there were in the same country shepherds abiding in the field, keeping watch over their flock by night.

And, lo, the angel of the Lord came upon them, and the glory of the Lord shone round about them: and they were sore afraid.

And the angel said unto them, Fear not: for, behold, I bring you good tidings of great joy, which shall be to all people.

For unto you is born this day in the city of David a Saviour, which is Christ the Lord.

*And this shall be a sign unto you; Ye shall find the babe wrapped
in swaddling clothes, lying in a manger.
　And suddenly there was with the angel a multitude of the
heavenly host praising God, and saying,
　Glory to God in the highest, and on earth peace, good will toward
men.*

LUKE 2:1–14

M<small>Y</small> dear brothers and sisters, now we have heard the Christmas
story. We heard about Caesar Augustus and the governor of
Syria, about Joseph and Mary and the birth of the baby in Bethlehem,
about the shepherds in the fields and the appearance of the angel of the
Lord in their midst, about the multitude of the heavenly host, praising
God and saying "Glory to God in the highest, and on earth peace among
men with whom he is pleased."

I surely would like to know what went on in your minds when you
heard this story. Perhaps two or three among you did not listen very
carefully—this happens quite often—and the story passed over their
heads like a cloud or a puff of smoke. Should I read the story again for
the benefit of these people of wandering thoughts? It is worth repeating
twice, even a hundred times! But for today we shall leave it at this.

Or perhaps there are those, men or women, who thought I was telling
a nice fairy tale, far removed from the realities of life? Too beautiful to
be true? What shall I tell them? Shall I debate with them? I shall gladly
do so at any other time. But presently ours is a more important task.

Perhaps also some among you, when they heard the story, were
reminded of the days of their youth long since gone by. They thought of
Sunday school where they were told this story for the first time, of the
Christmas tree, of the presents and the candies, of how beautiful things
were, but are no longer and never will be again. What shall I answer?
Shall I put on a serious face and say, forget about Christmas trees and
Christmas sentiments and concentrate on the Christmas story itself?
This will not be my reply either.

I only intended to show you, my dear friends, that these are our
human reactions to the Christmas story, which truly is the story of us all.
It is much more important, more true and more real than all the stories in
history books and novels and all the broadcast and printed news put
together. A little absentmindedness, a little unbelief and a little Christmas sentiment, these are our reactions, not only yours, but mine as well.

Until the *angel of the Lord* appears and shakes us up! The angel of the
Lord most certainly passed this night through the streets and the homes
and the squares of Basel. He was here for those who celebrated
Christmas Eve in loneliness and distress, or on the contrary in fun and
frivolity. He is here for all those who are still asleep and maybe have
something to sleep off. He is passing through the churches of our town
this morning. How does he tell the good news to all these people? How
do they listen to him or do not listen at all? However, let us not refer to
other people, but rather focus on ourselves. The angel of the Lord most

certainly is here in our midst to speak and to be heard. It only remains for me to make you aware of his presence and attentive to his words, so that together we may listen, and ponder what he has to say.

An angel! That is, a messenger, who has some news for us. You might quite simply think of the mailman bringing you some news. The angel of the Lord is God's messenger carrying the news of the Christmas story. You see, if *he* announces the news, absentmindedness, unbelief and lofty sentiments are swept away, for the angel of the Lord descends directly from God to us. I recently saw a picture where he precipitates straight from heaven to earth, almost like lightning. Granted, this is an image, and yet it is real. If the angel of the Lord is the carrier of the news, the lightning strikes and illumines the truth: the glory of the Lord shone around them and the night was as light as the day. As a Christmas hymn has it: "Eternal light from heaven descends, the earth all new and bright extends, and vanquished is the darkest night, we all may be children of light."

And now let us try to hear and understand part of what the angel of the Lord told the shepherds and tells us now: *For to you is born this day in the city of David a Saviour!* These words *you—this day—a Saviour* contain the whole Christmas story. We shall meditate on each one of them.

"To you is born this day a Saviour," says the angel of the Lord. This is already tremendously important.

First, the news of the birth of the child in Bethlehem is quite different from the news, let's say, of the arrival of the Emperor of Ethiopia in our country. You may have heard about this event. We were flattered that the emperor liked our country and that his hosts were equally impressed with their guest. But we hear this news—don't we?—thinking, "Why should I be concerned? This is entirely a matter between him and them." In contrast, the angel of the Lord points to Bethlehem, saying, "for *to you* is born this day a Saviour." For your sake God was not content to be God but willed to become man; for you he emptied himself that you may be exalted; for you he gave himself that you may be lifted up and drawn unto him. The wondrous deed brought him no gain, fulfilled no need of his. It was accomplished only for you, for us. The Christmas story then is a story that is enacted with us and for us.

The news of the birth of the child in Bethlehem is not to be likened to a statement made in a textbook. The angel of the Lord was no professor as I am. A professor would perhaps have said, "To mankind is born a Saviour." So what? We are apt to deduce that mankind in general does not include me, is only meant for others. It is like in a movie or a play where we are confronted with people who are not ourselves. In contrast, the angel of the Lord points to the shepherds and points to us. His news is directly addressed to us, *"To you* is born this day a Saviour." You, regardless of who you are, whether or not you understand the message, whether or not you are good and pious people. The news is meant for you. For your benefit the Christmas story happened. Again, it does not take place without us; we are involved in it.

The news of the birth of the child in Bethlehem affects us differently than the morning mail. When the mailman arrives, we eagerly ask, "Anything for me?" And seizing the letter, we withdraw to read it. We resent intruders peeping over our shoulder and want to read the letter alone, since this is a private matter. In contrast, the event of Bethlehem is no private matter. *"To you* is born this day a Saviour." True, the angel of the Lord points to you and to me, individually, yet he addresses us corporately. His news ties us together like brothers and sisters who share a wonderful present from their father. No one is first, no one is last, no one gets preference, no one gets shortchanged, and—most important—not a single one goes wanting. He who was born in Bethlehem is the eldest brother of us all. Therefore we pray in his name *"Our* Father." Therefore we do not pray, "Give me this day my daily bread," but rather, "Give us this day *our* daily bread. And forgive *us our* trespasses! And lead *us* not into temptation, but deliver *us* from evil!" Therefore also we go to the Lord's Supper as to the table of the Lord, and eat from *one* bread and drink from *one* cup. "Take and eat! Drink ye all!" Therefore the Christian life is one great communion, a fellowship with the Saviour and hence a fellowship among brothers. Where there is no communion with the Saviour, there is no communion among brothers, and where there is no communion among brothers, there is no communion with the Saviour. The one is not possible without the other. This is the content of the angel's call *to you,* and we should keep it in mind.

"To you . . . *this day,"* says the angel of the Lord. When Christ was born it was *this day.* A new day dawned in the middle of the night. Christ himself was and is the sun of this day and of everyday. The new day is not only Christmas Day, it is the day of our life.

This day refers not only to the past, to "once upon a time." Far from it. The angel of the Lord today announces the same news he then announced to the shepherds. We live in the new day which God has made. We hear of a possible new beginning in our human relations and conditions, in the history of our lives and even in the history of the world. We are told that yesterday's misery, guilt and fear, though still existing, have been mercifully covered and no longer harm us, because to us is born a Saviour. We may take courage, pull ourselves together and venture a new start. Human experience does not warrant such confidence, yet this is the assurance of the angel of the Lord. Because the Saviour is born, therefore a new day has dawned!

This day implies *not only tomorrow.* Certainly *also tomorrow.* He who was born on that first Christmas Day will not die ever again but lives and reigns eternally. Yet we ought not to dwell on the morrow. You know well enough the kind of people that love to repeat: *Morgen, morgen, nur nicht heute!* (German proverb, in translation: Tomorrow, tomorrow, but never today!) "Let's wait and see" is a dangerous saying. Who knows if we shall be around tomorrow? Surely the Saviour will be there, but what about us? Who knows whether we shall hear the good news once again tomorrow and shall be free to respond? The decision is not in our hands. Only yesterday I came across a word of our Swiss writer Jeremias Gotthelf: "Life is not a light, a light can be kindled again; life is a fire given by God to burn on earth just once and nevermore." My dear friends, let us pay heed lest we miss the hour of this fire right here and now. We are told elsewhere, "O that today you would hearken to his voice! Harden not your hearts!"

This is what the angel of the Lord has to tell us when he announces *this day*. And now we hear, "To you this day is born *a Saviour*." This is the very heart of the Christmas story. To you this day is born *a Saviour*. Of the many thoughts that come to mind here, I shall choose just one.

What does the word *Saviour* convey? The Saviour is he who brings us salvation, granting us all things needed and salutary. He is the helper, the liberator, the redeemer as no man, but God alone, can be and really is; he stands by us, he rescues us, he delivers us from the deadly plague. Now we live because he, the Saviour, is with us.

The Saviour is also he who has wrought salvation free of charge, without our deserving and without our assistance, and without our paying the bill. All we are asked to do is to stretch out our hands, to receive the gift and to be thankful.

The Saviour is he who brings salvation to all, without reservation or exception, simply because we all need him and because he is the Son of God who is the Father of us all. When he was made man, he became the brother of us all. *To you this day is born a Saviour,* says the angel of the Lord.

This, then, is the Christmas story. You see, we cannot possibly hear this story and not look away from ourselves, from our own life with its cares and burdens. There he is, our great God and Saviour, and here we are, human beings, and now it is true that he is for me, is for us. Impossible to hear his story without hearing our own. It is the great transformation that has been worked in us once and for all, the great joy it has released in us, and the great calling we have received to set out on the way he shows us.

What shall we do now? Shall we continue in our old ways, in absentmindedness, in disbelief, perhaps in some lofty Christian sentiments? Or shall we awake and rise, set out on our journey and turn about? The angel of the Lord does not compel anybody. Even less can I compel! A forced listening to the Christmas story, a forced participation in the story, is of no avail. We must willingly listen, and willingly participate.

And suddenly there was with the angel a multitude of the heavenly host praising God and saying, 'Glory to God in the highest, and on earth peace among men with whom he is well pleased.' Our place is not among the angels; we live here on earth, in this city, in this house. Yet when we hear about this song of praise and when we realize that God did not send one angel alone, but that the multitude of the heavenly host was present with their song of praise, might we not be carried away just as we fall in step when a good band plays or unconsciously hum or whistle a well-known tune that falls on our ears? That would be it! Then we would freely listen to and freely participate in the Christmas story. Amen.

O Lord, our God! Thou art great, exalted and holy above us and above all men. This is thy glory that thou dost not forget us, not abandon us, not reject us despite all that speaks against us. In thy dear Son Jesus Christ, our Lord, thou hast given us nothing less than thyself and all that is thine. We praise thee that we are invited as guests at the table of thy mercy throughout our life and beyond.

We spread before thee all that troubles us, our mistakes, our errors and our transgressions, our sorrows and cares, also our rebellion and our bitterness— our whole heart, our whole life, better known to thee than it is to ourselves. We commit all this into the faithful hands which thou hast outstretched in our Saviour. Take us as we are; strengthen us when we are weak; grant us, the poor, the bounties of thy blessings.

Let thy lovingkindness shine upon our loved ones, upon all prisoners, and those in the pangs of misery, illness or death. Bestow upon the judges the spirit of justice and upon the rulers of this world some measure of thy wisdom, that they may strive for peace on earth. Give a clear and courageous witness to all who are called to preach thy word here and abroad.

Gathering up all our concerns we call on thee as our Saviour has permitted and commanded us to do, *"Our Father . . ."*

Karl Barth (1886–1968) *One of the most famous theologians of the twentieth century, Dr. Barth taught and preached in the Reformed tradition. He lectured widely in Switzerland, Germany and the United States. His commentary on the book of Romans has become a standard for clergymen. The sermon selected here was preached to prisoners.*

Clovis Gilham Chappell/The Lost Book

And when they brought out the money that was brought into the house of the Lord, Hilkiah the priest found a book of the law of the Lord given by Moses.

2 CHRONICLES 34:14

HOUSECLEANING was going on in Jerusalem. The house that was being cleaned was the Temple. Among the multitudinous rubbish that was discovered was a book, a book that had been lost for so long that its message was in large measure forgotten. A book it was too whose finding at once made a difference in the lives of those who read it. Some sort of a reform was at once set in motion by it.

Now, this book is not the only one that has ever been lost. The truth of the matter is that we have been losing books ever since the birth of literature. Sometimes we lose them through some great disaster, like the burning of the Library of Alexandria. Here hundreds of thousands of volumes were lost in a very few hours. But books are not only lost through some great catastrophe—the process of losing them is one that goes on continuously. Books are in a measure like men—they are born, they speak their message and have their day, and cease to be. Emerson tells us that the lifetime of the average novel in his day was only nine months. They often live a still shorter time now. Books of science last but little longer; books of history and other kinds of literature, but little longer still. We outgrow our books as individuals and as a race somewhat as a child outgrows its toys.

We do not enjoy the games and the pastimes today that we enjoyed as small children. We do not cherish the same ambitions and ideals that we cherished then. We do not read the same books. We have outgrown them. We do not consult the same authorities when we want information. For it comes to pass again and again that in the ever-enlarging horizon of man's knowledge the wisdom of yesterday is the folly of today, and the knowledge of yesterday is the ignorance of today.

But there is one book that the world has never outgrown. It speaks to the needs of our day, and of all days, as if written peculiarly for that time. And yet it is one of the oldest of books. "It was born of divine seed, planted in human soil," many centuries ago. It waxed strong under the prophet's mantle and grew to its maturity on missionary journeys and upon the isle of apocalyptic vision. It is an old book, but though so old, it is the newest and the freshest and most vigorous single piece of literature in the world today. It has a message for the individual and for the race that is both timely and timeless. Men have never outgrown it. They never will. It is a book that no nation has ever been able to keep house adequately without.

In the story before us the Jews lost their Bible. Of course it was only a small fragment of the Bible we know, but that loss was disastrous in its results. During the days in which the Book was lost sin began to weave the scourges that finally whipped them away into exile. It was in these days of a forgotten and lost Book that sin began the placing of those bombs which in later years blasted the foundation from underneath the nation.

Mr. Moody calls attention to the fact that before the outbreak of the French Revolution France spent millions of money sowing down her people with atheistic literature. They thought the Bible stood in the way of their progress, and they threw it overboard. The Book came in very large measure to be a lost book, but with the loss of the Bible they lost much besides. That loss made it possible for half the children of Paris for a time to be born out of wedlock. That loss made it possible for as high as ten thousand newborn babies to be fished out of the sewers in one single year.

Now, while America is to some extent a Bible-reading and a Bible-guided country, there are multitudes even in America to whom the Bible is in large measure a lost book. The benefits they receive from it are indirect benefits. They no longer read it. They no longer make it the companion of their leisure hours. They no longer renew their energies by feeding upon its bracing truth. They no longer read it to their children. They do not study it in the Sunday school. Vast numbers do not attend, and multitudes of those who do attend do not study the lesson.

So it comes to pass that so far as many of us are individually concerned the Bible is a lost book. We have not read a chapter in it intelligently for the past six months. The ignorance of the ordinary individual about the Bible is one of the appalling facts of today. This ignorance is not confined to those who do not attend church and Sunday school. It is not confined to the ignorant and uneducated. It spreads its appalling darkness over all sorts and conditions of people.

In one of our state universities a freshman class of one hundred and thirty-nine members was given an examination on the Bible. The passing mark was seventy-five. The questions were of this nature:

1. What is the Pentateuch?
2. Name ten books of the Old Testament.
3. "Parading for a mess of pottage"—what is the reference?

4. Who was the Apostle to the Gentiles?

5. What was Jonah's gourd?

And other simple questions. Only twelve of the one hundred and thirty-nine passed. The average for the class was only 40 percent.

I am told that a certain literary society in England offered a prize some years ago for the best short story. One member of the club copied the Book of Esther word for word, changing only the names of the characters and the historic setting. He won the prize, and when the president presented the medal he marveled where the man developed such a wonderful literary style.

The average individual is ignorant of the Bible, appallingly ignorant. It is said that a college professor in the course of an English class came upon the word "epistles." "By the way," said he, "what are the epistles?" And for a moment all the air a solemn stillness held. Then one man raised his hand. "Good," said the professor, "I am glad somebody knows. Will you tell us, please?" Then came the answer: "I am not sure that I know myself, but I think they were the apostles' wives."

Every man ought to be interested in the Bible for at least three reasons. First, he ought to be interested in the Bible from the standpoint of literature. It is the greatest single piece of literature in existence. If you love biography, you ought to read the Bible. There are no biographies that make us so intimately acquainted with their heroes as do those of this Book. Boswell does not acquaint us any more fully with his great Dr. Johnson than does the Bible with Abraham, and with Jacob and David, and in a few short pages. We know these men better than we know our next-door neighbors. We know their virtues. All biographers will tell us that about their heroes. We also know their weaknesses, their vices, their failures, their sins. We know the men as they were, what they thought, how they felt, how they battled, how they sought God and found him, how they sinned against God and lost him. If you love biography, read the Bible.

If you love philosophy, read the Bible. Jean Jacques Rousseau says, "All other philosophy is contemptible in comparison with it." And he was a man of no natural partiality toward the Book.

Do you love oratory? Then read the Bible. Webster said, "If there is anything of eloquence in me, it is because I learned the Bible at my mother's knee." Some months ago I was called upon to speak before a school of oratory on "The Oratory of the Bible." I was amazed at the wealth of material I had at my disposal. Take the marvelous oration found in the twenty-sixth chapter of Acts. You would have to go far before you find one more gripping and more mighty.

Do you love drama? Then read the Bible. The most marvelous dramas ever written are to be found there. Take the story of the Rich Fool or the story of Dives and Lazarus, or above all else, the parable of the Prodigal Son. Edwin Booth said that this parable was the greatest drama ever written.

Do you love poetry? Then I commend this Book to you. The greatest epic ever written is in the Bible. That is not my opinion simply, but that of that great master of English, Thomas Carlyle. He said, "There is nothing in the Bible or out of it to compare with it. Sublime sorrow, sublime reconciliation, oldest choral melody as of the heart, quiet as the summer midnight, as the world with its seas and stars."

Do you love songs, songs expressive of the highest heights of human joy and of the deepest depths of woe? Then read the marvelous songs of the Bible. They have in them the sobbings of a desolate child that has lost its way. They have in them also the rapturous music of one who has found his way back into the light, and who is being undergirded with the Everlasting Arms. Oh, if you love great literature, and everybody should love it—then read the Bible.

Then you ought to be familiar with the Bible in the second place, because you cannot understand the best of modern literature without knowing it. The works of the greatest modern masters are literally saturated with the Bible. You could almost make a small Bible with the gleanings from Tennyson and Browning and Shakespeare and Ruskin and Carlyle. These men brought their choicest water from this mountain spring. They found their fairest flowers in this colorful garden. They dug for their most resplendent jewels in this inexhaustible mine. So much is this the case that to read them intelligently you must know something of the Bible.

But the third and last big reason why everybody ought to be familiar with the Bible is that it is a book of the heart. It is God's revelation of himself to the human soul. The Bible will make you wise about many things if you will study it carefully; but its big purpose is this, to make you wise unto salvation. It shows you who God is, what he thinks, how he feels about you and me, how he feels about sin and how he feels about righteousness. No man can read the Bible intelligently and candidly without turning away from it with a new conception of God.

This is the one great purpose of the book. This is what unifies it and combines its sixty-six volumes into one book. On the surface it is not a unit. It was written by some forty different men. These men belonged to every station in society from ploughmen and shepherds up to prime ministers and kings. These men were not only separated from each other by every possible social distinction, but they were separated by fifteen centuries in time. And yet the different volumes they give us combine into one great book.

When you open its pages, the fact of its unity does not at first impress you. In truth it seems anything but a unit. "We are plunged," as Dr. Watson tells us, "into an ocean of detail. The love affairs of a man and a maid and contracts of marriage; the quarrels between brothers with their treachery and their revenge; the bargains in business, wherein land is bought and sold, and covenants are made with witnesses; the feuds between rival tribes, enlivened by raids and captures; the choice of kings and their anointing amid the rejoicing of the people; the evildoing of kings and their assassination amid a people's hatred; the orations of statesmen as they warn their nation against offending God, or comfort them in days of tribulation; adroit arrangements of ecclesiastics, and the inner history of church councils; the collision of parties in the Christian church, and the bitter rivalries which distract congregations; the radiant record of deeds of chivalry, and the black story of acts of treachery; the romance of unselfish friendship, and the blind enmity of religious bigotry; the career of a successful man and the unmerited suffering of a martyr; the devotion of a mother to her child, and the jealousy of women fighting for the same man's love; the idyll of childhood; the strength of young manhood, the mellow wisdom of old age; nomads of the desert, dwellers in the city; prophets and sages, ploughmen and vinedressers, soldiers and traders, rich men and beggars, holy matrons and women who are sinners; patriarchs driving huge herds before them, and apostles going forth with nothing in their hands; priests offering sacrifice in the holy place, and publicans collecting their gains in the receipt of custom; scholars busy in their studies, and carpenters toiling in their shop—all pass across this stage in unarranged and natural procession. Nothing could be more artless, nothing more fascinating.

But as we read this many-volumed story there comes to us a growing vision of the face of God. We see him ever clearer till we pass out of the Old Testament into high uplands of the New, where he who in time past spake to us through the prophets, at last speaks to us through his Son. And as we see the face that looks out upon us from the Gospels, we know what God is like.

It is therefore a saving book. It saves by showing us God. And here, let me say, it stands alone. If God has not made a revelation to us through his book, we have no revelation. This is a wonderful world in which we live. Far be it from me to despise its multitudinous beauties. But when I ask it for knowledge about a loving and forgiving God, it gives me no answer.

The depths saith, "It is not in me." And the stars say, "It is not in me." And the flowers say, "It is not in me." Nature never forgives, and she has nothing to say to me of a God who forgives. I know that one has said,

> *Earth's crammed with Heaven,*
> *And every common bush aflame with God.*

I know there was one who could find in the "meanest flower that blows thoughts that lie too deep for tears." But these were people who carried minds saturated with the truth of the Bible to their seeing. Nature alone cannot tell us of God, or else it would not be true, as it is true, that "Where every prospect pleases only man is vile."

Oh, if you are hungry to know God, read the Bible. It is authority in that realm. That is the secret of its marvelous power. That is the reason why it is such a convicting power. If you want men to be convicted of sin, give them the Bible. It is the hammer that breaks the rock in pieces.

That is the secret of its converting power. If you want men reborn, give them the Bible—"Being born again not of corruptible seed, but of incorruptible by the Word of God which liveth and abideth forever."

That is the secret of its sustaining and upbuilding power—"I commend you to God and the word of his grace, which is able to build you up."

How weak and anemic many Christians are! How sickly and dyspeptic! They have no appetite for the Word. Therefore they do not feed on the Bible. But wherever you find a strong Christian you are going to find a Bible-reading Christian. Jeremiah, who had to stand alone for so many years, said, "Thy words were found and I did eat them, and they became the joy and rejoicing of my heart." Most of us are weak because we are literally starving for the Word.

This ignorance too accounts for the readiness of many of us to take up any new fad that comes parading by in the stolen garb of religion. This is the reason so many are ready to swallow any sort of nostrum that the modern religious quack chooses to dose out.

I beg you then to give this book a large place in your life. I beg you to appreciate it more, to love it better, to read it with greater diligence, to teach it to your children. You ought to appreciate it, in the first place, because of the cost of the book. It is cheap now. You can buy a Bible for a dollar easy enough, but it has come to you at a great price. God's sons have suffered for this book. They have suffered as you and I will never know. For this book has been hated as well as loved. If you turn its pages intelligently, you will see them stained with the blood of those who have died for the blessed volume. If you turn its pages, you will discover upon them the dank mold of dismal dungeons where men have rotted in their effort to give you this book. If you shake it you will see fall from its pages the gray ashes of those who have burned at the stake that this unspeakable gift might gather dust upon your center table. We ought to appreciate it more. It has come to us at a great price.

Clovis Gillham Chappell (1882–1971)   *This leading Methodist evangelist and pastor produced nearly a dozen books of sermons. A powerful biblical preacher, he served the congregation of the First Methodist Church in Charlotte, North Carolina.*

Albert Schweitzer/The Courage of Action

And the seventy returned again with joy, saying, Lord, even the devils are subject unto us through thy name. And as he said unto them, I beheld Satan as lightning fall from heaven. Behold, I give unto you power to tread on serpents and scorpions, and over all the power of the enemy: and nothing shall by any means hurt you. Notwithstanding in this rejoice not, that the spirits are subject unto you; but rather rejoice, because your names are written in heaven.

LUKE 10:17–21

I T was harvest time. Many men had gathered around Jesus and followed him from village to village. Now they were getting ready to go back home and gather the harvest. But from among them he chose seventy whom he knew well because they had often sat around him (this was after he had sent out the Twelve). He said to the seventy men, "Go out first and preach the Gospel, then come back and I will let you go."

Seventy, chosen symbolically for the number of the Gentile nations as they were counted in the Old Testament. None could have been less prepared than they, and yet he commanded them to go and preach. Jesus knew what they would gain by this activity, that something would be revealed to them by preaching the Gospel. Nor was he deceived. "We have fought and won," they cry out jubilantly on their return.

They had fought and won, and now they owned the secret of Christianity. They carried it within them, and no one could take it from them. For Christianity is conflict and victory through Jesus. That is why Jesus praised God in this hour for revealing to the simple the secret which was hidden from the wise and clever.

The revelation was not granted them because of their mere simplicity. They were chosen because they had acted and fought as ordinary people. Not by meditation and reflection does one grasp the great secret which hovers over the world and human life. The higher realization flowers only in work and action. For this highest realization there is no difference between the wise and the simple. The simple, if they act, are given insights kept from the wise.

In action lies wisdom and confidence. A man who does not act gets no further than the maxim, "Tife means conflict and tribulation." But a man who acts can attain the higher wisdom and know that life is conflict and victory. That is why God forces men to labor. That is why he gives them children to bring up. That is why he gives them duties. Through action, they may reach a deeper realization. They may have confidence and belief in the victory of Christ. You know the beautiful saying, "I lay in heavy chains until you came and set me free."

But how does Jesus approach those who are weighed down by sorrow or remorse? He lays before them a duty, a task. And in executing it they regain, not without hard fight, their confidence and faith. For in action they feel the power of God which preserves and revitalizes everything.

This realization of life is like a man who sits by his window, watching the March wind chase the dark clouds across the sky. "How sad, how desolate," he says, and he gets no further. Meanwhile, a man is working in the field. He sees the wind chasing the clouds, but he grasps more than that. He feels a living breath. He senses life stirring everywhere, the birth of a victorious power which cannot be held back. He alone has understood the March wind, for he was there as a worker in the fertile field. Only those who stand as workers in the field of life notice the life-giving breath and the victorious Spirit of God which rules the world. A man who is active cannot despair of victory of the divine over evil. You have heard of the philosopher Schopenhauer, who in his writings elevated to a supreme wisdom his belief that life is only suffering, conflict and misery. I can never read a page of his without asking myself what would have become of this man if—instead of being able to withdraw in splendid isolation from any profession—he had been obliged to become a schoolteacher in a small Alpine village where he would have been faced with the task of converting neglected children into useful citizens. He would never have written his famous books. People would never have lionized him or pressed laurel wreaths upon his silver locks. But Schopenhauer's brilliance made him only a wise man. The simple and ignorant men of Galilee whom Jesus had sent out to work possessed a wisdom higher than his. For to them had become manifest the secret that life is conflict and victory in Christ.

They bore this secret also in a more tangible form. They boasted with joy that they had realized it through Jesus' power and strength working in them. They had been able to do signs, to heal the sick and to cast out demons. Jesus rejoiced with them. Yes, certainly, he tells them, the time of conflict with the power of evil has begun and we shall be victorious. To help them understand, he speaks in the language of the time. "I saw Satan fall as lightning from heaven," he says. "Snakes and scorpions cannot poison you, for I have given you power. Nothing will harm you." Then, before giving them a final blessing and sending them back to their homes, he cast a veil over their all-too-confident joy by saying, "Don't rejoice because the spirits are subject unto you. Rather, rejoice because your names are written in heaven." What he meant by this higher, interior joy they did not comprehend.

But they were to understand it later. They returned home, and everyday life with all its trivialities and anxieties engrossed them once more. And there they found themselves in conflict with the power of evil, an evil much greater than the perils they had survived on their mission. It was not a battle against Satan, who dwells in the air and speaks words of blasphemy through the mouth of the possessed. No, it was a struggle against the power of evil which dwelt in their hearts. It was the war against sin, the endeavor to fulfill the saying, "Ye shall be perfect, as your Father in heaven is perfect." It was a fight for purity of heart, for trust in God, for hope in tribulation, for faith. And this silent battle within was difficult, for the eye of Jesus was no longer on them. He was far from them, no longer in this world. But now, in this inner struggle, they at last understood the meaning of his words when they had returned. He had spoken of interior joy. Those words, the last they heard him speak—"I have given you power, nothing will harm you, rejoice that your names are written in heaven—they now comprehended as eternal, interior, undying words. They understood them as we understand them, words of the Lord to those in conflict. And still today, in the hearts of those who fight, they shine as brightly as the stars in the sky. "I have given you power"—Christ is a power within the combatants. Who can explain this? Who can explain how his strength and power worked in those days in the missionaries he sent out in Galilee, enabling them to perform work like his? And yet, they experienced it in themselves. So, to this day, Christ is a power in all who from their hearts accept him as their Saviour. The power they have within is invisible from the outside, a mysterious power, a power to lead them forward and sustain them.

And this power becomes most evident in us when we accept inward or outward harm. Nothing shall hurt you. The Lord has said so. Nothing, not sorrow or tribulation, not sickness or pain or disappointment. From all these bitter conflicts you will arise strengthened and renewed, enriched in the inner man.

Nothing will harm you—neither the Fall nor sin, Jesus promises. "For whoever accepts me as his Saviour proceeds, through humiliation and remorse, to joy and forgiveness and a life begun anew."

Hence this eternal promise, "Rejoice, for your names are written in heaven—not as those who rest, or as those who suffer, but as those who fight with the promise of victory through Jesus Christ. Rejoice, for you cannot be lost. God holds his protecting hand over you."

As those Galileans went their homeward way, they dreamed of peace and the joy of peace. But in the "Rejoice" he called after them, which they did not understand, there was an echo, "I came not to bring peace but a sword." It was a prophetic saying. Later, in trial and tribulation, when the waves closed over their heads, they heard again this powerful word "Rejoice," spoken to those in the midst of conflict and strife. Now they understood it. Rejoice because your names are written in heaven! There was one who was not with them, the Apostle Paul; and he did not hear this word "Rejoice." But he proclaimed with the tongue of an angel all the glory that lies within this word. His interpretation of the call to rejoice in the midst of conflict is written in the eighth chapter of the Letter to the Romans:

> What shall we then say to these things? If God be for us who can be against us? He that spared not his own Son, but delivered him up for us all, how shall he not with him also freely give us all things? Who shall lay any thing to the charge of God's elect? It is God that justifieth. Who is he that condemneth? It is Christ that died, yea rather, that is risen again, who is even at the right hand of God, who also maketh intercession for us. Who shall separate us from the love of Christ? shall tribulation, or distress, or persecution, or famine, or nakedness, or peril, or sword? As it is written, For thy sake we are killed all the day long; we are accounted as sheep for the slaughter. Nay, in all these things we are more than conquerors through him that loved us. For I am persuaded, that neither death, nor life, nor angels, nor principalities, nor powers, nor things present, nor things to come, nor height, nor depth, nor any other creature, shall be able to separate us from the love of God, which is in Christ Jesus our Lord.

Albert Schweitzer (1875–1965)   *World-renowned theologian, musician, philosopher and physician, Albert Schweitzer linked Africa with the rest of the world. He won the hearts of millions through his concept of Reverence for Life. When he died at ninety, he was still working in his beloved hospital at Lamborene, Africa.*

Halford Luccock/A Dangerous Pentecost

For the promise is to you and to your children, and to all that are far off.

ACTS 2:39

DAVID Loth, in his *Lorenzo the Magnificent,* tells a story of the exploits of Lorenzo de' Medici as a pageant director. Lorenzo was a great showman. One of the chief interests of his life was furnishing to the citizens of Florence artistic and magnificent spectacles of many sorts. He produced many religious pageants with striking realism and effectiveness. On one occasion he surpassed himself in staging a pageant of Pentecost.The descent of the tongues of fire upon the apostles, however, was just a bit too realistic. Actual fire was used, the flimsy trimmings and stage hangings were set ablaze, and not only the stage but the whole church burned down.

This is a very suggestive story. It comes with the reminder that if we should be visited by a real descent of Pentecostal fire, a good many things in our churches would be burned up. And that is not a bad reminder. One of the spiritual risks connected with the subject is that of a flood of language about the Holy Spirit, language so general and vague that it approaches incoherence. There is a classic story in New England of the Cape Cod farmer who was shingling his house on a foggy day, and shingled right off into the fog. There is hardly any subject in the field of religion on which it is easier for the preacher to "shingle off into the fog" than the subject of the Holy Spirit and Pentecost. There have been so many expressions, desiring another Pentecost, that it is quite important for us to open our eyes to some of the costs and the inevitable results of a real Pentecostal experience for the Church in our day. One thing surely would happen—just what happened when Lorenzo de' Medici staged his realistic drama. There would be a big conflagration amid our ecclesiastical scenery and machinery.

The little incident from sixteenth-century Florence may serve as a starting point in our thought concerning the bringing of this first-century experience into our twentieth-century setting. With the coming of any genuine Pentecostal power, much of our neat, and cozy and comfortable ecclesiastical world would be upset. The question for us to ask is whether we are really ready for an actual Pentecost, whether we really want one. For it would be undoubtedly an upsetting and disturbing thing.

There are many who are indulging the conventional longing for Pentecost, who would give scant welcome to the real thing were it suddenly to to appear. Max Beerbohm has spoken for a large company of us when he confessed, "I am a Tory Anarchist. I am willing for anyone to do anything he wishes, as long as it does not disturb the things to which I have been accustomed." We could all be anarchists with that reservation! It is easy to be a Christian with that reservation. It is easy, and on the whole rather a satisfying thing, emotionally, to yearn for the coming of fresh tides of Pentecostal power—with the proviso, of course, that nothing to which we have been accustomed shall be disturbed!

All of this is just another reminder that it is a terribly serious thing to pray. The real seriousness comes not in the possibility that our prayer may not be answered; the appallingly serious thing is that it *may* be answered. A real answer to prayer will usually let us in for more than we ask. A man prays for strength, for instance, without much thought of the matter, as though strength could be wrapped up in a package like a pound of tea and handed to one. Strength must be grown; it comes from struggle against obstacles. The only way in which a prayer for strength can be answered is by putting a man into a place where he will have to struggle. We ought to take good care before we ask for strength! God may overhear us and answer us. So it is with the frequent prayer that we may have the spirit of Jesus. Many people make that prayer thoughtlessly without realizing that if they really had the spirit of Jesus it would knock themselves and their whole world upside down.

This is profoundly true of the gift of the Spirit of God, the impact and energy of God within us. If we ask for Pentecostal power, we ought to remember what the consequences and conditions will be.

If we study the first three chapters of the Book of Acts with some care, we will find that two things are closely allied: the new surge of power, that quickening of the being which came to the company of Christians gathered in Jerusalem, and their facing the social tasks of their time. The two things are tied up together. We will never understand what happened in the upper room in Jerusalem, unless we look at it in connection with the disciples' attitude to the world outside of the room.

The point most often forgotten is this: *the disciples received the Pentecostal power when they faced the Pentecostal task.* Pentecost began before they went to the upper room. It began when they ceased gazing upward into the skies on Mt. Olivet and made their way back to Jerusalem. In doing that they faced their world of need, of danger, of opportunity. Before that quickening experience, symbolized in the Book of Acts by the tongues of fire, that little company had made definite plans for a forward thrust to carry Christ into the contemporary world. The election of a disciple to take the place of Judas looked in that direction.

If the church as a whole could grasp this one simple truth, all the emphasis on Pentecost in any year would be infinitely repaid.

Now, of course, we must not read back into the apostolic age any of our modern social conceptions. When we say that little company faced the social task of their time, we do not mean that they made a community survey. We have no right to try to make the apostles speak the language of twentieth-century social reform. They spoke many languages at Pentecost, but they certainly did not speak that one. We do violence to dress them up in present-day sack suits. Such treatment is on a par with any other form of violence or dishonesty. Nevertheless, we fail to grasp the full meaning of the story unless we see that there was a definite determination to carry Christ out into the world, with a clear realization that that process would definitely change the world.

What the experience seems to teach is a lesson of enormous significance for the church of our day and of any day, that God gives power only to men who need it. He does not waste power. He gives it to those who have tackled something so big, so overwhelming, that their own resources are quite insufficient. Such a tackling of a task too big for human power is the opening of the door through which there comes the rushing of a mighty wind of the spirit.

It is in this way that a parent acts toward his child who comes to him for money. Some questions are put: "What do you want it for?" "What do you need it for?" "What are you going to do with it?" The same questions are heard at the bank. A man goes to the bank to borrow money and his first task is to show that he needs it. When we ask for power, these are the questions which God puts to us: "What are you going to do with it?" "Why do you need it?" "What have you squarely faced?" "With what have you gotten yourself so deeply into conflict that you utterly need it?" Often we must answer that question by saying, "What, indeed?" The previous question, determining whether we shall have a Pentecost or not, is, "Where are we in such a grapple with the anti-Christian forces of our pagan world that we need an inrush of divine power?" Does not the reason of our lack of the exhilaration and the conquering mood of Pentecost lie in the fact that we are not planning to do anything in particular?

Let us bring this a little more closely home by looking at the church of the Book of Acts. It was emphatically a church on a frontier. On many frontiers it was exploring new areas of social life and claiming them for the lordship of Jesus. For one thing, it was pioneering in thought, it was opening up for men a new and living way into the heart of the Father. In the second place, it was claiming a new moral realm, the relations of men and women, the whole perplexing field of sexual relations, for the authority of Jesus. Third, one of its first experiments was that of bringing the principle of love into economic relations. The exact form of the communistic experiment in Jerusalem is not important. What is important for all the centuries is that one of the first results of the coming of the Holy Spirit into the lives of men is that they tried to bring a better order into their economic relations one with another. Fourth, continually the church crossed racial frontiers, pioneering in the most perplexing social field in any century, be it the first or the twentieth, that of race. Fifth, the church was on a continually moving frontier as the westward horizon was sought. The church was only a few years old when the hearts of some within it were stirred with the dream of carrying the evangel of Jesus to the very limits of the world.

Turn from that picture of the first-century church on the moral frontiers of its time, needing power and getting it, to ourselves. What moral frontiers are we occupying?

Take the old and complex one of race. Are we out on the dangerous edges of that problem, or are we dug in behind a comforting stockade of platitudes and evasive generalities? Heywood Broun wrote, "You cannot satisfy a race which is crying for justice by tossing it a mammy song." Is that not what we have been doing so often? Do we not more often take the sentimental attitude, represented by the "mammy song," than the attitude of faith represented by the Negro spiritual, "All God's chillun got wings"? The church that has a visitation of Pentecostal power will be the one that faces this task of making brotherhood a reality.

How about another big question, essentially the same as that faced by the first-century church when it was confronting emperor worship? Our present equivalent of emperor worship is the widespread religion of prosperity of our day; that is, the ascendancy of the business philosophy and the point of view which draws from multitudes of people the attitudes of awe, reverence, devotion and loyalty, usually associated with an accepted religion. Just as many Christians were commanded to bow down to the emperor, so there is a demand today that we burn incense to the great god Prosperity. Prosperity is both a morality and a religion. It has its high sanctities—that the very ongoing of the business of the country depends on the acceptance of the profit motive as the only sufficient guarantee of the individualistic drive necessary to industry; that whatever is good for business is good for all; that the gaining of wealth is the chief end of man; that property rights precede human rights; that profit-making must never be interfered with, or at least must be very tenderly dealt with both by government and by religion; that any dispute of these dogmas is a blasphemy, a heresy to be stamped out.

One hundred years ago the Frenchman, Saint-Simon, prophetically hailed the captain of industry as "the future priest of humanity." To a very real extent that prophecy has been fulfilled. The priests are now conducting regular services in new cathedrals.

It has its commandments. Profit says, "Thou shalt have no other God before me, for I the Lord, thy God, am a jealous God."

Where is our struggle with this omnipresent Antichrist so clear-cut, and sharp and definite that we need a power which comes from the measureless energy of God to assist us? That is the previous question of Pentecost.

Let us turn back to the story of Lorenzo de' Medici with which we started. Let us ask ourselves seriously, what are some of the things which will be consumed by the descent of the Pentecostal fire? One of them certainly will be the thing which keeps us from getting out on frontiers where many conquests are to be made for Christ, exploring areas of life which hitherto have not yielded to his rule. We have a habit of barricading ourselves in. Francis Hackett, in his *Henry the Eighth,* has a penetrating observation of Catherine of Aragon, the first of the long and tragic succession of Henry's wives. He says, "Catherine was immured in her own squat righteousness. She wanted the environment to adapt itself to her, and if it refused she stood the siege until her walls became her tombstone."

Take that phrase into your imagination, "her walls became her tombstone." That is the insidious thing about walls; they so easily become tombs. Put up to preserve life, they strangle it. How many of the walls set up by the church to keep its Gospel enclosed in the churchyard have become the tomb of a dead Christ—dead because in the minds of his followers he does not count in the most significant areas of life?

Another encumbrance which will be consumed by the Spirit of God is the habit of accommodation, of adaptation of ourselves and our Gospel to the world. The church has taken over from secular education, without sufficient scrutiny, the idea that the purpose of life is successful adaptation to one's environment. In the deep sense the Christian purpose can never be adaptation to the world, but the transformation of the world. What prevents a real apostolic disturbance in our lives is this diabolical skill in adapting ourselves and our message to the world. By such adaptation, of course, we mean the kind involving denaturing and compromising the message. It was said of Francis Thompson that his tragedy was that he never felt at home in the world. It is our tragedy that we do. It is also Christ's tragedy that we do feel so thoroughly at home in an unchristian world that we are rarely torn with his heartbroken discontent.

It is easy to begin at the wrong end with this matter of Pentecostal power. The first step to get power is not to ask for it, but to put ourselves into such desperate conditions that we need it. If we face Christ's task in our day, we will find that the reality of that conflict will bring the zest which we feel in the New Testament. It will be in our day the opening of the door to the rushing of a mighty wind and the coming of the Spirit of God.

Halford Luccock (1885–1960)   *One of America's great preachers—and teachers of preachers—Luccock taught at Yale Divinity School for a quarter of a century. He is best known for his wealth of sermon illustrations and twenty-three books on preaching. At his death he was still publishing books as well as preparing articles for national magazines.*

Henry Drummond/**Going to the Father**

I go to my Father.
JOHN 14:12

DID you ever notice Christ's favorite words? If you have, you must have been struck by two things—their simplicity and their fewness. Some half-dozen words embalm all his theology; and these are, without exception, humble, elementary, simple monosyllables. They are such words as these: world, life, trust, love.

But none of these was the greatest word of Christ. His great word was new to religion. There was no word there, when he came, rich enough to carry the new truth he was bringing to men. So he imported into religion one of the grandest words of human language, and transfigured it, and gave it back to the world illuminated and transformed, as the watchword of the new religion. That word was Father.

Now the thing which steadied Christ's life was the thought that he was going to his Father. This one thing gave it unity, and harmony and success. During his whole life he never forgot his Word for a moment. There is no sermon of his where it does not occur; there is no prayer, however brief, where it is missed. In that first memorable sentence of his, which breaks the solemn spell of history and makes one word resound through thirty silent years, the one word is this; and all through the after years of toil and travail "the Great Name" was always hovering on his lips or bursting out of his heart. In its beginning and in its end, from the early time when he spoke of his Father's business till he finished the work that was given him to do, his life, disrobed of all circumstance, was simply this, "I go to my Father."

If we take this principle into our own lives, we shall find its influence tell upon us in three ways:

   1. It explains life.

2. It sustains life.

3. It completes life.

It explains life. Few men, I suppose, do not feel that life needs explaining. We think we see through some things in it—partially; but most of it, even to the wisest mind, is enigmatic. Those who know it best are the most bewildered by it, and they who stand upon the mere rim of the vortex confess that even for them it is overspread with cloud and shadow. What is my life? Whither do I go? Whence do I come? These are the questions which are not worn down yet, although the whole world has handled them.

To these questions there are but three answers—one by the poet, another by the atheist, the third by the Christian.

The poet tells us, and philosophy says the same only less intelligibly, that life is a sleep, a dream, a shadow. It is a vapor that appeareth for a little and vanisheth away; a meteor hovering for a moment between two unknown eternities; bubbles, which form and burst upon the river of time. This philosophy explains nothing. It is a taking refuge in mystery. Whither am I going? Virtually the poet answers, "I am going to the unknown."

The atheist's answer is just the opposite. He knows no unknown. He understands all, for there is nothing more than we can see or feel. Life is what matter is; the soul is phosphorus. Whither am I going? "I go to dust," he says, "death ends all." And this explains nothing. It is worse than mystery. It is contradiction. It is utter darkness.

But the Christian's answer explains something. Where is he going? "I go to my Father." This is not a definition of his death—there is no death in Christianity; it is a definition of the Christian life. All the time it is a going to the Father. Some travel swiftly, some are long upon the road, some meet many pleasant adventures by the way, others pass through fire and peril; but though the path be short or winding, and though the pace be quick or slow, it is a going to the Father.

When we see him, we must speak to him. We have that language to learn. And that is perhaps why God makes us pray so much. Then we are to walk with him in white. Our sanctification is a putting on this white. But there has to be much disrobing first, much putting off of filthy rags. This is why God makes man's beauty to consume away like the moth. He takes away the moth's wings, and gives the angel's, and man goes the quicker and the lovelier to the Father.

The other thing which this truth explains is why there is so much that is unexplained. After we have explained all, there is much left. All our knowledge, it is said, is but different degrees of darkness. But we know *why we do not know why.* It is because we are going to our Father. We are only going; we are not there yet. Therefore patience. "What I do thou knowest not now, but thou shalt know. Hereafter, thou shalt know." Hereafter, because the chief joy of life is to have something to look forward to. But, hereafter, for a deeper reason. Knowledge is only given for action. Knowing only exists for doing; and already nearly all men know to do more than they do do. So, till we do all that we know, God retains the balance till we can use it. In the larger life of the hereafter, more shall be given, proportionate to the vaster sphere and the more ardent energies.

Necessarily, therefore, much of life is still twilight. But our perfect refuge is to anticipate a little, and go in thought to our Father, and, like children tired out with efforts to put together the disturbed pieces of a puzzle, wait to take the fragments to our Father.

And yet, even that fails sometimes. He seems to hide from us, and the way is lost indeed. The footsteps which went before us up till then cease, and we are left in the chill, dark night alone. If we could only see the road, we should know it went to the Father. But we cannot say we are going to the Father; we can only say *we would like to go*. "Lord," we cry, "we know not whither thou goest, and how can we know the way?" "Whither I go," is the inexplicable answer, "ye know not now." Well is it for those who at such times are near enough to catch the rest: "But ye shall know hereafter."

Secondly, and in a few words, this sustains life.

A year or two ago some of the greatest and choicest minds of this country labored, in the pages of one of our magazines, to answer the question, "Is life worth living?" It was a triumph for religion, some thought, that the keenest intellects of the nineteenth century should be stirred with themes like this. It was not so; it was the surest proof of the utter heathenism of our age. Is life worth living? As well ask, "Is air worth breathing?" The real question is this, taking the definition of life here suggested, "Is it worthwhile going to the Father?"

There is nothing to sustain life but this thought. And it does sustain life. Take even an extreme case, and you will see how. Take the darkest, saddest, most pathetic life of the world's history. That was Jesus Christ's. See what this truth *practically* was to him. It gave him a life of absolute composure in a career of most tragic trials.

This is the Christian's only stay in life. It provides rest for his soul, work for his character, an object, an inconceivably sublime object, for his ambition. It does not stagger him to be a stranger here, to feel the world passing away. The Christian is like the pearl-diver, who is out of the sunshine for a little, spending his short day amid rocks and weeds and dangers at the bottom of the ocean. Does he desire to spend his life there? No, but his master does. Is his life there? No, his life is up above. A communication is open to the surface, and the fresh pure life comes down to him from God. Is he not wasting time there? He is gathering pearls for his Master's crown. Will he always stay there? When the last pearl is gathered, the "Come up higher" will beckon him away, and the weights which kept him down will become an exceeding weight of glory, and he will go, he and these he brings with him, to his Father.

Lastly, in a word, this completes life.

Life has been defined as a going to the Father. It is quite clear that there must come a time in the history of all those who live this life when they reach the Father. This is the most glorious moment of life. Angels attend at it. Those on the other side must hail the completing of another soul with ineffable rapture. When they are yet a great way off, the Father runs and falls on their neck and kisses them.

On this side we call that death. It means reaching the Father. It is not departure, it is arrival; not sleep, but waking. For life to those who live like Christ is not a funeral procession. It is a triumphal march to the Father, and the entry at the last in God's own chariot in the last hour of all. No, as we watch a life which is going to the Father, we cannot think of night, of gloom, of dusk and sunset. It is life which is the night, and death is sunrise.

"Pray moderately," says an old saint, "for the lives of Christ's people." *Pray moderately.* We may want them on our side, he means, but Christ may need them on his. He has seen them a great way off, and set his heart upon them, and asked the Father to make them come quickly. "I will," he says, "that such an one should be with me where I am." So it is better that they should go to the Father.

Henry Drummond (1851–1897) *Noted for his famous book* The Greatest Thing in the World, *Drummond was a science professor as well as an active preacher in the Free Church of Scotland. He was introduced to America by Dwight Moody.*

William Ashley Sunday/**Food for a Hungry World**

They need not depart; give ye them to eat.
MATTHEW 14:16

S OME folks do not believe in miracles. I do. A denial of miracles is a denial of the virgin birth of Jesus. The Christian religion stands or falls on the virgin birth of Christ. God created Adam and Eve without human agencies. He could and did create Jesus supernaturally. I place no limit on what God can do. If you begin to limit God, then there is no God.

I read of a preacher who said that the miracles of the Bible were more of a hindrance than a help. Then he proceeded to spout his insane blasphemy. He imagined Jesus talking to the five thousand and like many speakers overrunning his time limit. The disciples, seeing night coming, said, "Master, you have talked this crowd out of their supper and there is nothing to eat in this desert place; dismiss them so they can go into the towns and country and get food."

He imagined Jesus saying, "We have some lunch, haven't we?"

"Yes, but not enough to feed this crowd."

"Well, let's divide it up and see." So, Jesus proceeds to divide his lunch with the hungry crowd.

An old man, seeing Jesus busy, asked, "What's he doing?"

"Dividing his lunch."

"Huh," grunts this old knocker, "He is the first preacher I've ever seen who practices what he preaches."

Shamed by the example of Jesus, this old tightwad brought out his lunch basket and began to divide. Others caught the spirit and followed suit, and in this way the five thousand were fed. This heretic of a so-called preacher thought such an occurrence more reasonable than the Bible account. Every attempt to explain the miracles by natural laws gets the explainer into great difficulty and shows him up as ridiculous.

I wish to draw some practical lessons from this miracle of Jesus feeding the five thousand. The world is hungry. Jesus stood face to face with the problem of physical hunger just as we in our day face the problem of hunger, not only physical but spiritual. If one were to believe all the magnificent articles in current and religious literature, one would think the world is disgusted and indifferent to the religion of Jesus Christ. I believe exactly the opposite is true. In no century since the morning stars sang together has there been more real hunger for genuine religion than this. And yet, many a preacher, instead of trying to feed this spiritual hunger, is giving some book review, staking a claim out on Jupiter or talking evolution, trying to prove we came from a monkey with his prehensile tail wrapped around a limb shying coconuts at his neighbor across the alley. The world is not disgusted with religion, but is disgusted with the worldliness, rituals, ceremonies and nonessentials in which we have lost religion.

There are some kinds of religion the world is not hungry for:

A religion of formal observances. In Isaiah, first chapter, the Lord says; "To what purpose is the multitude of your sacrifices? I am full of the burnt offerings of rams and the fat of fed beasts. Incense is an abomination unto me; your new moons and your appointed feasts my soul hateth. When you make prayers, I will not hear them. Your hands are full of blood. Put away the evil of your doings; cease to do evil, learn to do well."

Their formalism didn't make a hit with the Lord. He saw through their smoke screen. Religion does not consist in doing a lot of special things, even if branded as religious, but in doing everything in a special way as the Lord directs. Whenever the church makes its observances and forms the end instead of the means to the end, the world will turn its back on it.

Praying is not an act of devotion—reading the Bible is not an act of devotion—going to church is not an act of devotion—partaking of the communion is not an act of devotion; these are aids to devotion. The actual religion lies not in prayer, reading the Bible, church attendance, but in the quality of life which these observances create in you. If the doing of these things does not change your life, then it profits you nothing to have them done. Thousands forget religion and allow the forms of religion to take the place of religion. They are substituting religiousness for righteousness. Jesus alone can save the world, but Jesus can't save the world alone. He needs our help.

The world is not hungry for a religion of theory. There was a time when people were interested intensely in fine-spun theological theories. You could announce a debate on the forms of baptism and pack the house with the S.R.O. sign hanging out. That day has passed; a debate on baptism or predestination would not draw a corporal's guard. The average man has not lost interest in the vital truths connected with these topics, but he has lost interest in the type of religion that spends its energy in argument, word battles, and windjamming. Religion should relate to life and conduct as well as theory.

There has never been a time in my memory when religion has been so reduced to forms and ritual as today. In the mind of Jesus, religion was not to build up the church, but the church was to build up religion. Religion was not the end but the means to the end. Jesus was so far removed from the formalism and traditions taught by the priests instead of teaching the commands of God that he was constantly at cross-purposes with them. A church of make-believers will soon beget a generation of nonbelievers.

The church in endeavoring to serve God and mammon is growing cross-eyed, losing her power to know good from evil. Jesus dealt with fundamentals; his quietest talk had a torpedo effect on his hearers. Some sermons instead of being a bugle call to service are showers of spiritual cocaine. I am satisfied that there has never been a time when it is harder to live a consistent Christian life than now. I believe the conflict between God and the devil, right and wrong, was never hotter. The allurements of sin have never been more fascinating. I do not believe there ever was a time since Adam and Eve were turned out of Eden when traps and pitfalls were more numerous and dangerous than today.

The world is not hungry for a religion of social service without Christ. I will go with you in any and all movements for the good of humanity providing you give Jesus Christ his rightful place. You cannot bathe anybody into the kingdom of God. You cannot change their hearts by changing their sanitation. If is an entirely good and Christian act to give a down-and-outer a bath, bed and a job. It is a Christian act to maintain schools and universities, but the road into the kingdom of God is not by the bathtub, the university, social service or gymnasium, but by the blood-red road of the cross of Jesus Christ.

The Bible declares that human nature is radically bad and the power to uplift and change is external; that power is not in any man, woman or system, but by repentance and faith in the sacrificial death of Jesus Christ. The church is the one institution divinely authorized to feed the spiritual hunger of this old sin-cursed world.

You will notice that Jesus did not feed the multitude. He created the food and asked his disciples to distribute it. Jesus was the chef, not the waiter, at this banquet. Jesus created salvation, the only food that will feed the spiritual hunger of the world; the task of distributing the food is in the hands of his human followers.

For every two nominal Christians, there are three who are not even nominal. Out of every two church members, one is a spiritual liability; four out of five with their names on our church records are doing nothing to bring the world to Jesus. There are twenty million young men in this country between the ages of sixteen and thirty. Nineteen million are not members of any church; nine million attend church occasionally; ten million never darken a church door. Seventy-four percent of our criminals are young men under twenty-one years of age. In the past twenty-five years the age of prostitutes has fallen from twenty-six years of age to seventeen years of age. Five hundred girls fifteen years old and under were divorced or widowed last year. Juvenile crime increased in one year from thirty-two percent to a hundred and thirty-eight percent.

There are many institutions that enter into competition with the church in preaching certain phases of religion, but not in preaching religion itself. Associate charities preach charity sometimes with stronger emphasis than the church. Some organizations talk about justice and square-dealing with more vehemence than the church. Some individuals thunder against vice and crime more than the pulpit. Many institutions and organizations preach one or more phases of religion; but it is to the church humanity must ever turn for the last word on salvation and eternal destiny.

People are dissatisfied with philosophy, science, new thought—all these amount to nothing when you have a dead child in the house. These do not solace the troubles and woes of the world. They will tell you that when they were sick and the door of the future was opening in their face, the only comfort they could find was in the Gospel of Jesus Christ. Christianity is the only sympathetic religion that ever came into the world, for it is the only religion that ever came from God.

Take your scientific consolation into a room where a mother has lost her child. Try your doctrine of the survival of the fittest with that brokenhearted woman. Tell her that the child that died was not as fit to live as the one left alive. Where does that scientific junk lift the burden from her heart? Go to some dying man and tell him to pluck up courage for the future. Try your philosophy on him; tell him to be confident in the great to be and the everlasting what is it. Go to that widow and tell her it was a geological necessity for her husband to croak. Tell her that in fifty million years we will all be scientific mummies on a shelf— petrified specimens of an extinct race. What does all this stuff get her? After you have gotten through with your science, philosophy, psychology, eugenics, social service, sociology, evolution, protoplasms and fortuitous concurrence of atoms, if she isn't bughouse I will take the Bible and read God's promise, and pray—and her tears will be dried and her soul flooded with calmness like a California sunset.

Is the church drawing the hungry world to its tables? There is no dodging or blinking or pussyfooting the fact that in drawing the hungry world to her tables, the church is facing a crisis. That there is a chasm between the church and the masses no one denies. If the gain of the church on the population is represented by eighty during the past thirty years, during the last twenty years it is represented by four, and during the past ten years it is represented by zero. The birth rate is going on a limited express while the new birth rate is going by way of freight.

Need the world turn to other tables than those of the church for spiritual food? Jesus said, "They need not depart; give ye them to eat." The church has the power and the food with which to feed the hungry world. It can feed the spiritual hunger of the world by doing what Jesus did when he fed the five thousand. By a wise use of what it has on hand with the blessing of God upon it, what has the church on hand with which to feed the hungry world? It has two things:

A set of principles which if put into practice in the life of the individual and society and business and politics will solve every difficulty and problem of city, state, nation and the world. There is no safer or saner method to settle all the world's problems than by the Sermon on the Mount. These principles are truth, justice and purity. It has a person who has the power to create and make powerful these principles in the lives of mén and women and that person is Jesus Christ, the Son of God.

Many skeptics have said, "Bill, if you will only preach the principles of Christianity instead of the Person, we will find no fault with you." Nothing doing, old top! Wherever a preacher or a church preaches a set of principles without the person Jesus Christ, that ministry, that church, becomes sterile and powerless. Truth is never powerful unless wrapped up in a person. I take truth and wrap it up in Christ and say, "Take it!" You say, "Give me truth but no Christ." Then you will be lost. You are not saved by truth but by the person Jesus Christ. Why take truth and reject Christ when it's Christ that inspires truth?

I take justice and wrap Christ up with it and say, "Here, take it." You say, "I will take justice. I deal squarely in business, pay my debts, give labor a square deal; I take justice but not your Christ." You are lost. Why take justice and cast Christ away when it is Christ that inspires justice?

I take purity and wrap it up with Jesus and say, "Here, take this." You say, "I will take the principle purity but not the person Jesus Christ." Then you are lost, for it is Christ that saves, not the principle of purity. "One thing thou lackest," the person Jesus.

Other religions have preached good things, but they have no Saviour who can take these things and implant them in the human heart and make them grow. All other religions are built around principles, but the Christian religion is built around a person—Jesus Christ, the Son of God, our Saviour. Every other religion on earth is a religion you must keep, but the Christian religion saves you, keeps you and presents you faultless before his throne. Oh, Christians! Have you any scars to show that you have fought in this conflict with the devil? When a war is over, heroes have scars to show; one rolls back his sleeve and shows a gunshot wound; another pulls down his collar and shows a wound on the neck; another says, "I never had use of that leg since Gettysburg"; another says, "I was wounded and gassed at the Marne in France." Christ has scars to show—scars on his brow, on his hands, on his feet; and when he pulls aside his robes of royalty, there will be seen the scar on his side.

When the Scottish chieftains wanted to raise an army, they would make a wooden cross, set it on fire and carry it through the mountains and the highlands among the people and wave the cross of flame; and the people would gather beneath the standard and fight for Scotland. I come out with the cross of the Son of God—it is a flaming cross, flaming with suffering, flaming with triumph, flaming with victory, flaming with glory, flaming with salvation for a lost world.

William Ashley Sunday (1862–1935) *Voted one of the most popular preachers in the United States in 1924, Billy Sunday became a powerful Presbyterian lay* *evangelist. He had been a successful professional baseball player and used the slang and theatrical language of his former life to communicate the Gospel to the thousands devoted to him. Vehemently against liquor and the saloon, Sunday's voice carried great weight in the passing of the 18th Amendment.*

George Washington Truett/
The Conquest of Fear

Fear not; I am the first and the last, and the Living One; and I was dead, and behold, I am alive forevermore, and I have the keys of death and of Hades.

REVELATION 1:17, 18

IN this hour of worship, let us think together on Jesus' greatest saying concerning the conquest of fear. It is given in these words in the first chapter of the last book of the New Testament. "Fear not; I am the first and the last, and the Living One; I was dead, and behold, I am alive forevermore, and I have the keys of death and of Hades."

It is both the mission and the message of Jesus to deliver mankind from servile, enervating, down-dragging fear. And certainly the problem of fear is a problem to be reckoned with in many lives. One of the most outstanding and surprising disclosures of our stressful, nervous, modern civilization, is the fact that many people are in the thralldom of fear. This fact obtains with all classes of people—the high and the low, the rich and the poor, the educated and ignorant, the old and the young, with all ages and classes. They have fears of all kinds—fear of themselves, of others, of the past, present and future, of sickness, of death, of poverty, and on and on.

A little while ago, it was my privilege to preach twice daily for a week to one of our most influential American colleges. Its student body is large and widely influential, and more mature in years than is the student body of most of our colleges. Before my arrival there, the president of the college sent a questionnaire to every student, asking that the students indicate any subjects upon which they would have the visiting minister speak. When the answers were tabulated, the president and faculty of the college, together with the visiting minister and others, were amazed by the fact that the majority of that large and mature student body had made this request: "Let the visiting minister tell us how we may conquer fear."

The Bible is the one book which answers that very question. There are two words which stand out in the Bible like mountain peaks—the words *Fear not!* With those words, God comforted Abraham, "Fear not, Abram; I am thy shield and exceeding great reward." With those same words he comforted Isaac at his lonely task of digging wells in the wilderness. With the same words he comforted Jacob, when his little Joseph was lost somewhere down in Egypt. So comforted he the Israelites at the Red Sea, "And Moses said unto the people, fear ye not, stand still and see the salvation of the Lord, which he will show you today." These two words, *Fear not!* standing out here and there in the Bible, are a part of our great inheritance as Christians. We shall do well to note tham very carefully, wherever they occur in the Bible, and to note their contextual relations.

The three supreme matters which concern mankind are life, death and eternity. Jesus here gives us an all-comprehensive statement concerning these three vast matters. He bids us to be unafraid of life, of death and of eternity. It is Jesus' greatest saying concerning the conquest of fear. It was spoken to John, who was banished to Patmos because of his fealty to Christ. Let us now earnestly summon ourselves to think on this vast message of Jesus.

And first, Jesus bids us to be unafraid of life. He reminds us that he is "the first and the last and the Living One." Is the fear of life real? It is poignantly so with many. The liability of fear is constant, and this fact is perhaps the explanation for many a suicide. I asked one who sought in a despondent hour to snuff out the candle of life, and was prevented from so doing, "Why did you wish to end your life?" And the pathetic answer was given, "I was afraid to go on with life." People are afraid, for one thing, because they are so dependent. They are utterly dependent upon God, and greatly dependent upon one another. Sometimes the proud expression is heard, "I am independent." Let such a one tell us of whom he is independent, and how and where and when. We are all bound together in the bundle of life. "For none of us liveth to himself, and no man dieth to himself."

Again, we are afraid because we are continually in the presence of great mysteries, such as the mystery of sin, of sorrow, of God, of one's own personality, and of the strange and ofttimes trying providences that come to us in the earthly life.

Still again, the responsibilities of life are such that serious men and women must often tremble. Piercing questions arise to probe our hearts to the depths. Often do we ask, "Will I make good in the stern battle of life?" "Will I disappoint the expectations of my loved ones and friends?" Even Moses trembled before his mighty responsibilities, thus voicing his fear, "O my Lord, I am not eloquent, neither heretofore, nor since thou hast spoken unto thy servant: but I am slow of speech, and of a slow tongue." And even Solomon shrank before his vast responsibility, saying, "And now, O Lord my God, thou hast made thy servant king instead of David my father; and I am but a little child: I know not how to go out or come in." Often come the testing hours in life, when we cry out with Paul, "Who is sufficient for these things?" Many times are we provoked to ask that very question, as we are called upon to make important decisions and meet the critically testing experiences of life. Verily, we are many times made to tremble before the immeasurably responsible facts of life. Jesus graciously comes to us, saying, "Do not be afraid of life." "I will never leave thee nor forsake thee."

Again, he bids us be unafraid of death. He reminds us, "I was dead, and behold, I am alive forevermore." The shuddering fear of death is a very real fact in many a life. Some are in bondage all their earthly lifetime, through fear of death. Maeterlinck confesses in his autobiography, "I am a frightened child in the presence of death." It is not to be wondered at that the thought of death casts its oppressive shadows about us, because death is an experience utterly strange to every one of us. "It is a bourne whence no traveler returns." "The black camel kneels at every gate." "With equal pace, impartial fate knocks at the palace and the cottage gate." It is not surprising that numbers of people have a strange fascination for prying into the secrets of death. This gruesome curiosity sometimes leads its possessor into strange quests and still stranger claims. What shall be said of these uncanny efforts to pry into the secrets of the dead? Such efforts are both profitless and presumptuous. Jesus has told us all that we need to know about death. He knows all about the grave, for he has explored its every chamber, and he has met this Waterloo of death and won. He is not now in the grave. He is alive, he is the Living One who is now bringing to bear the resources of his wisdom, mercy, power and love upon our needy world, and his will is bound to prevail. We are told that "ideas rule the world." Very well, compare the ideas proclaimed by Jesus with all others, and at once we see how preeminent his ideas are. The hands on his clock never turn backward. "For he must reign, till he hath put all enemies under his feet." Some day, thank God, war will be under his feet forever. And so will be all forms of intemperance, and selfishness and sin. And so will be death itself, because it is divinely decreed that "the last enemy that shall be destroyed is death." "O death, where is thy sting? O grave, where is thy victory? . . . But thanks be to God who giveth us the victory through our Lord Jesus Christ."

And still further—Jesus is with his people when they come to die. The evidences of this fact are countless and glorious. Often and joyfully did John Wesley declare, "Our people die well." Many of us, even in our limited and very humble sphere, can give the same glad testimony. "Our people die well." Indeed, when we see how well they can die, how unafraid and triumphant they are when they face the last enemy, we are fortified afresh for our work of testifying to the sufficiency of Christ's help in every possible human experience.

Not long ago, I saw a timid mother die. Hers was a very humble home, the husband was a carpenter, the children were very modestly clothed, and the limitations imposed by a meager income for the home were markedly in evidence. With a calmness, fearlessness and joyfulness indescribable, that modest woman faced the final chapter of the earthly journey. She gave her sublime Christian testimony to her sorrowing husband and children; she confidently bound them to the heart of God, in a prayer that can never be forgotten by those who heard it; and then she passed into the valley of the shadows, smilingly whispering the victorious words, "Yea, though I walk through the valley of the shadow of death, I will fear no evil, for thou art with me; thy rod and thy staff they comfort me." The next day, I saw a strong husband and father pass to the great beyond. He requested that the pastor pray that the whole household might unreservedly accept God's will. When the prayer was concluded, the strong man who was rapidly hurrying down to death sublimely said to the poignantly sorrowing wife and sons, "This is God's way; he doeth all things well; I accept his will without a question; tell me, O my dear wife and children, will you not likewise accept his will in this hour, and through all the unfolding future?" And with one voice, they said, "We will." And then, the strong man was gone, and the peace and calm of Heaven filled all that house. A third day came, and I was called to witness the passing of an unusually timid girl in the Sunday school. The modest child of little more than a dozen years of age anxiously said to her mother, "Everything is getting dark, Mamma. Come close to me, I'm afraid." And the gentle mother said to the little daughter, "Jesus is with us in the dark, my child, as well as in the light, and he will surely take care of all who put their trust in him." And the child's face was immediately lighted up with a joyful smile, as she said, "I am trusting him, and I'll just keep on trusting him, and he will stay close to me, for he said he would, and he always does what he says he will do." And a little later, even in life's closing moments, her voice could be heard singing, "There'll be no dark valley when Jesus comes to gather his children home." Such illustrations of triumph in the hour of death could be indefinitely multiplied. The pastors of your churches are privileged to witness such triumphs week by week; and they are able, therefore, to stand in their pulpits and victoriously shout with Paul, "But thanks be to God, who giveth us the victory through our Lord Jesus Christ."

Not only does Jesus bid us be unafraid of life and of death, but he also bids us to be unafraid of eternity. The word he speaks here in his great promise is, "I have the keys of death and of Hades." That little word "keys" carries with it a large meaning. It means guidance, it means authority, it means control. Just as Jesus cares for his people in life and in death, even so will he care for them in eternity. "I go to prepare a place for you. And if I go and prepare a place for you, I will come again, and receive you unto myself; that where I am, there ye may be also."

Belief in God and in immortality go together. The age-old question, "If a man die, shall he live again?" is a question that will not be hushed. It is no wonder that such a question has been eagerly asked by myriads in the recent years. The Great War laid millions of young men under sod and sea, and has sent other millions to stagger on with broken health, even down to the grave. Suffering hearts all around the encircling globe have asked and are continually asking if death is an eternal sleep, and if the grave ends all. To such questions we must give our most positive answer. The grave does not end all. The doctrine of immortality is not a dead creed, an empty speculation, an intellectual curiosity, an interesting question. The doctrine of immortality is a fact, a force, a great moral dynamic, which lifts life to high levels and drives it to great ends. Yes, we are to live again, beyond the sunset and the night, to live on consciously, personally and forever.

The nature of man demands immortality. The instinct of immortality is the prophecy of its fulfilment. Where in all nature can you find instinct falsified? The wings of the bird mean that it was made to fly. The fins of the fish mean that it was made to swim. The deathless yearnings of the heart imperiously cry out for immortality. On the modest monument that marks the last resting place in France of President Roosevelt's son, who fell in the Great War, is inscribed this death-defying sentence, "He has outsoared the shadow of our night." The human heart refuses to be hushed in its cry for immortality.

The character of God presages immortality. When Job thought of men, he said, "If a man die, shall he live again?" When he thought of God, he said, "I know that my Redeemer liveth." Then Job went on to voice the deathless cry of the heart for immortality. God is infinitely interested in us, he cares for us, he provides for us. If he cares for the birds, as he does, surely he cares also for us. He bids us to put fear away, reminding us, "But the very hairs of your head are all numbered." "Fear ye not, therefore, ye are of more value than many sparrows." Abraham was "the friend of God." Death has not dissolved that friendship. "Enoch walked with God; and he was not, for God took him." A little girl who heard a preacher's sermon on this sentence gave this report of the sermon to a little neighbor girl who did not hear the sermon, "The preacher said that Enoch took a long walk with God; and they walked, and they walked, and they walked; and at last, God told Enoch that he need not go back to live at his house anymore, but he could just go on home with God, to live with him, in his house, forever." Surely, the little girl's interpretation is what our hearts demand, and it is what we steadfastly and joyfully believe to be the plan of God for his friends.

But the crowning argument for immortality is the experience of Jesus. He has incontestably proved it. He came to earth, and really lived, and died, and was buried, and rose again, just as he said he would do. Long years ago, the men of the Old World wondered if there was some other land, beyond the waters, to the far west. One day, a bolder spirit than others had been set sail toward the west. And by and by, Columbus set his feet upon the shores of a new land. Even so, Jesus was the divine Columbus who has explored all the chambers of the grave, and has come back therefrom, the victorious Conqueror of death. He comforts his friends with the gracious words, "I am the resurrection and the life; he that believeth in me, though he were dead, yet shall he live. And whosoever liveth and believeth in me shall never die." In that incomparable chapter of guidance and comfort, the fourteenth chapter of John, Jesus would anchor us, once for all, with his divinely assuring words, "Because I live, ye shall live also."

Low in the grave He lay—Jesus my Saviour!
Waiting the coming day, Jesus my Lord!
Up from the grave, He arose,
With a mighty triumph o'er His foes;
He arose a Victor from the dark domain,
And He lives forever, with His saints to reign,
He arose! He arose! Hallelujah! Christ arose!

With our faith in that victorious Saviour, we may sing with Whittier, in his exquisite poem, "Snowbound."

Alas for him who never sees
The stars shine through his cypress trees!
Who, hopeless, lays his dead away,
Nor looks to see the breaking day,
Across the mournful marbles play!
Who hath not learned, in hours of faith,
The truth to flesh and sense unknown,
That Life is ever lord of Death,
And Love can never lose its own!

Are you trusting in Christ as your personal Saviour, and do you gladly bow to him as your rightful Master? If your hearts answer "Yes," go your many scattered ways, I pray you, without hesitation or fear. Your personal relations to Christ will determine your relations to the three vast matters—life, death and eternity—concerning which he would have us put all our fears away, now and forever more. He is our Pilot, our Righteousness, our Saviour, our Advocate, our promised and infallible Guide, even unto death, and throughout the vast beyond, forever. Well do we often sing, "He leadeth me." As we sing it now, who wishes openly to confess him and follow him?

George Washington Truett (1867–1944)   *Dr. Truett served as pastor of the First Baptist Church in Dallas, Texas, for almost fifty years. One of the most famous preachers of his time, he held the presidency of Southern Baptist Convention as well as of the Baptist World Alliance.*

Walter Arthur Maier/Thanks Be unto God for His Unspeakable Gift!

Thanks be unto God for his unspeakable gift!
2 CORINTHIANS 9:15

MAY the Christmas grace of giving glory to God in the highest, the inner peace granted at Bethlehem, and the Christ-child's good-will toward our fellowmen be and remain with every one of you today and always!

As I extend these greetings to you, not only in behalf of myself but also in the name of a hundred workers associated with me in this radio mission for Christ, I remind you that, while we are now gathered from coast to coast for this afternoon's glorification of the Christ-child, Christmas is almost ended in Bethlehem. The hush of midnight has drawn its silent curtain over the little town with its seven thousand inhabitants and the many visitors who crowd its time-grooved streets. On the other side of the world, westward in the blue Pacific, in this very moment Christmas is still young. On many of the coral islands eager children and happy parents are meeting for Christmas worship in their little palm-thatched churches amid the fragrance and beauty of a tropical December. Should it not be so—Christmas ending, yet always beginning—Christmas everywhere, Christmas for everyone?

Incomparably more personal and blessed than the widespread and continued Christmas rejoicing is the benediction of the Christ-child in our own lives. Before this busy, blessed day of the Saviour's birth draws to its close, let us remind ourselves of the glorious gift with which God would enrich every one of us today. It is the most precious and blessed bestowal that you can ever receive, even though you may be showered with costly and lavish remembrances almost without number. It is the priceless gift, more valuable than all the mountain of earthly presents and honors that you may accumulate during the rest of your life, including Nobel prizes, Rhodes fellowships, Congressional awards, royal grants, extra dividends and lavish bonuses. Ranking high among the most costly manuscripts in the world is the Sinai Codex, a Bible manuscript written in the fourth century. British children saved their pennies and finally purchased the parchment from the Soviet government for $500,000. If you have a New Testament and believe it, particularly the 263 simple words of Saint Luke's Christmas story, you have a treasure which in the sight of God far exceeds $500,000.

Among the most valuable paintings in all the art galleries of the world is Raphael's glorification of the Christ-child and his mother. Five million dollars, we are told, could not purchase this picture. If you receive and believe God's Christmas gift, and have Christ imprinted in the fibers of your heart, you have a blessing that makes five million dollars seem paltry. One of the most costly pieces of property in the world is the site of the Church of the Nativity in Bethlehem. No amount of money could purchase this reputed spot of our Saviour's birth; streams of blood have flown from ten thousand wounds as many have tried to seize or to protect this place. Yet if you have God's Christmas gift, and kneel in spirit at the Christ-child's manger, even if you are out of work, out of funds, out of supplies, you are richer than if you held the title to that church at Bethlehem; for when Christ is born in your hearts, you have a living, victorious assurance that can never come from any disputed traditional spot of the Saviour's birth.

What is it, we may well ask, then, that gives this incomparable greatness to Christmas and how are we to reflect its inestimable glory? As you in the East begin to light your Christmas trees at the approach of evening darkness, and you in the West rise from your holiday dinners, let me show you before another Christmas has passed all too quickly into the irrevocable gulf of the past, that the joy of this day is much more definite than a mere hazy feeling of goodwill, a sense of material happiness through good times, good business, good friends. Above the sparkle of the Christmas lights, the fragrance of the Christmas greens, the brightness of the Christmas colors, the echo of the carols, the heaped gifts, there must be, if this day is to bring its blessings to you and to your home, that Christ-directed faith, that Christ-centered joy, that Christ-focused confidence, which makes us join in that eight-word yet all-comprehensive Christmas hymn intoned by the apostle, "Thanks be unto God for his unspeakable gift!"

When Saint Paul calls Christ God's "unspeakable gift," he is not toying with exaggerated superlatives, polishing his style with impressive phraseology. The blessing of the Saviour's Gospel was as inexplicable to him as it must be to us. The apostle uses a term here which means, one "cannot bring out" or "express" the blessing, the fullness, the glory, the riches, the value of this divine gift. If Saint Paul, acknowledged even by the Christless world as a master of logic, expression and rhetoric, asserts that God's Christmas gift to the world defies all description, where shall we find words or pictures, poetry or painting, that can reproduce in full majesty the limitless love of our Lord Jesus? No sacred oratorio, not even the unforgettable strains of Handel's *Messiah* and its climax in the stirring "Hallelujah Chorus," or the artistry of Bach's *Christmas Oratorio,* can be classed with the angel chorus reechoing over Bethlehem; and even those angel voices could not sing the full glory of Christ. All the hands of genius painting nativity scenes, the fifty-six Madonnas of Raphael, or an art gallery graced with the masterpieces of the ages that have depicted the Christ-child, cannot truly delineate the personal blessings of Bethlehem. No poetry, not even the sacred lines of our hymnals, the measured stateliness of any nativity ode, not even the ancient psalms of inspired prophecy, can fully express the height and depth of God's love in Christ. The heart of Christmas remains unspeakable in its beauty, immeasurable in its power, unutterable in its glory.

All other gifts, from the festively decorated packages beneath your Christmas trees to the most elaborate grants ever recorded in history, can be measured and valued. A crowned churchman once drew a line through North and South America and presented the eastern section of this hemisphere to one country, and the entire west, today consisting of dozens of nations, multiplied millions of black-skinned, red-skinned, white-skinned men, to another country. Surveyors and assessors can describe in voluminous detail the contents, the value, the extent, of this grant, perhaps the greatest gift in all history; yet not all the corps of experts and the intricacies of higher mathematics can provide a gauge to mark the extent of Christ's blessing in individual hearts and in the history of nations. Even in an age where billions are common figures of high finance, the Christ of Christmas remains incomputable. Study the nativity Gospel from whatever angle you wish, and you will repeat Saint Paul's "unspeakable." Reason falters, logic fails, orators stammer and authors grope for words when confronted by the "unspeakable" mystery of Christmas—the Incarnation of God, God-made man; the divine mortal; the Creator, a creature; the Son of God, the Son of the virgin; the King of Heaven's throne, a Babe of Bethlehem's stall. No scientific treatises can explain the unfathomable miracle concealed behind Saint John's simple summary of the Christmas evangel, "The Word was made flesh and dwelt among us; and we beheld his glory, the glory as of the only-begotten of the Father." No master minds can discover any deeper truth concerning the Incarnation of Christ than the confidence which has enriched the simple trust of millions, the assurance that the Son of Mary is the "Son of the Highest," that, as the angels caroled, the Babe "wrapped in swaddling-clothes" is "Christ, the Lord." His birth, which brought heaven to earth, remains the unspeakable mystery before which, humbled and awestruck, mighty intellects have worshiped with joy and childlike trust.

While the Christmas mystery of God manifest in the flesh transcends our poor powers of analysis, its truth remains as unchangeable as heaven itself. Even if unbelief and denial combine, as they do today across the waters in the strongholds of atheism, and in our own country, to shower harsh words of blasphemous attacks on the Holy Child; even if doubt and skepticism unite to shrug shoulders in suspicion, and question the Christmas Gospel; even if infidelity and apostasy join hands and voices in churches which a century ago exalted the Incarnation of God in the Christ-child, but which today are trying to palm off an all-too-human Jesus as the true son of Joseph instead of the true Son of God, as the Christ of Bethlehem, but not of heaven—if you value your soul, if you think thoughts of Eternity and weigh the alternatives of endless living with Christ or endless dying without him, do not let any influences on earth or in hell move your trust from that basic conviction of Christmas faith in which you declare, "I believe that Jesus Christ, true God, born of the Father from Eternity, and also true Man, born of the Virgin Mary, is my Lord." Don't say, "Explain the birth of Christ, and I will accept it"! This, the apostle reminds us, belongs to the "unspeakable" glory of Christmas; and instead of probing into these mysteries, we are to trust them; instead of questioning, to affirm them; instead of debating, to declare them. If we take the word of man for a thousand mysteries of life, why not take God at his word for this supreme mystery of our faith, and, beholding the Child born unto us and the Son given to us, crown him—and I pray you will—"the mighty God"?

Equally "unspeakable" is the mercy granted to us in the birth of Jesus. It has been the custom to remember with our gifts today those who are near and dear to us, to whom we are bound by ties of friendship or indebted by obligation. The great gift of Christ is granted not to God's friends, but to his enemies, to those who in their sins have risen up against God and declared war against the Almighty. To every one of us, suffering, as we and our world are, under the destructive powers of sin, God offers his gift of "unspeakable" grace. Christmas does not offer rejoicing to a selected few; it cries out, "Joy to the world!" We stand before that supreme and saving truth, the holy of holies of our Christian faith, the blessed assurance that "Christ Jesus came into the world," not to build big and costly churches, not to give his followers earthly power and rule, but—and this is why the angels sang their praise—"to save sinners." He came, not to establish social service, social consciousness, social justice; but first and foremost he came to seal our salvation. No wonder that the apostle calls the mercy of God as shown by the gift of Christ "unspeakable"; it goes beyond the limit of human speech. Just as beholding the glare of the sun, men lose their power of vision, so raising our eyes to the brilliance of Jesus, the Sun of Righteousness, we are blinded by the splendor of the greatest gift that God himself could bestow. Christ came to save—blessed assurance! But more, he came to "save . . . to the uttermost," so that no sin is too great, no sinner too vile, to be blessed, when penitent and believing, by this gift. Christ came to save; but more, he came to save freely. No conditions are attached to this gift of God in Christ; nor is it offered to those who have earned or deserved it. It is the free, gracious, unearned, unmerited gift of God to those who with the humility of the shepherds and the reverence of the Magi believe with a personal and trusting faith that Jesus is the ransom of their souls and that he "shall save his people from their sins." Christ came to save; but more, he came to bring with his salvation positive, doubt-destroying conviction. The gift of his grace is not a matter of speculation, not a theory of conjecture. It is the absolute and final truth, which does not leave men in suspense, in question or in doubt as to their salvation. It does more than teach men to yearn and pray and hope for their deliverance from sin; it gives them that exultant conviction by which nothing in life or death itself "shall be able to separate us from the love of God which is in Christ Jesus."

Christ, our Christmas gift, is "unspeakable" because of his everlasting triumph and eternal blessing. All other gifts decay and perish; all other love, even the most deep-rooted devotion that binds husband and wife, parents and children, must end; but the love with which Christ loved us never weakens, never changes, never ends. Octavius, whom we usually refer to as Augustus, ruled the world when Christ was born at Bethlehem; today only a few statues, some crumbling columns of broken temples, remain as the tottering evidence of his departed glory. The helpless Babe in the manger, crowded out of the inn, hunted by Herod, exiled from his homeland, towers over the wrecks of time. That Child changed our calendar, our race, our world, because he changed the hearts and lives of millions as he displaced fear with confidence, despair with hope, doubt with trust, punishment with pardon, terror with peace, hell with heaven, and death with eternal life—all the rich blessings of our "unspeakable gift."

Need we wonder, then, that the great apostle, contemplating the mystery of our Saviour's advent into the flesh, breaks forth in this heart-deep "Thanks be unto God"? Who today, having refused to desecrate the birthday of our King by drunkenness, gluttony or gross sin, knowing what Christmas truly means, will not reecho this hymn of gratitude for Christ, our Christmas gift, "Thanks be unto God"? Only the smug and self-satisfied who boast that they need no Saviour; only blatant sinners who raise their clenched fists against God and resolve to continue in sin; only the blasé, the spiritually dying and the dead whose greedy hearts and covetous eyes have been focused on the treasures and trinkets of the season, the dollars and cents of Christmas profit or loss—can refrain from joining the chorus of gratitude raised by hundreds of millions of Christians today, "Thanks be unto God!"

This gratitude must not be restricted to words. You who have now heard the blessed essence of Christmas must show your thanks. No praise means so much in the sight of our heavenly Father as your trusting acceptance of the "unspeakable gift"; and it is my prayer on this Christmas, a day divinely appointed to call men to Christ and his salvation, that many of you will make his historical birthday your spiritual birthday and blend your hearts and voices in this Christmas *Te Deum*.

To this end I ask you, have you received this "unspeakable gift"? Have you thanked God for the first Christmas and its ageless blessing to you? I know that some of you may feel like asking me, "How can I give thanks when I have so many reverses and hardships in my life; when I have no Christmas bonuses and dividends, as hundreds and thousands of others have; when, at best, I have received only a few straggling gifts?" To you Christmas comes with a personally directed message of hope, and teaches you the blessings of compensation in Christ; for if you are his and he is yours, you are unspeakably rich. Then the apostle reminds you, "Ye know the grace of our Lord Jesus Christ that, though he was rich, yet for your sakes he became poor, that ye through his poverty might be rich." Your Christ is a sympathetic Saviour, who was poor, too, so poor that, though the earth and its fullness are his, the first moments of his life were lived in a manger and the last on a crude, gory cross. Clinging to Christ, you can draw on the resources of heaven and find the peace that men of fabulous wealth who have rejected his atoning love can never purchase. If you have Christ, you can behold this "unspeakable gift" and exult, "He that spared not his own Son, but delivered him up for us all, how shall he not with him also freely give us all things?"— believing that the God who gave the greater gift, his Son, will in his way and at his time grant you the incomparably smaller gifts required for the support of your body, your home, your family.

With Christ you know that all these sorrows serve a remedial, purifying, building purpose. I recently read an account of the 1864 Christmas in the Confederate States. The price on flour on that Christmas was $600 a barrel, sugar $30 a pound, beef $40 a pound; a ham cost $300. The vegetables for a Christmas dinner—cabbage, potatoes and hominy—represented an outlay of $100. There was no dessert in this typical plantation dinner; instead, black molasses, which cost $60 a gallon. Yet out of that harrowing war and privation there emerged, as you on the other side of the Mason-Dixon Line personally realize, a better and happier South. In a much higher degree God often checks our ambitions, reverses our plans, destroys our programs, so that we may be saved for the everlasting blessings.

Perhaps some of you have greeted this Christmas morning on sickbeds; and you who are wasting away in wearying illness, let me bring you a special Christmas comfort by stressing the fact that Jesus, too, suffered, bore agonies that no man can endure, the punishment for all sin, that we might look with him to the homeland, where there shall be no suffering. Some years ago a young man of only twenty-three years, recovering from a siege of sickness, thought of Christ and, subduing his impatience, penned the lines that many of you will sing, even on sickbeds.

As with gladness men of old
Did the guiding star behold;
As with joy they hailed its light,
Leading onward, beaming bright.
So, most gracious Lord, may we
Evermore be led to Thee.

That was William Chatterton Dix, born just a hundred years ago. May your pain thus help to bring you closer to Christ!

Some of you are lonesome on this Christmas Day, separated by great distances from your loved ones; and some of you are misunderstood, oppressed. Take heart, however, as you recall that the beginning of our Saviour's life was marked by Herod's brutal murder and its end with the cruelty of the crucifixion. During the ravages of the Thirty Years' War, Paul Gerhardt, one of the greatest hymn-writers of the church, met with harsh opposition and hatred. Yet when Christmas came, he could sing:

All my heart this night rejoices,
As I hear, far and near,
Sweetest angel voices;
"Christ is born," their choirs are singing,
Till the air, everywhere,
Now with joy is ringing.

God grant that with Christ born in you again today you will experience his sacred companionship even through heartaches and heartbreaks, sorrow and loneliness, misunderstanding and family quarrels.

Since the "unspeakable gift" was freely given for all, the appeal that surges up in our hearts now calls, "O come, let us adore him!" Fathers should understand that Christmas is the most appropriate Father's Day, revealing as it does the fatherhood of God with his divine love for wayward children; mothers should remember that Christmas, with its unequaled exaltation of motherhood, is the best and truest Mother's Day. Let the aged rejoice that the Christmas truth enables them to shake off the uncertainty of life and the fear of death to join aged Simeon in his psalm of everlasting praise, "Lord, now lettest thou thy servant depart in peace, . . . for mine eyes have seen thy Salvation"; and let children be happy on Christmas, which as no other day brings the full glory of childhood, since the Saviour of mankind, the true Son of God, becomes a wee, small Babe. The rich, the learned and the mighty, who can follow the star of faith and, like the Wise Men from the distant East, find in the service of Christ the goal toward which their money, time, talents, influence, but above all their faith must be devoted; the great masses in America, the common working people, for whom Christmas always brings a special blessing, since we recall that the first Nativity message was proclaimed not to kings but to commoners, not to aristocrats but to workingmen, not to princes of finance but to shepherds who were guarding their flocks—all to whom this gift of all ages, all mercy, all blessing, has been freely granted on this day, come now.

It is not too late. Your sins are not too numerous and not too grievous. You need bring no gift to win the favor of the Christ-child, for he loved you before you were. Come now, and as you attune your faith to the angelic song, "Glory to God in the highest," repeat with me this resolute promise of your Christmas gratitude in hovels and mansions, in darkened sickrooms and radiant sitting rooms, in dingy basements and towering apartments, in old folks' homes and orphanages, in asylums and prisons, on land, on the sea, and in the air, in crowded cities and snowbound villages, the strong in courage and the weak in faith, those who have always known Christ and those in whose hearts even now the first flickering flame of faith begins to banish darkness—O shout it from Maine to California, from Canada to Mexico, this chorus of Christ-centered praise, "Thanks be unto God for his unspeakable gift!" God grant you this Christmas gratitude for Jesus' sake. Amen.

Walter Arthur Maier (1893–1950)   *This prominent Lutheran clergyman taught at Concordia Seminary and became known throughout the world as the forceful biblical preacher on the Lutheran Hour on radio. He wrote more than a dozen books during his ministry.*

Leslie Dixon Weatherhead/
Why People Do Go to Church

WE hear a great deal of complaint in these days that people don't go to church, and in the preceding sermon I discussed some reasons for this. Let us look now at the reasons for which people *do* go to church.

Half a century ago it might have been true to say that many people went to church because it was the conventional thing to do. The men put on terrible frock coats and top hats, and the ladies were appropriately garbed—I will not attempt a fuller description of their dress—and they would have been shocked at the very thought of not attending church at least once on a Sunday. That is certainly not true now. I don't suppose there are many persons today who attend church from a purely conventional motive. There may be one or two reluctant husbands dragged by their wives, but that kind of compulsion doesn't account for much churchgoing these days. The truth is that those who now attend, though fewer in number, are of more sincere motive. They are truly seeking something or Someone, even if the goal of their quest is a little uncertain even to themselves. Let us ask ourselves why we attend, for if we are clear about what we are seeking, we are much more likely to find it.

Here, then, are four reasons why people go to church:

The first—and by far the most important—is that you go to worship God. You do not, I trust, go to hear a preacher, or hear lovely music, save as both do what they are meant to do, help you to worship God. And what does worshiping God mean? It means all that prayer means— adoration, thanksgiving, confession, petition, intercession, meditation, dedication—and we cannot, of course, discuss them all now. But I do feel very sorry for a person who has excluded God from his life, who neither in joy nor in sorrow has any sense of "otherness" about his life, who as he wakes up after a night's refreshing sleep and finds himself healthy in body and mind has no one to thank. I pity even more a person who in the depths of sorrow has no one to offer him comfort; and still more the person who, crushed beneath a burden of sin and self-loathing, has no one to whom he can turn, no philosophy of life except a bleak humanism, no resources of strength save his own. One of my friends was driven to a belief in God by the sheer intolerableness of supposing that man was alone in the universe with no outside help whatever and with no hopes at all save those which arise from man's self-born striving.

I came across two sentences in my reading lately which express that forlorn attitude. Here is the first: "Man is a low form of cellular life on his way to the manure heap." Here is the second: "Man is fighting a lone fight against a vast indifference."

I believe that you go to church, in spite of all the alluring voices calling you elsewhere, because you believe in Someone, strong, loving, serene, and holy, who is the personification of all those qualities which you believe matter most to man. They are of priceless worth, and I need not remind you that the word "worship," the word "worth" and the word "worthy" all come from the same root. As you look up from your humanity to God, your spirit is already climbing up to realize that in him there are, and that in you there may be increasingly, those qualities in life which are of greatest worth.

It is not my intention to go into that vexed question as to whether God is so self-sufficient that he does not need our worship at all. I think, if I were pressed, I should say that, of his own ordaining, he has decreed that his entire perfection lacks something if it is denied human response. But I cannot, at any rate, escape the belief that God is pleased with our worship. Suppose that you had enough money and time to make a very lovely garden. You would set it about with trees and lawns, flower beds and shady pools, and you would welcome into it little children. It would be true to say that every flower in the garden was already yours. But if some little child whom you loved plucked a flower and brought it to you and said, "I picked this for you," would you not be pleased? You would not say, "They are all mine, anyhow." Of course they are all yours, but if you loved the child, it would give you joy to think that he picked something that was beautiful and gave it to you. You would be delighted that his little mind linked up together the beauty of something and the desirability and suitability of giving it to you. God has made a lively spiritual garden in which are thoughts and feelings and acts, as well as the translation of his thoughts into the things we see and hear and touch. All are his already. But if you go into this garden of thinking and feeling and willing and offer him your little blossom of worship, saying, "I have brought this to you," he will not say, "I need it not." The offering will bring him joy, and, if the figure of speech may be pressed, he will wear your flower in his bosom. Said Tennyson, "Our wills are ours to make them thine." So are our thoughts and feelings and every power of our personality.

But apart from that, apart from what worship may mean to God, I am quite sure that it can mean something very important to us; and it is because of that that we do go to church. Our minds lay hold on those qualities which we believe he not only possesses but *is,* and as our minds lay hold on the thought of what he is, to some tiny extent we become like that ourselves. "As he thinketh in his heart, so is he." I suppose the psychology of it runs somewhat thus: whenever you express an emotion, you strengthen the emotion. When, therefore, you express the emotion of admiration for those things which God is—and worship is partly such an expression—admiration for the qualities concerned is increased; and it is a commonplace to say that we tend to become what we admire. In a more profound sense than perhaps the words have sometimes meant to us, man is made in the image of God. The man who looks up to God in worship is constantly being remade in the image of God. The sneer has often been uttered that man makes God in his own image, and I admit the danger and comparative truth in that sneer; but in worship, as our hearts go up to him in adoration, God remakes us in his own image. To some tiny extent we become like the God we worship. Even, therefore, if a man goes to church in a bad mood, the music, the hush, the beauty of the building, the grandeur of the hymns, the majesty of God's Word and the message of the preacher may so remind him of the things of God in whose image he is made that, as it were, he will put out the hands of his spirit and draw down into himself something which his best self has always admired; and he will strengthen, not only the emotion of admiration, but the will to possess the admired quality. That, then, is our first point. People go to church to worship God.

People also go to church to find forgiveness. Don't be shocked if I say that nine times out of ten that doesn't make sense at all. They don't find pardon, because they don't seek it. They have such a faint sense of sin. How many people ever notice the petition in the monotoned Lord's Prayer, "Forgive us our trespasses"? It is no good pretending. We just let the petition slide over us. Unless we have a real sense of sin, felt either as a personal burden or a share in the corporate guilt for the evils in the world, we find no reality in the offer of forgiveness. And the truth is that, more and more, the modern man tends to give sin a more attractive title. It is not sin; it is his inhibitions or complexes or perversions. It is his heredity or environment or the treatment of his nurse in infant days. It is moral disease, for which, it is said, he is no more to be blamed than for measles. It is due to evolution, the legacy of the jungle for which he cannot be held responsible. A friend wrote me recently of a girl for whose illegitimate baby he wanted me to find parents. The father was unknown. The girl wanted to be rid of the baby. But, in the writer's view, the girl hadn't sinned. She had, in his phrase, "slipped up." She had been "unlucky." It was a mere peccadillo, a youthful adventure that turned out badly. There was no thought of a little life pushed out into the world with neither father nor mother, of a holy thing made cheap and shameful—no case needing forgiveness. There was no sense of sin.

If there is not even a sense of guilt in regard to the gross sins, when will men wake up to a sense of sin in regard to the evils Jesus condemned, such as unkindness, spiritual pride, the unforgiving spirit, gossip, failure to do our duty to those who pay us to do it, the neglect of the suffering of others, and causing the weak to stumble? Forgiveness is unreal because, in the main, the sense of sin is weak; and, even where it exists, God is thought of as a sentimental indulgent father who will pat us on the back and say, "There, there, I'm sure you didn't mean it."

But sometimes there steals into the place of worship some burdened spirit, some depressed heart, some crushed soul, writhing sometimes in a torment of agony and self-loathing; and then what has been a truth of the intellect becomes what Shelley called "a truth of the emotions." A truth to which the reason assented becomes a truth that burns in the heart like a living flame. We might use the illustration of the automobile and say that the energy expressing itself in the revolving flywheel suddenly becomes geared in so that the car moves forward. Something that has always been true becomes a power to drive and to satisfy. When that happens, we are caught up into that unity with God which is one of the most amazing experiences we can know. I am not talking now to anyone who has no sense of sin at all, who is not burdened in that way—though I would in parenthesis suggest that truly to look upon the spotless purity of God would, if we let it do so, produce a deep and healthy sense of sin. I am talking to the one who feels unworthy, overburdened, sick of himself; and I am offering in the name of Christ that miracle, much more amazing to me than many of the miracles in the Gospels, by which we can be rid of the burden. It really can fall off our shoulders. We can reach that unity of God which the birds, who have never known sin, express; which the flowers, that worship in un-blemished splendor, reveal; which the stars, shining in a majesty unassailed by evil, manifest—a unity deeper than they can ever know, the unity of the sons of God. We can be caught up joyously, gladly, volitionally, into that perfect harmony with God. There is no greater experience in the world than that. You may have "known" all your life that God forgives sins, and then in a time of worship "know" it in a completely different sense. I am aware that you may find this pardon outside the church, but every part of the worship of the church is there to remind you of God and of the endless offer of his forgiveness.

I remember this happening to me during the last war. I wasn't a chaplain then, but a staff officer riding from one Arab sheik to another on government business. I had not been able to attend a service for weeks. One Easter Sunday night I remember going into a crowded Y.M.C.A. tent to a service. I cannot remember a word of the sermon or who preached it, but we sang that great hymn "Christ the Lord is risen today," and suddenly his presence became a fact. His forgiving love became real. I think I felt something of what John Wesley felt when, having *known* the fact of forgiveness for years, having preached about forgiveness, having gone as a missionary to Georgia and offered forgive-ness to others, he afterward sat in a little room in Aldersgate Street and *experienced* forgiveness for himself. "I *knew,*" he wrote, "that Christ had forgiven my sins, even mine, and saved me from the law of sin and death."

The rapture of this experience no one knows until he has had it. It was of this that Masefield was writing when he made Saul Kane say:

O glory of the lighted mind,
How dead I'd been, how dumb, how blind.
The station brook, to my new eyes,
Was babbling out of Paradise;
The waters rushing from the rain
Were singing, "Christ has risen again."
I thought all earthly creatures knelt
From rapture of the joy I felt.
The narrow station wall's brick ledge,
The wild hop withering in the hedge,
The lights in huntsman's upper story,
Were parts of an eternal glory,
Were God's eternal garden flowers.
I stood in bliss at this for hours.[1]

Our second point, then, is that people go to church to restore a broken relationship, to find forgiveness of God, and that they should go out, whatever they may have done in the past, looking up into the face of God and saying to him, "There is nothing between us now."

Men go to church to find fellowship. One of the things that used to please me most about the City Temple in the days when great crowds thronged it was the fact that people would write again and again—not only our own members and regular worshipers, but visitors—to say something like this: "As soon as I crossed the threshold I felt that I was among friends." If we church members pray more and love more, if we gossip less and find fault less, eager, not to see where others are wrong, but to see and draw out their best, if we go to church determined not only to get good for ourselves but to make it easier for others to find God and to find love and friendship, then even strangers and wayfarers will find something worth coming to seek. I am quite sure that the synagogue at Capernaum was quite different when Jesus was present. I do not mean when he was preaching or reading the Scriptures, but when he was worshiping there. If we go to church in the right spirit to pour out our hearts in prayer and intercession, to ask God to unite us with all others present and give us loving thoughts about them, then the whole service can become a unity of fellowship, so that the downhearted and unhappy, the lonely and the sad, the mentally tortured and the spiritually dead, will be caught up into fellowship and thus into the life of God.

I have been rather disturbed in my correspondence lately because so many people have talked about taking their own lives. I know that my correspondence is unusual and that I am therefore liable to get a distorted view of life, which for the great majority is probably still happy. I know that I spend most of my time with people who are ill in either body or mind or else unhappy and in some kind of distress. The

---

[1] "The Everlasting Mercy," *Poems.* By permission of The Macmillan Co.

war has something to do with it, not because the war can destroy the Christian faith, but because so often it proves that we have no real hold on the Christian faith, that what we thought was faith was merely assent, or else faith in something false. But, insanity and nervous illness apart, people would never talk about taking their lives if they had the security that comes from belonging to a fellowship in which one is loved. One can be desperately unhappy, worried, and restless, but a fellowship should be strong enough to hold one, however great the individual agony. I think the suicide is the person who, at the dread moment, believes that nobody cares or that nobody cares enough. The Christian church should offer a fellowship that goes down underneath that tendency toward disintegration, as though to say, "We love you, and we will hold on to you."

I believe that the very memory of what Christian fellowship can mean can become a strong factor in a man's life. A man I know had been a victim of sex temptation and had successfully resisted it over a long number of years. Only his very best friends knew what a battle this particular problem was for him. One evening he found himself on business in Berlin with time on his hands. As he strolled down the Friedrichstrasse, his attention was caught by a large framed photograph of nude women. You can guess the kind of place that was thus advertised. He was greatly tempted to go in. No one would have known. His character would not have been damaged in the eyes of his friends. His respectability would have been unsoiled at home. Then suddenly, with great resolution, he walked away. A hundred yards from the place he had an immense sense of relief and spiritual power. When asked how he had found strength to make that great decision, he answered without hesitation, "My church at home." Even the memory of the fellowship, even the thought that he belonged to a company who loved him and who, with him, were seeking together the high and the lovely and the true and the beautiful things, strengthened him in the hour of temptation.

But the fellowship of the church involves not merely "my church at home." It is a fellowship that goes right across the world into all lands, where men are worshiping in jungle villages, in desert towns, in ice-bound solitudes, in tropical forests. It is a fellowship that goes back throughout all the centuries, a line of witnessing in an unbroken chain, so that as we imagine it we note that the last man in the chain has his hand in the hand of Christ in a little upper room at Jerusalem. It is a fellowship indeed that goes not only across the world and back through the centuries but up into the unseen. "Therefore with angels and archangels, and with all the company of heaven, we laud and magnify thy glorious name, evermore praising thee, and saying, Holy, Holy, Holy."

Our third point, then, is that men come to church to find fellowship.

Lastly, people come to church to find power—spiritual power for this difficult task of living. Here again I suppose the psychology of it is this: power is released in the will through the emotions whenever the mind takes hold on truth. I would ask you to ponder that statement. Whenever the mind is really possessed by truth to such an extent that we *feel* it to be true as well as give it our intellectual assent, then power is released in the will. The will alone is not enough. The feeling alone is not enough. One might risk the illustration that feeling is to the will what gasoline is to the machinery of an automobile.

It is all very well for people to tell us that everything depends on will power. I was reminded, by a sermon of Dr. Fosdick, of the following hymn:

> *Awake, my soul, stretch every nerve,*
> *And press with vigor on;*
> *A heavenly race demands thy zeal,*
> *And an immortal crown.*

Philip Doddridge wrote five hundred hymns, including "O God of Bethel," but "Awake, My Soul" is not one of his best. Certainly when he wrote it he was not in any deep trouble. I can imagine very few situations in which I should wish it to be my message. The people I talk to are not much interested in an immortal crown. They are wondering whether they can get through today and tomorrow without defeat, and I for one would not dare to say to anyone, "Stretch every nerve." The people I deal with have their nerves stretched to the breaking point.

I know a young woman who wanted very badly to be a surgeon. She took the long and arduous medical course necessary, passed with distinction in surgery, and was ready to set out on that grand career. But in a bomb explosion glass was flung in her face, and for a long time it seemed as though all hope of her ever being able to see had gone. She has had thirty-five operations, and there is left to her only the glimmer of sight in one eye. Shall I say to her, "Stretch every nerve, and press with vigor on"?

In a family of my acquaintance there are two daughters, one fifteen and one twenty. The girl of fifteen is what a girl should be at that age— healthy, happy, full of life. But what shall I say about a lovely girl of twenty, at the very threshold of life, whose brain has been infected by germs which have destroyed her controls so that she cannot be left day or night? I have consulted a specialist on her behalf, and his opinion is that there is no hope whatever. Twice she has tried to take her own life, and there always exists the danger of her attacking others. The sentence of the most eminent medical opinion is that she must remain in a mental hospital for the rest of her life. That may be fifty years. Yet for periods she is entirely sane and pleads to be taken home. Shall I say to her and to her stricken family, "Stretch every nerve, and press with vigor on"?

I will not harrow your feelings by talking thus. If you and I were meeting in a little room, you would say to me, "Yes, I know a case where ..." and I would only have to open my own diary at any week in the year to tell you of case after case of deep human need, so deep that no human resourcefulness is an adequate reply. All last winter, when the horror of bombing went on night after night, I found it almost unbearable to listen to some new story each day. There are many people to whom I minister who have lost their boys, lost their home, lost their business, lost everything except their faith. I would not like to ask them to say to themselves:

Awake, my soul, stretch every nerve,
And press with vigor on.

I would not presume to offer them the petty shallowness of any word of human wisdom, the pagan triviality of being told to endure, the irritating irrelevance that others suffer similarly, the heartless torture which falsely teaches that all suffering is punishment for sin.

But I think I know why such people go to church. Those people go to church because the only comfort for them is God—not God explaining himself in arguments, for no explanation I have ever met satisfies the need of the mind, let alone the hunger of the heart; not God remote and far away; but God coming down into human life and into human suffering; God who is himself crucified and who still remains serene, calm, loving. That God, who doesn't try to answer our questions, answers our need; and I believe in a God who brings his children through their dread sufferings with finally nothing lost, but with something gained which is of immortal worth.

Since I have criticized one hymn, let me offer you another:

See, from his head, his hands, his feet,
Sorrow and love flow mingled down:
Did e'er such love and sorrow meet,
Or thorns compose so rich a crown?

Those who go to church and find the real God, answer for themselves the question with which we started, "Why do men go to church?" They go to worship; they go to find pardon; they go to enter a fellowship; they go to get power. No! No! We need not divide it thus. They go to find all their deepest longings satisfied when they find God himself. He is the goal toward which our spirits move. He is the reality behind all men's dreams. He is the answer to all our prayers. Jesus, who was the supreme Master of the art of living, could not live without God. Can you?

Leslie Dixon Weatherhead (1893–1976) *A true prince of the English pulpit, Leslie Weatherhead was an outstanding student of psychology. He served as a chaplain in World War I, and then in various British churches. His last pastorate was at City Temple, London, where his magnetic preaching drew capacity crowds throughout his ministry.*

Epilogue/A View from the Pew

DAVID POLING

THAT faithful pursuer of preaching and outstanding pulpit minis-
tries, S. E. Frost, Jr., once discussed the reason for "greatness" in
preaching. He was asking the question that some readers here may have
raised: what truly makes a sermon great? What is it that one required in
seeking greatness, especially when we are so far removed in time and
place from the first delivery and presentation of these gathered sermons? The obvious answer, for Frost and many of us, was the literary
value of the sermons. Whether historic or fairly recent, the sermons
prized had at least to read well, to have structure and direction, to
incorporate style and composition.

But more than this literary qualification, Frost argued that the true
signs of greatness in any sermon would be found in that special ability to
"satisfy the fundamental cravings of mankind." These he identified as
the yearning for knowledge, the plea for hope and comfort, the aware-
ness of sin and the condemnation of personal transgression. Great
preaching always touches the human condition. And for the millions
who have come away filled and strengthened from times of inspiration,
forgiveness, and love expressed by powerful preaching, sermons are life
itself.

Fifty years ago Charles Clayton Morrison and his colleagues at *The
Christian Century* polled nearly ninety thousand clergymen in North
America, asking them to name the outstanding preachers of that day. A
collection of sermons followed, with twenty-five being published in
1925. The twenty-five preachers selected were asked to contribute "a
sermon which expresses a characteristic note of your ministry." A fine
book resulted *(The American Pulpit):* yet here the selection of preachers
and of the material also was by clergymen. Therefore, it seemed
appropriate in this volume that the final word be from the laity—a view
from the pew on preaching and sermons.

A decade ago a fine little classic was published in England entitled

God's Frozen People, by Mark Gibbs and T. Ralph Morton. The theme of the book was rather basic—that the laity of the Christian Church were a frozen asset, underemployed and underrated by the present functioning of the religious authorities. Each were off doing their own thing, clergy and laity. If they would be faithful to the Gospel, they should be seeking goals for Christ together. Regarding preaching, the authors said:

> The ministry of the Word is not the right of uninterrupted utterance from a pulpit but the duty of seeing that the Word has free course among men. The minister is ordained not that he alone may talk but that others may hear and understand and act.

Read that extraordinary paragraph twice, for it points to the heart of faith.

In this connection, pulpit and pew both stand under the Word of God. One party may be offering the Word, the other, receiving; yet both are *sharing* in that which is life-changing and life-directing. It was Andrew W. Blackwood, famous pastor, preacher and professor who argued long that we should not seek for "great" sermons but solicit good sermons. And good sermons? Those were the ones that truly "did good" in the lives of the people.

In preparation for this section we communicated with concerned lay people around the world. From them we hoped to gain a broad and fresh insight into the meaning of preaching today as well as the importance of the sermon to those who worship week in and week out. It was not a little surprising to find a clear spiritual consensus on these matters from men and women in all walks of life, *who had no opportunity to discuss this theme together and who speak from a variety of theological persuasions.*

Senator Mark O. Hatfield gave a generous response to our invitation to discuss the view from the pew. A thoughtful and active Christian, he has come to be regarded by many as one of the leading laymen in our national government. His participation in the Christian community is widely known and enthusiastically followed. He writes:

> There are two considerations that seem to men to be vital to the effectiveness of a sermon: authority and application. It is not that I enter a church looking for these characteristics, but rather that I find the impact of sermons minimal when both ingredients are lacking.
>
> By authority—I mean that I want the minister to have a strong biblical base for his preaching.

In his recent book, *Sent from God,* Dr. David H. C. Read underlines this thought by saying: "The preacher is not a religious free lance, but stands under the Bible's authority. It is the Word in Scripture that underlies all true preaching."

Continues Hatfield:

> Our primary witness to the Word is God has been passed along to us through Scripture. Preaching that neglects this as its foundation soon finds itself on a very shaky base—which can often be strongly influenced by the spirit of the times.

Hatfield is correct, for without a biblical base, regular preaching not only loses its contact with God's Word but also yields its moral dimension. Five hundred years ago John Calvin reminded his congregation in Geneva:

> When I first came here there was almost no organization, the gospel was preached and that was all. Everything was in upheaval. I have lived through many marvelous conflicts. . . . I have been greeted in mockery in the evening before my door with fifty or sixty shots. . . . Then I was hunted out of town. People set their dogs on me. . . . Concerning my doctrine, I have taught faithfully and have not corrupted a single passage of Scripture nor knowingly twisted it.

So Hatfield observes:

> The prevailing moral consensus of a society can be often antithetical to biblical revelation. Any sermon that does not begin with the Bible is nothing more than a personal opinion, often educated and informed, but subject to no more consideration than judgments offered by other philosophers of the human condition.
>
> The sermon, however, should not be simply an exegetical exercise that dissects every word of every verse to the exclusion of the reality of the present world. After I have heard the Word of God, I am anxious to understand its relation to the world in which I find myself today. The biblical witness of Jesus Christ is not confined to a remote area two thousand years ago. If our faith is valid, then it has something to say to the problems of violence and poverty and all the other maladies that confront this and every age.

On this theme of the Gospel and social responsibility, Dr. Karl Menninger points us to his words (in his book *Whatever Became of Sin?*) that are almost parallel to Senator Hatfield's:

> The preacher can declaim; he can deplore; he can denounce; he can reprove and exhort and inspire. He can point out the responsibility of us all for the failure of us all. He can remind us of the priestly function of every member and he can recall to us the reality of sin and the validity of social morality. But until I recognize and acknowledge that I am my brother's keeper, the tide of human self-destructiveness will not be stemmed. We will not have achieved either moral or mental health, and it is the minister's task to keep telling us that.

In responding to my questions concerning preaching and what one looks for in a sermon, Dr. Menninger directed me to this further thought from his book:

> Millions of words have been set down regarding what the parishioners should hear: reassurance about the existence of God, His mercifulness, His grace, His goodness, His expectations of mankind to forgive and to love, His sure forgiveness of repented sin, the assurance of life everlasting. These worthy themes support the faith.

But then America's most famous psychiatrist pushes us to a different point by asserting that such themes

> will not reach the heart of some listeners for whom the roar and rumble of guilt drown out the reassurances. If, occasionally, a congregation is gently

scolded, is it for absenteeism, violation of the Sabbath, or niggardly support of the church budget?

If Dr. Menninger has a word from the pew, it is that the pulpit must sound off in powerful and ringing notes.

"How often," says the head of the Menninger Foundation, "How often does a modern sermon deal with sin? Sin in general or in particular? The civil rights struggle in our country certainly had its brave clergy spokesmen and leaders— perhaps more in action than in preaching—but they were a pitiful minority of the profession. Many were threatened and deterred by reactionary congregations."

This is a theme that won't go away for Karl Menninger, so he persists by writing: "Has the reader ever heard a sermon, for example, in which cigarette smoking or wildlife destruction, or political lying or business dishonesty were dealt with as sins?"

Whatever Became of Sin? has been a banner book ever since it first appeared in 1973. The author keeps a sharp focus on the role of the preacher and the place of the sermon in our entire Western culture. He urges the pastor not "to minimize sin and his proper role in our culture." If he, or we ourselves, "say we have not sin, we deceive ourselves, and the truth is not in us." We need him as our umpire to direct us, to accuse us, to reproach us, to exhort us, to intercede for us, to shrive us. Failure to do so is *his* sin."

Those who responded to the questions of this chapter were quite concerned about the present situation of mankind. Said Mark Hatfield,

It is my sincere belief that our world thirsts for the revelation of hope, for without it we are consumed in a drought of fear and despair. The sermon must speak to the needs of the people today—with the authority of the Word of God.

We noted earlier in this section the conditions for great sermons set down by Dr. Frost. He argued that enduring sermons and powerful preaching met people in their need. In a recent book, *Locked in a Room with Open Doors,* my friend Dr. Ernest T. Campbell of Riverside Church made this observation:

Seventy-five years ago Christian congregations in the Western world could be characterized by a general sense of guilt. Ten years ago those same congregations could be characterized by a general sense of doubt. Today the temperature has dropped still further. A minister may now presume, no matter where he preaches, that the congregation gathered before him is beset with a sense of discouragement.

I think if anyone had cause for despair or discouragement, it was Elisabeth Elliot. The whole Christian world followed the saga of this young missionary wife and mother when the story of her husband's death came to full discovery in the best-selling book, *Through Gates of Splendor.* Here was a young woman faced with the uncertainties and alarms of the Ecuadorian jungle, the savage Auca Indian tribe, and the perils of survival itself. Through the years—and the writings that followed—we have been given a large glimpse of what it means to be a Christian in times of unbearable stress and unexpected tragedy.

While in correspondence with Miss Elliot concerning the theme of this chapter, I read her later book, *A Slow and Certain Light,* and came across this passage:

> I have never heard any voices or seen any visions from heaven, but I have been reminded "out of the blue," on more occasions than I can count, of some word from the Bible which exactly suited my need.

Her reflections on preaching coincide clearly with her convictions about life:

> Preaching always requires a personality. If it were not so, we could get all we need from reading. But God has so arranged things that his Word is to be ministered not only through Scripture but also through men—men saturated with the written word and empowered by the Holy Spirit. I hope to hear a message which is the product not only of careful study and conscientious preparation, but of a life lived with God himself. The "words" come out of the "Word," they are the expression of a living reality, bought by the suffering which a life laid down for Jesus Christ and for others entails.

Over and over the friends and acquaintances who responded to the discussion of the "view from the pew" asked that the sermon speak powerfully to their need and fill them with the message of the Bible.

And these friends were from almost every segment of our national experience. Almost a decade ago I met David Hartman on a television show in Cincinnati, Ohio. We were guests who became friends. This motion picture star who has made such an impact in his own television seris, *Lucas Tanner,* portrays a high school teacher who is also a coach. The series is pure Hartman, for here is a man who has a solid interest in people, a genuine concern that they find fulfillment in life and joy in their relationships. Presently he hosts "Good Morning, America."

The son of a Methodist minister, David Hartman is a show-business celebrity who has never been ashamed of his Christian beginnings and the faith that follows a belief in Jesus Christ. His thoughtful and sensitive role as a physician in *The Bold Ones* (which ran for more than four years on network television) generated thousands of letters from viewers seeking counsel, advice, and direction from one they felt could be trusted. Part of his own "ministry" is to answer each inquiry personally and carefully. Concerning sermons and preaching, David Hartman contributes these thoughts as his view from the pew:

> I expect the sermon to challenge my thinking and my attitudes. Life is a difficult and demanding experience for everybody. I look for a personal lift, a powerful, shaping word from Scripture. We must have this in our lives. It is not optional. Our souls must be fed and the Bible teaches us to expect good and great things from God. This is the way I understand Jesus. He taught the full meaning of love. Our lives need to be loving and caring if we are honest to his teaching and faithful to his Gospel.

Hartman argues that Christianity is one of the most powerful things in the universe. If we are out of touch with God's power—and if this does not come through preaching—we are subject to nagging fears and defeatist moods. He searches for the preachers who lift up rather than put down: since so many forces in the world are negative and sour, the Church must have the voice of love, forgiveness, hope, and trust.

> Preachers are important in my life. It may surprise you to know that I faithfully watch Norman Vincent Peale and Robert Schuller on television when I am away from my home. For me, they sound the upbeat, the positive, the hopeful signals of the Good News of Christ. We must have Good News and the willingness to take seriously the promise that God loves us. If we don't love ourselves, we surely cannot be affectionate to others. Preaching really must teach us how to cope, to believe that we "can do" in this long, often difficult task of living twenty-four hours a day. I need a twenty-four-hour faith and great preaching gives me the clues for such a track.

Hartman contends that most people yield to patterns of failure, ignorant of successful ideals and hopes. He said, "If I fail, I fail Christ. He does not call me to defeat or failure but to achievement and accomplishment. We ought to hear this from the pulpit."

Another Hollywood star with thoughtful participation in the life of the Christian Church is Marge Champion. Her dancing talents have been appreciated and followed for years by a large public here and overseas. Her performance in films and her talent seen on television has brought us close to the beauty and joy of the dance.

With Marilee Zdenek she produced *Catch the New Wind*, a lively and helpful volume on the new dimensions of worship which includes her interpretations of modern dance. Hundreds of congregations have been using this tool to enrich their worship and enliven their understanding of response to God's love.

It is not surprising for her to respond to our questions by saying:

> It is very difficult for me to think of a sermon as a separate part of a worship service today. My expectations and needs in worship are to feel—and I do mean *feel*—that the entire service is the sermon. I am not saying that I want to eliminate the message, the spoken Word with which I can be inspired, challenged, educated, or entertained. But when the total service is the *sermon,* when each and every element is used to delineate some aspect of the theme, the spoken Word can be woven in and out of the music, the dance, the touching, the corporate and individual prayer.

Marge Champion then hits on some flaws of worshipers who center *only* on the sermon:

> It is not my need to get through all that other stuff including the collection before being allowed to be inspired by the minister, priest, or rabbi. That puts too big a burden on him and frequently leaves me feeling uninvolved—really a spectator. I look forward to hearing his words, learning from his theological expertise, but I don't want him feeling the crunch of being the star of the show every week.

Then Miss Champion delivers an understanding of worship that would rank high in the major seminaries of the Christian world:

> We are all called to worship with our whole being. I want my minister to know that I take that responsibility as seriously as he takes his—and I want

him to give me the chance to exercise it. I want to be inspired by his professionally trained insights, but I need space to share and care with my own talents and *those of my brothers and sisters in the congregation.* I want him to act as a catalyst so we can all contribute to *make the service the sermon.*

In summary, the word and view from the pew is that preaching reaches and changes the lives of listeners. It is hoped that in printed form, these messages from Christian champions would shape and alter lives, causing a deepening of the spirit and clarity of the soul.

R. E. C. Browne in his incandescent little book, *The Ministry of the Word,* has offered this thought for every generation:

> The language of a generation grows out of its faith, its disbeliefs, its preoccupations, its anxieties, its achievements, its amusements, its hopes and fears. Great ministers of the Word have always preached in a way that is both peculiar to themselves and to the times in which they preached. What they say so aptly for one special occasion is for all occasions . . . though a great sermon is made at one point in time, it is for all time; though its language may have an archaic ring, its significance is clear because it deals with perennial human concerns and can, therefore, be recognized as significant at any time.

Let me add a personal note. During the preparation of this manuscript, visiting five major libraries in four states, reading and considering hundreds of sermons by almost as many preachers, I came to the quiet, steady decision that I should return to the pulpit ministry. After nearly a decade of religious publishing, followed by three years of organizational work in the church, the impact and persuasive thought of *This Great Company* seemed to nudge and then stir my own thinking toward the pastoral ministry—and the pulpit—after an absence of a decade for work in other branches of the Christian community. Ideas and words have power, especially when linked with God's Word which never grows old.

In closing we salute those who have contributed so much of their thought and concern to make this section possible—to give us a view from the pew, without which pulpits would be useless. And a last word comes from Dr. Charles R. Brown, who said more than fifty years ago something that is helpful today—

> We are not called to produce great sermons, or to become great preachers—we are commissioned to produce, by our work as preachers, some great Christians.

References

The World's Great Sermons, by S. E. Frost, Jr. Garden City, N.Y.: Doubleday & Co., Inc., 1943.

The American Pulpit, edited by Charles Clayton Morrison. New York City: Macmillan Publishing Co., Inc., 1925.

God's Frozen People, by Mark Gibbs and T. Ralph Morton. London: Fontana Books, 1964.

Sent from God, by David H. C. Reed. Nashville, Tenn.: Abingdon Press, 1974.

Whatever Became of Sin? by Karl Menninger, M.D. New York City: Hawthorn Books, Inc., 1973.

Locked in a Room with Open Doors, by Ernest T. Campbell. Waco, Texas: Word Books, Inc., 1974.

Through Gates of Splendor, by Elisabeth Elliot. New York City: Pyramid Books, 1970.

A Slow and Certain Light, by Elisabeth Elliot. Waco, Texas: Word Books, Inc., 1974.

Catch the New Wind, by Marilee Zdenek and Marge Champion. Waco, Texas: Word Books, Inc., 1973.

The Ministry of the Word, by R. E. C. Browne. SCM Press, 1958.